MODERN WORLD HISTORY

FOR EDEXCEL SPECIFICATION A

Nigel Kelly

FOUNDATION

Heinemann

Heinemann Educational Publishers

Halley Court, Jordan Hill, Oxford, OX2 8EJ

a division of Reed Educational & Professional Publishing Ltd

Heinemann is a registered trademark of Reed Educational & Professional Publishing Ltd

OXFORD MELBOURNE AUCKLAND
JOHANNESBURG BLANTYRE GABORONE
IBADAN PORTSMOUTH NH (USA) CHICAGO

© Nigel Kelly 2001

First published 2001

ISBN 0 435 31142 5

03 02 01

10 9 8 7 6 5 4 3 2 1

Designed and typeset by Visual Image

Illustrated by Greig Sutton and Paul Bale

Printed and bound in Italy by Printer Trento s.r.l

Index compiled by Indexing Specialists

Photographic Acknowledgements
The author and publisher would like to thank the following for permission to reproduce photographs:

AKG Photo London: 12, 76, 78, 84, 87, 89, 90, 95, 96

Archive Photos: 140
Associated Press: 163, 217
Associated Press / Topham Picturepoint: 185
Birmingham (Alabama) Public Library: 215
Birmingham Gazette: 196
Camera Press: 142, 161
Corbis: 60, 61, 70, 119, 146, 159, 170, 206, 208, 211, 214, 220, 226, 230, 231, 259 (bottom), 261, 263, 293
David King Collection: 28, 33, 34, 35, 39, 41, 43, 51, 237, 238, 243, 244, 245, 246, 249
Dinodia Picture Agency / Vithalbhai Collection: 184
Ewan MacNaughton / Centre for the Study of Cartoon and Caricature: 171
Hulton Deutsch: 178 (top)
Hulton Getty: 45, 82, 92 (both), 100, 102, 107, 110, 124, 133, 177, 178 (bottom), 186, 187, 188, 192, 193, 195 (both), 197, 198, 200, 201, 203, 205, 253, 268, 279, 281
Hulton Picture Archive (Papercopy): 11, 58
Illustrated London News: 112
Kobal Collection: 255
Link / Orde Eliason: 175
Low / Centre for the Study of Cartoon and Caricature: 270
Novosti: 262
Peter Newark: 57, 212, 221, 222, 223
Popperfoto: 38, 151, 157, 277, 287, 289
Popperfoto / Reuters: 46, 66, 152, 156
Punch: 274
Solo Syndication / Centre for the Study of Cartoon and Caricature: 286
Suddeutscher Verlag Bilderdienst: 83
Telegraph Colour Library: 225, 227
Topham Picturepoint: 130, 136, 138, 143, 149, 153, 191, 207, 229, 233, 234, 251, 259 (top), 278, 288
United Nations: 165

Material for the three outline study units–*The Road to War; Europe, 1870–1914,The Emergence of Modern China 1911–76* and *Conflict and the Quest for Peace in the Middle East, 1948–95*–can be found at www.heinemann.co.uk/history/GCSE.
You will need to use a password to gain access to these units. The passwords are:
for *The Road to War; Europe, 1870–1914*: **road**
for *The Emergence of Modern China 1911–76*: **china**
for *Conflict and the Quest for Peace in the Middle East, 1948–95*. **middle**

CHAPTER 1

The war to end wars: 1914~19

Essential Information

On 28 June 1914 a Serbian student called Gavrilo Princip shot Archduke Franz Ferdinand. The Archduke was heir to the throne of Austria–Hungary. Not surprisingly the Austrians reacted angrily to the assassination. They sent the Serbian government an ultimatum. Amongst other things it said that the Serbians should allow the Austrian police into Serbia to investigate the shooting. The Serbians would not allow this, so on 28 July Austria–Hungary declared war on Serbia.

Over the next few days various countries joined in the war, so that the shooting of the Archduke led to what became known as the 'Great War' – the 'First World War' as we usually call it today.

There was a great deal of enthusiasm for the war in the various countries. In every country there was a belief that their own army was fighting a just war, and that victory would be won quickly and easily. Men rushed to join these armies. Britain did not join in the war until August but when it did, in the first month of the war, over 400,000 men volunteered to join the British Army.

The failure of the Schlieffen Plan

The Plan
The Germans had a plan to win the war very quickly. It had been drawn up by the German Chief Of Staff, Count Alfred von Schlieffen, as long ago as 1905. He said the plan would bring Germany victory in just six weeks. The plan said:

- When war broke out Germany could expect to fight on two **fronts**, against France in the West and against Russia in the East.

Who fought against whom?
The war was between the major powers of Europe. On the one side there were the **Allied Powers** (led by Britain, France, Russia and Italy). On the other side were the **Central Powers** (Germany, Austria–Hungary – later Turkey – and Bulgaria)

- Russia would take longer to get ready, so it was important to knock France out of the war before the Russians were ready to advance on Germany.

- The French expected an attack and had their troops drawn up along the French border. So the Germans should send a huge force (1.5 million men) into Belgium and down to the French capital, Paris.

- The French would be caught by surprise and would surrender. Then the Russians could be dealt with.

What went wrong?
Count von Schlieffen had set up a plan which made great demands on his soldiers. He wanted them to march hundreds of kilometres (in hot summer sun) and capture the French capital in just six weeks. They could not do this because they were exhausted. They soon fell behind schedule.

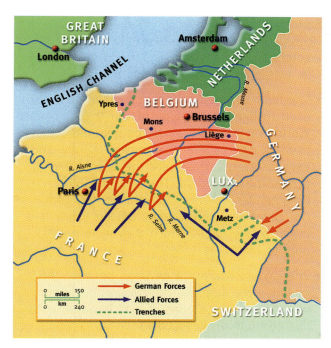

▲ The Schlieffen Plan in action.

The troops set off

On 4 August 1914 the German Army declared war on Belgium and began marching through its countryside. The Belgians asked the British for help. As far back as 1839 Britain had promised, in a treaty, to protect Belgium against attack. The Germans did not think that this promise still stood all these years later, but the 1839 Treaty gave Britain an excuse to go to war against its rival, Germany. The **Kaiser** was horrified to hear that the British had joined in the war over 'a scrap of paper'.

Belgian resistance

Within three weeks the **British Expeditionary Force** of 80,000 men was in Belgium helping to fight the Germans. Even without British help, the Belgians had resisted the powerful German Army for much longer than expected. When the British arrived with their new Lee Enfield Mark III guns they made the German advance much more difficult. One German officer complained that 'it seemed as though there was a machine gun behind every bush'.

The German advance to Paris was supposed to take six weeks but, three weeks after setting off, they were still in Belgium. They also heard that the Russians had got their troops ready much quicker than expected. So troops had to be taken from Belgium and sent to the other side of Germany to fight Russia. Everything seemed to be going wrong!

Stalemate, trench warfare and Haig

The German Army was so strong that, by the end of August, it was into France and heading for Paris. On 5 September, the French and British launched a major attack along the river Marne. After eight days of fighting, the German advance was stopped and the German troops retreated to the river Aisne (see map). To protect themselves, the German soldiers dug **trenches**. The French and British did the same.

The race to the sea

Each side wanted to go round the edge of the enemy's trenches. They tried to do so, by sending troops towards the North Sea. They also wanted to capture the ports on the Channel. In the end, the Germans took the cities of Bruges and Ostend, but ports like Calais and Dunkirk stayed in French hands.

The race to the sea had resulted in two lines of trenches facing each other, running from Ypres in the North to Switzerland in the South. This was the infamous '**Western Front**'. Despite millions of men being sent into battle (and millions of deaths), neither side ever managed to advance much more than 10 miles (16 kilometres) into enemy territory. When the final year of the war (1918) began, the trenches were largely in the same place that they had been in 1914.

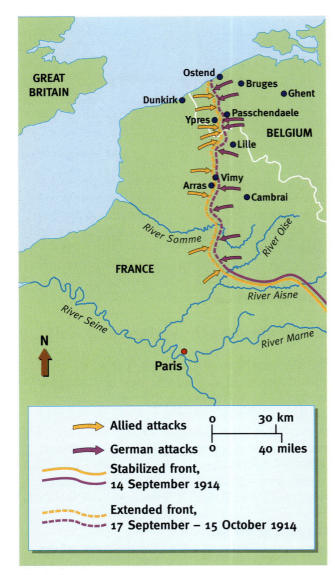

▲ The 'race to the sea'.

How did the Germans think they could beat France and Russia at the same time?

Why did the Schlieffen Plan fail?

What was the 'race to the sea'?

Stalemate

Historians have called the situation on the Western Front a stalemate. This means neither side was able to win. Why was this?

- The main problem was that neither side was used to fighting the type of war that the First World War soon became. The generals were used to wars where men moved rapidly, and **cavalry** attacks often sent the enemy fleeing across the battlefield. The two British Commanders-in-Chief, Sir John French and Douglas Haig, were cavalry officers. They had large cavalry forces which they were never able to use.

- The cavalry could not be used because the enemy were dug into trenches with barbed wire and machine guns. It was impossible to charge them on horseback!

So what did the generals do?

Neither side was happy at sitting in trenches looking at heavily protected enemy trenches just a few hundred metres away. So they had to work out how to attack. One way was to fire artillery shells at the enemy trenches until they were badly damaged. Then soldiers could be sent out of their trenches (they called this going **'over the top'**) and across **No Man's Land** to capture the enemy trenches. The problem was that the artillery was not very accurate and the enemy trenches were only partly damaged. So when the attacking soldiers came out of their trenches they were usually mown down by enemy machine guns. In battles such as Verdun and the Somme (see page 8) losses were appalling.

Mud

Another problem the generals faced at the North end of the Western Front was mud. The area to the south of Ypres (or 'Wipers' as the British soldiers called it) was called Flanders. It is a flat and very wet area with thousands of drainage ditches to take away the water.

Source 1

STORY A
WOOD J.E., D.C.M.

LANCE SERJEANT
KILPATRICK J.W.
MARDELL W.
MATHERS T.

CORPORAL
ANDERSON R.
BEADLE G.H.
BOLTON J.W.
CROSS S.
DAVISON F.
GADD W.
GILL W.B.
GORMAN J
HAMLIN A
HARRISON J
HART J.E.
HILL P.H.
HOGAN J
JAMES E
ROWLANDS J.J.
ROBINSON H.F.

RUDER C.C.
SOWEN W.
SPENCE N.C.
SERVED AS GOOD J.
STEELE M.J.
STEWART E.D.
TURNER C.J.
WINTON J.
WOODS G.H.

PRIVATE
ACKLAM T.
ADAMS R.F.
AGAR W.E.

AMOS A.
ARNOLD A.G.
ASHTON W.
ATKINSON J.
AUSTIN A.J.
BAILEY A.J.
BAILEY W.J.
BALCOMBE C.H.J.
BARR H.
BARTON J.W.
BATES J.
BATTARBEE H.
BEACH E.F.
BEAL J.H.

BLADON J.H.
BLYTH C.
BOARDMAN F.
BOND J.W.
BONNEY J.S.
BONSER J.
BOWDEN J.R.
BOWLES C.A.
BOWMAN A.
BOWMAN W.
BOX A.
BRADY W.
BRANTON A.

▲ **The names of soldiers who have no grave are recorded at the Menin Gate in Ypres.**

Artillery bombardments destroyed these ditches and produced churned up areas of mud and craters full of water. Soldiers had to walk on duckboards to avoid sinking into the mud. At the Battle of Passchendaele in 1917 many of the deaths were the result of drowning in the mud and water on the battlefield.

The Menin Gate
One of the main roads into Ypres passes through the **Menin Gate**. It is a memorial on which are carved the names of 55,000 soldiers who were killed in the war, but whose bodies have not been found. Another 35,000 names are recorded on the wall of Tyne Cot cemetery just a few miles away. Many of these missing men simply disappeared in the mud of Flanders.

Trench warfare
Life in the trenches could be really uncomfortable, as this poem by a soldier shows:

> *Far from Wipers I long to be*
> *Where the Germans can't get me*
> *Cold is my dugout; damp are my feet*
> *Waiting for a whizzbang to put me to sleep*

(**Dugouts** were small shelters dug into the side of trenches. **Whizzbangs** were artillery shells that made a whizzing noise before you heard them explode.)

Soldiers faced other dangers in the trenches too. Snipers would wait for the opportunity to pick off any soldier who did not stay under cover. At Hooge, near Ypres, the trenches were just 15 metres apart and 500 British soldiers were killed when the Germans dug a tunnel and exploded a massive mine under the British trenches.

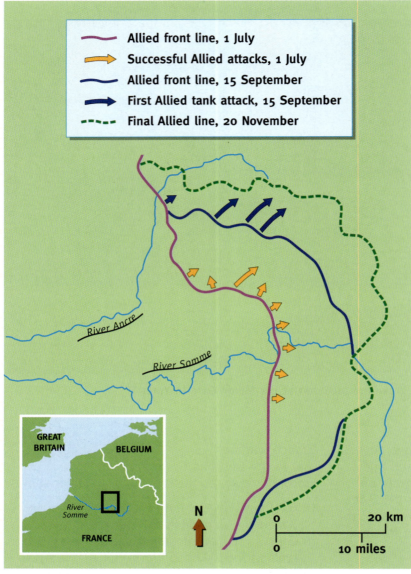

Legend:
- Allied front line, 1 July
- Successful Allied attacks, 1 July
- Allied front line, 15 September
- First Allied tank attack, 15 September
- Final Allied line, 20 November

River Ancre

River Somme

GREAT BRITAIN
BELGIUM
River Somme
FRANCE

N

0 — 20 km
0 — 10 miles

▲ The Battle of the Somme, 1916.

Daily routine

Although life in the trenches could be terrifying (and some men went mad), often it was very different, even boring. If no fighting was taking place, then the enemy changed. It was rats, fleas, mud, dirty water or illness such as bronchitis or pneumonia. One particularly unpleasant problem soldiers had to deal with was 'trench foot'. This was caused by feet being continually cold and wet. Soldiers' feet would swell up and blister. The condition was so painful that men would cry out in agony.

But if soldiers could remain healthy and were stationed in an area where there was no fighting, then their biggest problem could be boredom. The day would consist of trench maintenance and weapon cleaning. Perhaps they hated being bored. Perhaps they were grateful for it.

If a soldier was in an area where an attack was being launched, he knew what to expect. When a soldier was sent over the top, there was a 30 per cent chance of being killed and a 40 per cent change of being wounded. That meant it was twice as likely that he would not come back healthy as it was that he would!

General Haig

Douglas Haig became Commander-in-Chief of the British forces on the Western Front in December 1915. He believed that the war could be won by getting huge numbers of men to launch an attack on the German trenches at the same time. This was called the '**Big Push**'.

On 1 July 1916, Haig launched his big push at the Battle of the Somme. For almost a week British artillery had bombarded the German trenches. Then the British troops left their trenches and walked across No Man's Land. They walked because they were told that the artillery bombardment would have made sure that 'there won't even be a rat alive' in the German trenches.

What do we mean by 'stalemate' on the Western Front?

How did this stalemate happen?

But the artillery bombardment did not destroy the German trenches. As the soldiers advanced, the German machine guns opened fire. There were 70,000 British casualties on the first day.

The misery continues

The Battle of the Somme went on until the November rains made it impossible to advance across the battlefields. The British troops had advanced for about 5 miles (8 kilometres), but the Germans won the land back by the next spring. The cost had been terrible. The table below shows the number of soldiers killed, missing or wounded.

German	650,000
British	420,000
French	200,000
Total	1,270,000

That is about 158 casualties for every metre of land gained. Or to put it another way, there were one and a half casualties for each centimetre of land gained.

Haig was heavily criticised for the losses at the Somme, but argued that he had wanted a force twice the size to fight the battle. In 1917 he ordered another big push at Passchendaele, just North of Ypres. This time 4 miles (6.4 kilometres) was gained, across a battlefield of thick mud. When Haig visited the battlefield he said 'My God, did I send men to fight in that?'

The war at sea

Before the war, Germany and Britain had been involved in a 'Naval Arms Race' as each of them tried to build a bigger and stronger navy than the other. It is interesting to see that, when the fighting started, neither country wanted to risk losing their navy by having a major battle.

Jutland

The **British Grand Fleet** and the **German High Seas Fleet** met only once in open battle. This was at Jutland in 1916. During the battle more British ships were sunk or damaged than German ships. However, it was the Germans who first broke off the battle and returned to port.

The German fleet never left port again. So both sides were able to claim that they had won the battle!

Various other tactics were used to win control of the sea. The Germans used 'raiders'. These were cruisers which attacked British merchant shipping. (Remember that much of Britain's food came from abroad). After the Battle of Jutland, the Germans also adopted a policy of **unrestricted submarine warfare**. Any British ship, whether it was a warship or a merchant ship, was a legitimate target. One attack which caused tremendous protest was the sinking of the passenger liner, the *Lusitania* in 1915. Nearly 1200 people were drowned. The Germans said that the ship had been carrying weapons (see pages 10–11).

The British Prime Minister, Lloyd-George, had to introduce a convoy system with warships as escorts to protect merchant ships. But the British also used their warships to hit Germany's food supplies. They **blockaded** German ports so that German imports could not reach their destination. The complaints from the German people about food shortages were a major factor in persuading the German government to end the war in 1918.

The Gallipoli Campaign

Turkey had joined the war on Germany's side. Some British leaders, like Winston Churchill, thought that there was more chance of defeating Turkey than winning victory on the Western Front. Once Turkey was defeated, Germany's other major ally, Austria–Hungary, could be attacked. Then supplies could be sent to help Russia.

So, in April 1915, troops were landed on the Gallipoli peninsula in Turkey. They were mostly from Australia and New Zealand. Before the landings the British Navy had destroyed four Turkish forts at the entrance to the Dardanelles, a narrow opening into the Black Sea. But the landings did not happen promptly and the Turks had time to rebuild their defences.

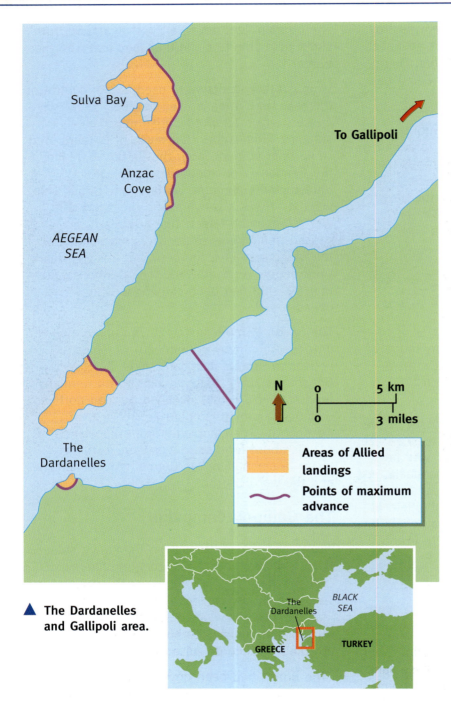

▲ **The Dardanelles and Gallipoli area.**

make much progress against the heavily fortified Turkish defences.

In the end, it was decided to withdraw the entire force. The evacuation was planned brilliantly and all the troops were safely withdrawn without a single death. It was really the only success in a disastrous campaign which had cost the lives of 150,000 troops through sickness or fighting.

The impact of new technology

The fact that it was so difficult to win the war on the Western Front made both sides look at new technology. They wanted to see if weapons could be invented that would help win the war somewhere away from the Western Front – saving the lives of hundreds of thousands of men. Or whether new weapons would make attacks on enemy trenches possible, without such heavy casualties.

Submarines

The Germans were concerned that the British Grand Fleet was too powerful to beat. But they knew that they had more submarines and hoped these could be used to sink merchant shipping, starving the British into surrendering.

When the landings happened at **Anzac Cove** the troops were a mile away from the planned landing site. Instead of a gentle slope, the attackers were faced by high cliffs. So the troops made little progress inland.

In August 1915 there was a second landing at Sulva Bay. Once again the troops were unable to

In 1914 German submarines sank three British warships in the North Sea. This gave them the confidence to launch their policy of unrestricted submarine warfare. In May they sank the *Lusitania*. The German Embassy in Washington had warned that the *Lusitania* would be attacked, but no-one believed it. Some 1198 passengers, including 124 Americans, were drowned.

▲ **A British tank crossing trenches in Flanders, September 1917.**

There was a tremendous outcry and the Kaiser decided that no more passenger ships should be attacked. The memory of the *Lusitania*, however, was one of the reasons for the USA joining the war on the Allies side in 1917.

Stop the submarines

By 1917 the Germans had 120 submarines and in the first three months of that year these sank more than 875,000 tonnes of Allied shipping. From May the British had to use their warships to protect convoys of merchant ships. They also laid mines across the English Channel. In addition, a number of armed ships (called 'Q-ships') were disguised as merchant ships to catch out German submarines. By the end of the year almost half the German submarines had been sunk and the danger was over.

Tanks

In 1916 the British introduced a new weapon to the Western Front. They hoped that this would make it easier for their soldiers to cross No Man's Land. On 15 September, 18 tanks took part in the Battle of the Somme. They were called 'tanks' because they had been smuggled to the front line disguised as water tanks.

The British had been developing the tank for some time, but some generals opposed their use. They said that these machines would frighten the cavalry horses. At the Somme, it was the German soldiers who were frightened. But not for too long. The muddy battlefield proved too difficult for the tanks, all of which eventually broke down.

▲ A painting of a German Zeppelin squadron.

More effective tanks

Tanks were first used successfully at the Battle of Cambrai in November 1917. The British used 380 tanks which broke through the terrified Germans' trenches. But the tanks had advanced so quickly that the troops could not keep up.

Later, in August 1918, 450 tanks drove the Germans back 8 miles (13 kilometres) at Amiens. This marked the beginning of a major German retreat until the war ended a few months later. But there were still problems with the tanks. Only 25 of the 450 were still working four days later. There was still a long way to go before tanks were as efficient as they are today.

Aircraft

In 1914 the aircraft was still a new form of transport and few people realised how important it would be in war. At first planes were used for **reconnaissance** (finding out about enemy positions etc). At this stage they were very flimsy machines, made out of wood and canvas. Soon, however, they were able to carry bombs, and civilians found themselves under attack from the sky. From late 1916 the Germans sent Gotha IV bombers to raid Britain. All together there were some 108 German raids, killing around 1400 people.

As well as bombers, the people also had to worry about German **Zeppelins**. These were huge air ships which floated across British skies and dropped bombs. It was not until 1916 that the first of these was shot down.

Dogfights

Dogfights began in France in 1915. These were aerial battles between fighter planes. The pilots of the fighter planes were called aces and some of them, such as the German Baron von Richthofen (the Red Baron) became very famous.

At first the Germans had the advantage in these fights because they had a device which meant that their guns could shoot through the propellor. But soon the British and French caught up. These dogfights marked the beginning of the aerial fighting that was to be so important in other wars.

Helping the soldiers

Army commanders realised that aircraft were very useful for identifying enemy positions and troop movement. For example, at the Battle of Vimy Ridge in 1917 aircraft had pinpointed almost all the Germany artillery positions. So, at the beginning of the battle, the Allies were able to knock out 80 per cent of the German guns.

Gas

On 22 April 1915 near Ypres the Germans first used a deadly new weapon. As it was so dangerous to send men across No Mans Land, how much better it would be if the enemy could be killed without your side having to do any fighting. This was what gas could do. The German gas attack in 1915 killed 9000 Allied soldiers. It looked like a deadly solution to the stalemate, but it soon turned out to be of limited value.

At first the only protection against gas was to urinate on a handkerchief and place it over your nose. Then **gas masks** were developed which solved the problem – as long as the masks were fitted in time. Gas was unpredictable because it relied on the wind. Sometimes the wind changed and blew the gas back on the attacking forces.

What problems did soldiers face in the trenches?

Why was the first day of the Somme such a disaster for the British?

The effectiveness of the gas mask and the problems with judging wind direction meant that, later in the war, gas was used only in surprise attacks. One of the last victims of gas was Adolf Hitler, who was temporarily blinded by gas in October 1918 and spent the last few weeks of the war in hospital.

US intervention: the collapse of Russia

The USA

The USA declared war on Germany in 1917. Many Americans, including President Wilson, had wanted to keep the USA out of the war. There were many hundreds of people from Britain, France, Germany and Austria–Hungary in the USA. Joining the war was bound to offend some of them. By 1917, however, the submarine attacks and attempts by Germany to get Mexico to attack the USA persuaded the Americans to support the Allies.

Russia

The US entry occurred just before the Russian departure. In 1917 there were revolutions in Russia which brought about the overthrow of the Tsar. The **Bolsheviks**, led by Lenin, took control. But they were opposed by the '**Whites**' in a bloody civil war. The Bolsheviks could not fight the Whites and the Germans at the same time. So they made a peace treaty with the Germans (The Treaty of Brest–Litovsk, March 1918). This was bad news for the Allies because the Germans were able to move a million men from Russia to fight on the Western Front.

The end approaches

The Germans on the Western Front had reinforcements from Russia and they knew that the USA would soon be sending forces to Europe. So they gambled on a last 'big push' to win the war quickly. In March 1918 they launched '**Operation Michael**'. The huge attack drove the Allies back 50 miles (80 kilometres), but the advance was halted in June by French and American troops.

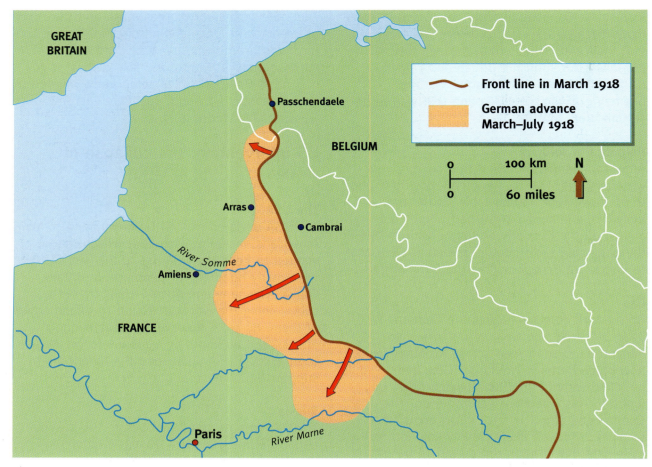

▲ The advance of German forces during Operation Michael.

The defeat of Germany and the Peace Settlement

After helping halt the German advance in 1918, the USA played a major part in the battles of September and October, which brought Germany close to surrender. The 1.25 million US soldiers provided a major boost to the Allied forces. In August 1918 the Allies attacked the Germans at Amiens and defeated them so heavily that the Germans called it a **'Black Day'**. For the next three months the Allied forces advanced steadily and, by September, the German commanders were convinced that defeat was inevitable.

However, in October 1918, Ludendorff took command of the German forces on the Western Front. He believed that the Germans should hold out until the spring of 1919 and then launch another attack. Despite this, the German government began talking to the Allies about terms for an **Armistice** (end to fighting). President Wilson had drawn up a list of **Fourteen Points** which he hoped would be the basis for helping keep peace in the world in the future. The Germans were sure that, at the end of the war, these Fourteen Points would be used to help draw up the peace treaty.

Whatever Ludendorff thought, by the winter of 1918 the situation in Germany was desperate. The Allied naval blockade meant that people were starving and there were demonstrations in the streets. On 7 November there was an attempted Communist revolution. The Germans knew that they had to surrender, but that this might be difficult for the Kaiser to do. So he stood down and went to live in exile.

The Terms of the Treaty of Versailles

- **Land**
  Germany lost about 10 per cent of its land. Alsace-Lorraine was given to France and the 'Polish Corridor' was set up to give the new country of Poland access to the sea. This cut Germany in two. Land was also lost to Belgium and Denmark. The Saar coalfield was given to France for 15 years. Germany was not allowed to ally with Austria–Hungary.

- **Colonies**
  All Germany's colonies were taken away and handed to Britain and France to look after until they were ready for independence.

- **Armed forces**
  The German army was reduced to just 100,000 men and conscription was banned. The Air Force was destroyed and the Navy reduced to six ships (and no submarines). The Rhineland area (next to France) was **demilitarised**. No German forces were allowed within 30 miles (50 kilometres) of the border.

- **War guilt and reparations**
  Germany was made to agree that it was to blame for War (Article 231). Therefore, it had to pay **reparations** to those countries which had suffered damage. In 1921 it was decided that this cost was £6600 million which was to be paid in installments throughout the twentieth century.

The German government then surrendered and at 11 am on 11 November 1918. The war ended.

The Treaty of Versailles

After the war, the victorious Allies met at the palace of Versailles to decide what should go in the peace treaty. The main decision-makers at Versailles were the '**Big Three**'. These were:

- President Woodrow Wilson of the USA

- David Lloyd-George, Prime Minister of Britain

- Georges Clemenceau, Prime Minister of France

The Germans were not allowed to attend any of the meetings. They had been defeated and had no say in what would happen to them after the war. When they first saw the terms of the Treaty of Versailles they were horrified. President Wilson's Fourteen Points had not been used to decide the terms for peace. Instead the treaty-makers had been most influenced by Clemenceau. His attitude was that Germany should be punished for what had happened in the war.

The Germans were so angry about the Treaty that they thought about restarting the war, but this was impossible.

In what ways were aircraft used during the First World War?

Why did the USA declare war on Germany in April 1917?

Why did Germany collapse so quickly in 1918?

Why were the Germans horrified at the terms of the Treaty of Versailles?

The failure of the Schlieffen Plan

Source A

The Germans advanced in companies of 150 men five deep, and our rifle has a flat trajectory up to 600 yards. Guess the result. We could steady our rifles on the trench and take deliberate aim. The first company was simply blasted away to Heaven, and in their insane formation every bullet was bound to kill two men. The other companies kept advancing very slowly, using the bodies of their dead comrades as cover, but they had absolutely no chance.

▲ A British soldier describes the opening of the Battle of Mons on 23 August 1914.

Source B

One must face facts. Our Army Corps, in spite of the numerical superiority, which was assured to them, have not shown on the battlefield those offensive qualities, which we had hoped for ... We are therefore compelled to resort to the defensive ... Our object must be to last out as long as possible, trying to wear out the enemy, and to resume the offensive when the time comes.

▲ From a report written by the French General, Joffre, to the French Minister of War on 24 August 1914.

Source C

I had come to the conclusion that the great decisive battle in the West had been fought and decided in Germany's favour. I had intended to take these reinforcements from the Seventh Army, which had made as little progress towards the Moselle as the Sixth. Both these armies, however, consistently reported that they were opposed by superior numbers of the enemy, also that losses had been so heavy that no units of the Seventh Army were fit for employment elsewhere until they had been brought up to strength again. For these reasons, it was decided to send two Corps from the right wing ... to the Eastern Front. I admit that this was a mistake and one that was fully paid for on the Marne.

▲ From the memoirs of Von Moltke, describing his actions on 25–26 August 1914, when he sent reinforcements from the West to the Eastern Front.

Source D

Year	Right flank in Belgium	Left flank in Alsace-Lorraine
1905	54	8
1912	75	11
1914	54	17

▲ The numbers of German infantry divisions in the Schlieffen Plan.

Source E

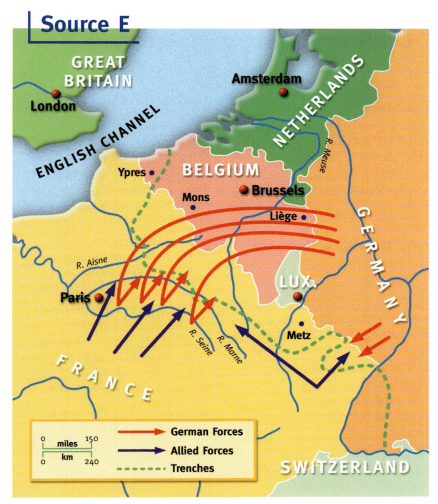

▲ The routes taken by the German Army in August and September 1914.

Map legend:
- German Forces (red arrow)
- Allied Forces (blue arrow)
- Trenches (green dashed line)

Scale: 0–150 miles, 0–240 km

Source F

The numerically superior German units made deep inroads into the Allied lines, but never succeeded in breaking through. Their final defeat in the middle of November was principally a British victory. The English infantrymen, all professional soldiers, had mastered rapid rifle shooting to such an extent that the Germans suspected great numbers of British machine guns where there were hardly any. Many British marksmen could discharge 30 rounds a minute. The Allies were also helped by the determined stand of the Belgian King, Albert, who did not hesitate to have the lock gates of the canalised Yser River opened at Nieuport.

▲ From a modern history book.

Study Source A

a What can you learn from Source A about the German advance into Belgium in August 1914? (4)

Study Sources A, B and C

b Does the evidence of Source C support the evidence of Sources A and B about the German attacks in August 1914? Explain your answer. (6)

Study Sources D and E

c How useful are these sources in helping you to understand why the Schlieffen Plan failed? (8)

Study all of the sources

d 'The Schlieffen Plan failed because the Germans were outnumbered and made tactical errors.' Use the sources and your own knowledge to explain whether you agree with this view. (12)

Stalemate, trench warfare and Haig

Source A

The three main objectives with which we had commenced our offensive in July had already been achieved ... Verdun had been relieved; the main German forces had been held on the Western Front; and the enemy's strength had been very considerably worn down.

▲ From the despatch written by Haig after the Battle of the Somme.

Source B

Far from the German loss being the greater, the British army was being worn down – numerically – more than twice as fast, and the loss is not just to be measured by bare numbers.
The troops who bore the brunt of the Somme fighting were the cream of the British population – the new volunteer army ...
A general who wears down 180,000 of his enemy by expending 400,000 men has something to answer for.

▲ From the *Official History of Australia in the War*, by C.E.W. Bean.

Source C

It is not too much to say that when the Great War broke out our Generals had the most important lessons to learn. They knew nothing except by hearsay about the actual fighting of a battle under modern conditions. Haig ordered many bloody battles in this war. He only took part in two. He never even saw the ground on which his greatest battles were fought, either before or during the fight.

▲ From the war memoirs of David Lloyd George.

Source D

▲ A British trench in the Somme.

Source E

Before going in to this next affair, at the same dreadful spot, I want to tell you, so that it may be on record, that I honestly believe Goldy [his brother] and many other officers were murdered on the night you know of, through the incompetence, callousness and personal vanity of those in high authority. I realise the seriousness of what I say, but I am so bitter, and the facts are so palpable that it must be said.

▲ From the last letter written by Lieutenant John Raws to his mother on 19 August 1916, during the Battle of the Somme. He was killed later in the same month.

Source F

	Haig's estimates	Actually available
Divisions	36	18
Guns	828	400
Roads	29	13
Railways	7	3

▲ A comparison of Haig's original estimates of men and equipment needed for the Battle of the Somme and what was actually available on 1 July 1916. Haig's estimates are taken from papers he wrote during 1915.

Study Source A

a   What can you learn from Source A about Haig's view of the Battle of the Somme? (4)

Study Sources A, B and C

b   Does the evidence of Source C support the evidence of Sources A and B? Explain your answer. (6)

Study Sources D and E

c   How useful are these sources as evidence about Haig's role in the Battle of the Somme? (8)

Study all of the sources

d   'The failure of the Battle of the Somme was the result of bad planning by Haig.' Use the sources and your own knowledge to explain whether you agree with this view. (12)

The war at sea / The Gallipoli campaign

Source A

The departure from Mudros was to the accompaniment of wild cheering ... The troops were then told to rest; there was no wild excitement, but an air of quiet confidence. Very early on the morning of 25 April the men were roused and given a hearty meal before struggling into their kit ... Each man carried about 80 pounds, but instructions were to remove packs after landing and stack them in company piles ... Not a shot was to be fired ... Absolute silence was ordered until ashore, when only the bayonet was to be used.

▲ **From a description of the landings at Anzac Cove written by Private Fred Fox.**

Source B

The flotilla was nearly on shore when the senior naval officer realised a grave error had been made. The brigade was one full mile north of its intended landing place when at 4.25, with dawn clearly breaking ... they were only 50 yards from the beach, and at this moment the Turks saw them ... Instead of the gentle slope the troops had been led to expect, and the bank behind which they were going to form up and leave their packs, they were confronted by what appeared to be a steep cliff rising immediately off a narrow sandy beach.

▲ **Another description of the landings on 25/26 April 1915, from a modern book on Gallipoli.**

Source C

▲ **A photograph of Anzac Cove.**

Source D

'Y Beach', the Scottish Borderer cried

While panting up the steep hillside,

'Y Beach!

To call this thing a beach is stiff,

It's nothing but a b----- cliff.

Why beach?'

▲ A verse that appeared in the *Dardanelles Driveller*, a newspaper, on 17 May 1915.

Source E

How GHQ thought that to land the whole of the 11th Division in the dark on a strange shore and a few hours afterward land two brigades of the 10th Division on top of them could possibly be successful, passes the comprehension of even a junior officer ... At the actual landing my battalion lost the senior major, two captains and the adjutant killed and twelve officers wounded. I never saw my colonel for two days.

▲ A description of the landing at Sulva Bay in August 1915.

Source F

A week lost was about the same as a division. Three divisions in February would have occupied the Gallipoli peninsula with little fighting. Five would have captured it after 18 March. Seven were insufficient by the end of April, but nine might just have done it. Eleven might have sufficed at the beginning of July. Fourteen were to prove insufficient in August.

▲ From a book written by Winston Churchill after the war.

Study Source A

a What can you learn from Source A about the landings on Gallipoli in April 1915? (4)

Study Sources A, B and C

b Do Sources B and C support the evidence of Source A about the landings on Gallipoli? In your answer refer to all three sources. (6)

Study Sources D and E

c How useful are these sources in helping you to understand the problems faced by the Allied troops at Gallipoli? (8)

Study all of the sources

d 'The Gallipoli landings failed because the plans were badly carried out.' Use the sources and your own knowledge to explain whether you agree with this view. (12)

The impact of new technology

Source A

The monsters approached slowly. Nothing impeded them. Someone in the trenches said, 'The Devil is coming.' Tongues of flame leapt from the sides of the iron caterpillars. The English infantry came in waves behind.

▲ From a German description of the use of tanks at the Battle of Cambrai on 20 November 1917.

Source B

The news continues to be good, the tanks seem to have done good work and fairly put the wind up the Hun, who was seen to run like hell in front of them, shouting, 'This isn't war, it's murder.'

▲ From a letter written by a British officer in 1917.

Source C

▲ A painting of a tank crossing a trench.

Source D

Four hundred tanks in line of battle. Good going, firm ground, wheel to wheel and blazing brilliant weather. They crash through the barbed wire and bridge the trenches dealing death and retribution on the way.

The front line now, we swing her round, broadside on, a canister of shrapnel is poured into the huddling German troops. We trip merrily on, the six-pounder volleying shell after shell into the trench. The machine gunners firing as the Germans run for it.

▲ From an article in *The Fighting Forces Magazine*, describing a tank attack at the Battle of Amiens on 8 August 1918.

Source E

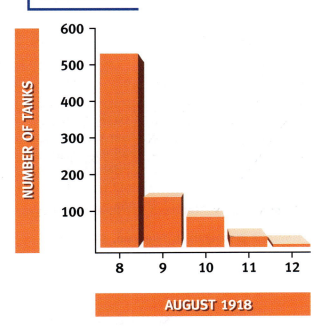

The numbers of tanks in working order at the Battle of Amiens, 8–12 August 1918.

Source F

Their effect was largely on morale. They did a good service in crushing machine-gun posts and in village fighting. The infantry liked to see them, and as the enemy has invariably exaggerated the numbers employed, and has often reported their presence when there was none, he evidently stood in fear of them.

▲ A British general describing the impact of tanks in 1918.

Study Source A

a What can you learn from Source A about the impact of tanks on German troops in November 1917? (4)

Study Sources A, B and C

b Do Sources B and C support the evidence of Source A about the impact of tanks? (6)

Study Sources D and E

c How useful are these sources in helping you to understand the impact of tanks in 1918? (8)

Study all of the sources

d 'Tanks were a decisive weapon in the final battles of the First World War.' Use the sources and your own knowledge to explain whether you agree with this view. (12)

US intervention: the collapse of Russia

Source A

We have no quarrel with the German people. We have no selfish ends to serve. We desire no conquest. We are but one of the champions of the rights of mankind. We shall fight for democracy, for the rights and liberties of small nations.

▲ From a speech made by Woodrow Wilson on 2 April 1917.

Source B

If this attempt is not successful, we propose an alliance on the following basis with Mexico: that we shall make war together and together make peace. We shall give general financial support, and it is understood that Mexico is to reconquer the lost territory in New Mexico, Texas and Arizona.

▲ From the Zimmermann Telegram, sent to the German Embassy in Mexico City in February 1917.

Source C

The rear was brought up by an enormous motor-bus load of the first American soldiers to pass through the streets of Paris. The crowds overflowed the sidewalks. From the crowded balconies and windows overlooking the route, women and children tossed down showers of flowers and bits of coloured paper.

Old grey-haired fathers of French fighting men bared their heads and with tears streaming down their cheeks shouted greetings to the tall, thin, grey-moustached American commander.

▲ From *And they thought we wouldn't fight,* a book written by a US soldier in the First World War.

Source D

▲ A photograph of US troops in 1918.

Source E

The sudden and dramatic entrance of the 2nd and 3rd Divisions into the shattered and broken fighting lines and their dash and courage in battle produced a favourable effect on the French soldiers. Although in battle for the first time, our men maintained their positions and effectively stopped the German advance on Paris. The Germans, who had been filled with propaganda about the poor quality of our training and war effort, must have been surprised at the strong resistance offered by the Americans.

▲ From the war memoirs of General John J. Pershing, the Commander of the US forces during the First World War. He is describing the first US actions in the spring of 1918.

Source F

From the Allied point of view, the US entered the war just in time. France had fought herself to a standstill. Britain, reeling from the shock of losing virtually an entire generation of young men, was desperately short of both soldiers and munitions. Worse still, the Tsar's government had been overthrown by revolution in March 1917.

▲ From a modern history textbook.

Study Source A

a What can you learn from Source A about the reasons why the USA declared war on Germany in 1917? (4)

Study Sources A and B

b In what ways does Source B add to the evidence of Source A about the reasons for the US declaration of war? (6)

Study Sources C and D

c How useful are Sources C and D as evidence about the impact of the US forces in France? (8)

Study all of the sources

d 'It was the entry of the USA into the First World War that brought about the final defeat of Germany.' Use the sources and your own knowledge to explain whether you agree with this view. (12)

The defeat of Germany and the Peace Settlement

Source A

July was a glorious month for the Allies, and August is even better. It began with the recovery of Soissons; a week later it was the turn of the British ... The 8th of August was a bad day for Germany for it showed that the counter-offensive was not to be confined to one sector, that from now on no respite would be allowed from hammer-blows.

▲ From an article in *Punch*, August 1918.

Source B

As the sun set on 8 August on the battlefield, the greatest defeat which the German Army had suffered since the beginning of the war was an accomplished fact. The positions between the Avre and the Somme, which had been struck by the enemy attack, were nearly completely annihilated.

▲ From the official German Army report on 8 August 1918.

Source C

August was the blackest day of the German army in the history of this war. This was the worst experience that I had to go through, except for the events that, from 15 September onwards, took place on the Bulgarian Front.

We had to resign ourselves now to the prospect of a continuation of the enemy's offensive. Their success had been too easily gained. Their wireless was jubilant, and announced – and with truth – that the morale of the German Army was no longer what it had been.

▲ From the war memoirs of General Erich Ludendorff.

Source D

These Armistice negotiations are having very bad consequences, since my soldiers can't see why they should continue fighting if they have to give up Belgium and Alsace-Lorraine. If we had battalions of full strength, the situation would be saved.

Yesterday we had a battle at Ypres. We were driven back, but came out well. It is true that gaps of four kilometres were broken in our line, but the enemy did not push through and we held the front. How much reinforcements from home would have meant to us.

▲ From a report by General Erich Ludendorff to the German Cabinet in Berlin on 17 October 1918.

Source E

The morale of the troops has suffered considerably and their power of resistance is declining steadily. The men are surrendering in droves during enemy attacks ... We have no more dug-in positions and cannot build them any longer ... I want to emphasise that already at this moment our position is an extremely dangerous one, and according to circumstances, may turn into a catastrophe overnight. Ludendorff does not realise the seriousness of the situation.

▲ From a letter written by Prince Rupprecht of Bavaria, the commander of the German Sixth Army, to Prince Max von Baden, the German Chancellor, on 18 October 1918.

Source F

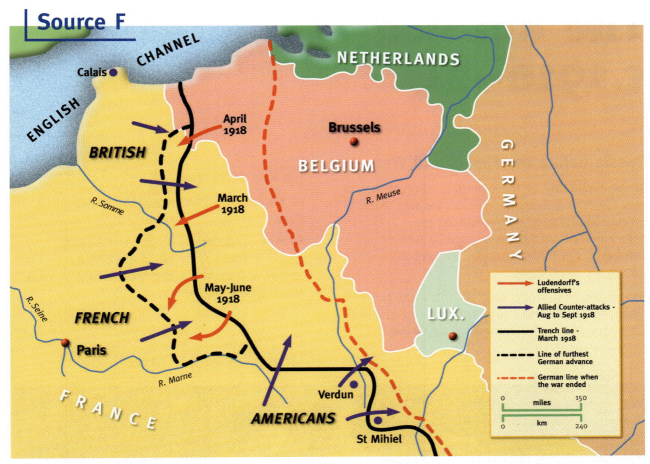

▲ A map showing the movements of the armies from August to November 1918.

Map legend:
- → Ludendorff's offensives
- → Allied Counter-attacks - Aug to Sept 1918
- ▬ Trench line - March 1918
- ▪▪▪ Line of furthest German advance
- ▪▪▪ German line when the war ended

0 ___ miles ___ 150
0 ___ km ___ 240

Study Source A

a What can you learn from Source A about the Allied attacks on 8 August 1918? (4)

Study Sources A, B and C

b Does the evidence of Source C support the evidence of Sources A and B? Explain your answer. (6)

Study Sources D and E

c How useful are these sources as evidence about the German Army in late 1918? (8)

Study all of the sources

d 'The German Army was defeated in 1918 through sheer weight of numbers.' Use the sources and your own knowledge to explain whether you agree with this view. (12)

CHAPTER 2

The Russian Revolution: C.1910~24

Essential Information

Russia before the First World War

At the beginning of the twentieth century Russia was ruled by a **Tsar**, Nicholas II. He was a kind, loving, family man, but he lacked the determination and perseverance to rule an Empire of 130 million people, and he was eventually overthrown.

Before the First World War, Nicholas had total power in Russia. He could appoint and dismiss members of the government as he wished.

The Rule of the Tsar

All power in Russia was in the hands of the Tsar.

He was an **autocrat**. He appointed and dismissed ministers, decided on when to go to war and used a secret police to deal with any criticism of the way he ruled.

Source 1

▲ Tsar Nicholas II and his family.

In 1905 a revolution had broken out in St. Petersburg, after which Nicholas had been forced to set up a **Duma** (parliament). But he didn't let it have any real power. Soon Nicholas began to ignore the Duma all together.

Autocracy

Nicholas believed that he was ruler of Russia because God had chosen him. It was his duty to maintain the power of the Tsar and pass it on to his son. So he soon began to ignore the Duma. He also appointed the hard-line Peter Stolypin as Prime Minister and took harsh measures against troublemakers. Russia remained a country where there were extreme differences between rich and poor, and where only the Tsar and a handful of chosen ministers had any say in how the country was run.

More than 80 per cent of its citizens were peasants, most of whom could not read and write. But they were very loyal to the Tsar, whom they addressed as 'Papa'. When war broke out in 1914 vast numbers of these peasants showed their loyalty to 'Mother Russia' by volunteering to join the Army.

Changes in Russia

However, things were not quite as they seemed. Russia was changing.

- Between 1800 and 1890 the population of Moscow doubled. As people moved to the cities, conditions got worse and there were food shortages. Russia grew enough food for its population, but did not have the transport to get it to where it was needed.

- Opposition to the Tsar was also starting to grow. In a country where the government cannot be changed by voting, the opposition often has to resort to violence. Nicholas's grandfather, Alexander II, had been killed in a bomb attack. So Nicholas knew how dangerous the opposition groups could be.

Opposition to Tsarist rule

There were three main opposition groups in Russia:

1. The **Social Revolutionaries** had the support of most of the peasants. Between 1900 and 1905 the group carried out more than 2000 murders.

2. The **Social Democrats** (SD) were popular in the cities where bad working and living conditions made the workers discontented. In 1903 the SD split into two groups – the Mensheviks and the Bolsheviks (led by Lenin).

3. The **Constitutional Democrats** (or Kadets or Octobrists) were mainly middle-class professionals, like lawyers and teachers. They wanted to work with the Tsar and the Duma to bring gradual change.

All of these opposition groups followed the beliefs of Karl Marx (so we call them **Marxist**). He believed that property should be shared more equally and each person should be paid what his or her work was worth to the community.

The Bolsheviks, led by Lenin, were the most committed and most disciplined of the opposition groups. This was one of the reasons why they were able to overthrow the Tsar and seize power in 1917.

But, at the outbreak of war in 1914, no-one would have guessed that this would happen. The Tsar's secret police (the **Okhrana**) had broken up the opposition groups, many of whom had fled into exile. Lenin himself was in Switzerland, waiting for the chance to return to Russia.

The Constitutional Democrats had been founded in 1905. They did not have revolutionary ideas, and feared what Lenin and the Bolsheviks wanted to do. They believed that the Tsar could be persuaded to make changes which would improve conditions in Russia and give people more involvement in the government of their country.

They strongly supported what Nicholas had promised in the **October Manifesto**. This is why they were sometimes know as 'Octobrists'. They worked hard to get their members elected to the Duma and to campaign for change through the new parliament. In the years 1905–1914 the Tsar took less and less notice of what the Duma said, the Octobrists did not have very much influence in Russia. This was particularly true in the years 1911–14 when the Russian economy grew rapidly and there was a period of increased prosperity. Then came war.

The impact of the First World War

In 1914 Nicholas declared war on Germany. Two weeks later Russian troops invaded Germany and caught the Germans by surprise. It looked like victory was going to be easy and that the Tsar would win great glory for his country's achievements in war.

But the Russian success did not last long. The Germans soon counter-attacked and revealed serious weaknesses in the Russian armed forces. Generals did not co-operate and were often more concerned with personal glory than gaining victory. Maps were years out of date and messages were sent without code – so the Germans heard them too!

Russia was not really equipped for a modern war. By the end of 1914 there were 6.5 million men in the Army, but only 4.5 million rifles. Not surprisingly, when the Germans attacked, the Russians were quickly defeated and forced back into their own country.

The Tsar takes command
Russia's huge Army needed supplies of food and ammunition, but the railway system was incapable of transporting it all to the war zone. It was also incapable of bringing back the vast numbers of casualties. The Tsar saw how bad the situation was and in September 1915 made a brave decision. He would go to the Front and take personal command of the forces. The troops' morale would be lifted by having their Tsar at the Front.

The October Manifesto

In 1905 Russia was heavily defeated in a war against Japan. This led to strikes and demonstrations in Russia, especially in the capital, St. Petersburg. Nicholas had to agree to issue a document called the October Manifesto. It gave the Russian people freedom of speech, the vote and a parliament. Soon Nicholas began to ignore the manifesto.

What do we mean when we say Nicholas was an 'autocrat'?

Why do you think so many peasants loved Nicholas?

But the Tsar's decision was not a wise one:

- As he would be in charge of the Army, if there were more defeats, he would have to take the blame for them.

- As he would be away from the capital, he could not govern effectively. He would have to leave others in charge and rely on them for accurate information on what was happening.

At first things seemed to go well for the Tsar. More railway was built, and food and supplies reached the Army. The Russian forces went on to attack and took 300,000 Austrian prisoners. However, they could not break through into Germany. A stalemate developed on the **Eastern Front**, just like the one in the West.

In Petrograd (as St. Petersburg was now called – the original name sounded too German) the government was becoming increasingly unpopular. The Tsar's wife, Tsarina Alexandra was German and there were rumours that she was a spy.

The Tsarina was also relying on a strange 'holy man', Grigori Rasputin. He claimed to be able to cure the Tsar's son's haemophilia and the Tsarina listened to every word he said. Soon he was telling her which ministers to appoint or suggesting how the Tsar should fight the war.

Both Rasputin and the Tsarina became detested by the ruling class in Petrograd and in December 1916 Rasputin was murdered. But his murder was really just a sideshow. The country was facing much more serious problems. Inefficient running of the railways meant that at the end of 1916, Petrograd was running out of food. Workers were needing to work harder and harder to produce goods for the war, but were receiving less food and were living in terrible conditions. Conditions were just right for a revolution.

1917: the fall of the Tsar

By January 1917 the situation in Petrograd had become desperate. Prices were rising, there were food shortages and the Tsarina was rumoured to be a German spy. Nicholas was sent regular reports by the President of the Duma telling him how bad things were. But Nicholas also received letters from the Tsarina telling him that things were not as bad as people said. There were minor incidents, but they would soon pass. The Tsar believed his wife. It was a mistake.

During February 1917 there were strikes and demonstrations which brought Petrograd to a standstill. At first the crowds were kept under control by soldiers. As the crowds grew and became more undisciplined, the soldiers were ordered to fire on them. They were not prepared to do this and began to mutiny. Soon a worker's council called the **Petrograd Soviet** was giving orders and the soldiers were obeying it, not the government.

Furthest line of Russian advance into Germany

Furthest line of German advance into Russia (by 1918)

Russian territory lost 1914–16

RUSSIA

BALTIC SEA

Masurian Lakes

Tannenberg

GERMANY

POLAND

AUSTRIA-HUNGARY

0   160 km

0   100 miles

N

▲ **Map showing the battles of 1914.**

Within days, the authority of the Tsar had collapsed. He considered using his troops to attack Petrograd, but doubted that they would remain loyal. So on 2 March 1917 he **abdicated**. The rule of the Tsars had come to an end in what has become known as the '**February Revolution**'.

The Provisional Government

Immediately after the abdication, a **Provisional** (temporary) **Government** took command. It was made up of members of the Duma. But it had little authority outside Petrograd. Even within Petrograd it had a rival in the Petrograd Soviet. So it had a very difficult task ahead of it – and it soon made some serious errors. The people wanted an end to the war, more food and land of their own to farm. The Provisional Government could not supply any of these things.

More revolution!

In April 1917 Lenin returned to Russia from Switzerland. Lenin was helped back by the Germans who hoped that he would cause unrest, making it harder for the Russians to fight in the war against Germany. They might even drop out.

Lenin knew what the people wanted and issued a document called the '**April Theses**'. He said that he and his followers would provide the Russian people with 'Peace, Bread and Land', though he did not say how he would do this. The Bolsheviks tried to overthrow the Provisional Government in May 1917 and later in July. They were unsuccessful. For his own safety Lenin had to flee, in disguise, to Finland.

Kerensky

In July 1917 Alexander Kerensky became the Prime Minister of the Provisional Government. In September an army general, Kornilov, tried to overthrow the Provisional Government and put himself in charge. Kerensky was desperate for help. He turned to the Bolsheviks. Those in prison were let out and were given arms to fight Kornilov. He was easily defeated.

But Kerensky had another problem now. Support for the Bolsheviks was growing and they had won control of the Petrograd Soviet and of other soviets in other cities in Russia. They were just waiting for the best time to seize power.

The Bolshevik takeover

In September, when Lenin was still in Finland, it was Trotsky who played the most important part in preparing for the Bolshevik takeover.

Source 2

▲ A demonstration against poor living conditions in Petrograd, 1917.

Trotsky's importance increased when he became chairman of the Military Committee of the Petrograd Soviet. Lenin returned to Russia on 16 October and on 24/25 October the Bolsheviks seized power. They cut telegraph wires and took control of the railway stations and other key buildings. They were then ready to attack the government headquarters in the Winter Palace.

In later years, Bolshevik propaganda made out that the revolution was a glorious victory against the forces of the Provisional Government. In fact things were a little different. The government was so unpopular that, when Kerensky appealed to the Army for help, only a few hundred soldiers turned up. Amongst these were students, 140 women and 40 soldiers who had been crippled by wounds. It was no great surprise that within two days the Bolsheviks were in control in Petrograd.

The failure of the Provisional Government

- The Provisional Government was largely ignored outside Petrograd and had a powerful rival – the Petrograd Soviet.

- It did not end the War with Germany.

- It did not take land from the wealthy and give it to the peasants.

- It did nothing to end food shortages.

Bolshevik rule and its impact

It was Trotsky who led the forces which took control of Petrograd but, once the Bolsheviks had seized power, their leader returned. Lenin set up a temporary government and appointed himself Prime Minister. He straight away issued two **decrees**.

1. The **Peace Decree** said that the war was over and negotiations with Germany would begin immediately.

2. The **Land Decree** said that all land belonging to the Church or government was to be handed over to the peasants immediately. They could also take any land belonging to landlords that was not being used for farming.

The Petrograd Soviet

This was a committee, set up in 1917, to represent workers and soldiers in the city.

Its leaders were elected – which was very unusual in Russia at the time!

It made sure that any measures proposed by the Provisional Government which it did not like did not happen.

When the Bolsheviks took power in October 1917, the Soviet was taken over by them.

Source 3

▲ **A painting of Lenin's return to Petrograd in April 1917.**

By doing this, Lenin showed he realised that the war and failure to give the peasants land had helped bring down the Provisional Government. He was not going to make the same mistake.

On 12 November 1917 the first ever General Election took place in Russia. The people of Russia voted for members to form a new parliament called the **Constituent Assembly**. The results are shown below.

Why did the Tsar have so little understanding of what was going on in Russia in early 1917?

Why do you think soldiers refused to shoot on the demonstrators in Petrograd in 1917?

What problems did the Provisional Government face?

Why did the Germans help Lenin return to Russia in 1917?

Here are the results of the General Election, 12 November 1917.

POLITICAL PARTY	SHARE OF VOTE WON	NUMBER OF SEATS WON
Bolsheviks	24% of the vote	175 seats
Social Revolutionaries	40% of the vote	340 seats

This was not what Lenin wanted. His political rivals had won the election!

Taking control

Lenin was now faced with two choices:

1. To hand over power to the Social Revolutionaries

2. To ignore the election result and go on governing.

He put off the decision until 5 January 1918. On that day the Assembly met for the first time. When it would not accept Bolshevik control, Lenin closed it down. Any opposition to the closure was met with force. The Bolsheviks had not staged a revolution just to hand over power to the Social Revolutionaries.

Lenin took other steps to ensure he had control of Russia. A decree on the press banned all newspapers except those published by the Bolsheviks. Then Lenin set up the '**Cheka**'. This was his secret police force which dealt with any opposition to the Bolsheviks (or **Communists** as they renamed themselves in 1918). Some people said that Lenin's rule was just as autocratic as that of Nicholas. They called him 'the Red Tsar' – but not in public!

Source 4

▲ Films have been made about the Bolshevik seizure of power – this scene shows the storming of the Winter Palace.

Economic changes

At first Lenin introduced committees of workers to run factories and businesses. Sometimes the entire workforce just took control. As they had so little experience, they were usually not very good at running things effectively and the economy suffered. Soon there were food shortages and Lenin was forced to introduce a policy called '**War Communism**' (see page 37).

Civil War

Although the Bolsheviks had taken over in Petrograd and much of Western Russia, there were still huge areas where they were not in control. These areas were dominated by the Bolsheviks' opponents. These might be supporters of the Tsar, supporters of the Provisional Government or just people who did not approve of Bolsheviks.

Also opposing the Bolsheviks were foreign countries such as Britain, the USA and France. They did not approve of Lenin taking Russia out of the war (because it would free up German troops in the East to fight on the Western Front) – and they did not approve of Lenin's decision to cancel repayment of all loans made to Russia before the revolution. So these countries sent aid to the **Whites** in Russia (as opponents of Lenin's **Red Army** were called) to fight in a civil war to see who would govern Russia.

Turning the tide

At first it looked like the Whites might win the civil war. They had experienced commanders and support from foreign countries, but the Bolsheviks were soon able to gain the upper hand. Why was this?

- The Bolsheviks had a great organiser in Trotsky who was responsible for making the Red Army an efficient fighting force.

- Trotsky used captured White officers to run the Red Army (of course he threatened them and their families if they didn't command properly). He also used **conscription** to make the Red Army 2 million men strong. This was much larger than the Whites' forces.

- The Bolsheviks did not control the majority of Russia, but they did have Petrograd and Moscow, the main centres of industry, and control of the railways.

The events of 1917

March
Tsar abdicates
Formation of Provisional Government
Election of Petrograd Soviet

April
Lenin returns from Switzerland
April Theses

May
Unsuccessful Bolshevik takeover

June
Provisional Government orders attack on Germany

July
'July Days' second failed Bolshevik takeover
Lenin flees

August
Kornilov tries to overthrow the Provisional Government

September
Trotsky becomes a member of MCOPS

October
Lenin returns to Russia
Bolsheviks seize power

November
First ever General Election in Russia

- The Bolsheviks were one group who knew what they believed in. The Whites were different groups with different beliefs and often quarrelled amongst themselves.

- The Bolsheviks also introduced War Communism to help win the war. Everything and everybody came second to the needs of the Red Army. It had first call on food, raw materials and industrial goods. This caused terrible hardship for civilians, but it helped win the civil war.

- The Cheka ensured that there was little opposition in Bolshevik controlled areas. More than 50,000 people were shot without trial.

- Some of the Whites lost heart when the Tsar and the rest of the royal family were executed in July 1918. Their bodies were thrown down a mine shaft and not recovered until the 1990s.

These factors all helped the Bolsheviks to win the civil war, but it was at a terrible cost. It has been estimated that by the time the war finished in 1921, 5 million people had starved to death.

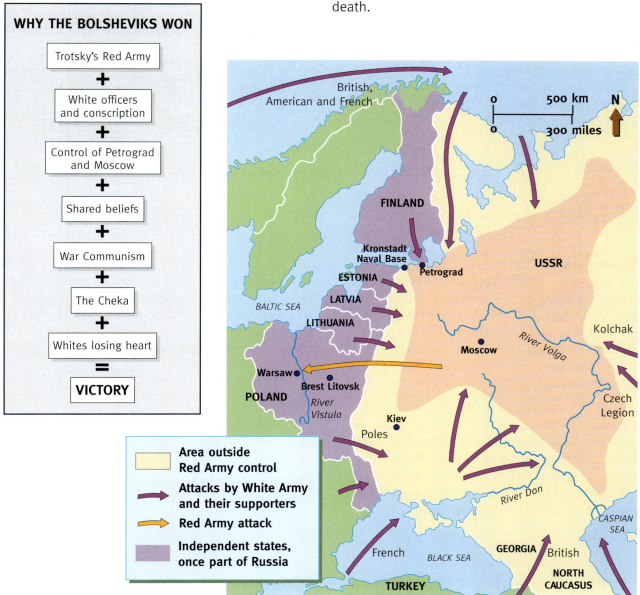

WHY THE BOLSHEVIKS WON

Trotsky's Red Army

+

White officers and conscription

+

Control of Petrograd and Moscow

+

Shared beliefs

+

War Communism

+

The Cheka

+

Whites losing heart

=

VICTORY

Legend:
- Area outside Red Army control
- Attacks by White Army and their supporters
- Red Army attack
- Independent states, once part of Russia

▲ This map shows how, at first, the Whites held all the advantages.

Officers for the Army

In 1918 Trotsky took charge of the Red Army.

His most important contribution was to get experienced officers for the Army.

He took these from the White Army. He spared their lives (and those of their families) in return for their services in the Red Army.

A special Bolshevik **Commissar** watched them to check that they behaved.

Source 5

▲ The house in Ekaterinburg where the Tsar and his family were killed.

Keeping power

War Communism and the civil war had brought terrible hardship to the people of Russia. The Bolsheviks had given priority to winning the civil war and they had been successful. But the price of success was so high that it threatened to make them even more unpopular than the Tsar's government had been in its final months.

In 1921 the sailors at Krondstadt naval base **mutinied**. These sailors had been amongst the most loyal supporters of the Bolsheviks since 1917. Now they had seen enough and were rebelling against Bolshevik rule. The mutiny was put down, but Lenin was shaken by what he saw and decided to make changes.

Now that the civil war was won, he could soften his approach. War Communism was scrapped and was replaced with the **New Economic Policy**. This new policy was a step back from communism and state control.

Source 6

▲ A flourishing market in Moscow during the New Economic Policy.

The New Economic Policy said that:

- Small businesses with up to 25 workers were allowed, instead of the state controlling all business.

- The government would no longer seize agricultural produce, instead workers would keep produce and pay taxes.

- Workers and peasants were allowed to make profits.

This new policy led to the rise of 'Nepmen', traders who made profits out of the relaxation of controls in the New Economic Policy. This was especially true in agriculture where hundreds of thousands of peasants developed their farms, produced more crops and sold them for a profit. These richer peasants became known as 'kulaks'.

Some communists criticised Lenin for taking a step back towards **capitalism**, but he knew that he had to win back the support of the peasants. When he died in 1924 Russia was well on the way to economic recovery – and the Bolsheviks' popularity had been restored.

Why did some people call Lenin 'the Red Tsar'?

Why did countries such as Britain and France oppose the Bolsheviks?

Make a list of the reasons why the Bolsheviks won the Civil War.

Russia before the First World War

Source A

His Majesty is an absolute monarch, who is not obliged to answer for his actions to anyone in the world but has the power and the authority to govern his states as a Christian sovereign, in accord with his desire and goodwill.

To the Emperor of All the Russias belongs the Supreme Autocratic power. God himself commands that he be obeyed, not only from fear of God's wrath, but also for the sake of one's conscience.

▲ From the Military Regulations of Peter the Great, 1716; this defined the power of the Tsar.

Source B

The Tsar's authority is unlimited – like a father's. This autocracy is only an extension of a father's authority. From the base to the summit, the Empire ... rests on one foundation: the authority of a father.

▲ A description of the power of the Tsar written in Russia in 1898.

Source C

The current attitude seemed to suggest that the government was a barrier between the people and the Tsar ... The Tsar's closest friends became convinced that the Sovereign could do anything by relying upon the unbounded love and utter loyalty of the people. The ministers of the government, on the other hand, did not hold to this sort of autocracy; nor did the Duma. Both were of the opinion that the Sovereign should recognise that conditions had changed since the day the Romanovs became Tsars of Moscow.

▲ A description of the Imperial Court of Nicholas II, written in 1913 by Count Kokovtsev, who succeeded Peter Stolypin as Prime Minister.

Source D

You are mistaken, my dear grandmama; Russia is not England. Here we do not need to earn the love of the people. The Russian people love their Tsars as divine beings, from whom all charity and fortune derive. As far as St Petersburg society is concerned, that can be completely disregarded.

▲ From a letter written by the Tsarina Alexandra to her grandmother, Queen Victoria.

Source E

From his youth he had been trained to believe that his welfare and the welfare of Russia were one and the same thing ... 'disloyal' workmen, peasants and students who were shot down, executed or exiled seemed to him mere monsters who must be destroyed for the sake of the country.

▲ From a description of Tsar Nicholas II written by Alexander Kerensky in 1917.

Source F

▲ The Romanov family, attending the celebrations of the 300th anniversary of Romanov rule.

Study Source A

a What can you learn from Source A about the power of the Tsar in Russia? (4)

Study Sources A and B

b Does Source B support the evidence about the power of the Tsar in Russia? In your answer refer to both sources. (6)

Study Sources D and F

c How useful are these sources as evidence about the position of the Tsar in Russia? (8)

Study all of the sources

d 'It would have been difficult for the Tsar to have an understanding of the problems faced by the ordinary people of Russia, and, even if he did, he would not have felt the need to act to solve them.' Use the sources and your own knowledge to explain whether you agree with this view. (12)

Opposition to Tsarist rule

Source A

The armies of the secret police are continuously growing in numbers. The prisons and penal colonies are overcrowded with thousands of convicts and political prisoners ... In all the cities ... the soldiers are employed and equipped with live ammunition ... yet this strenuous and terrible activity of the government results only in the growing impoverishment of the rural population ... A similar condition is the general dissatisfaction of all classes with the government and their open hostility to it.

▲ From an open address by the writer Leo Tolstoy to Tsar Nicholas II in 1902.

Source B

Peasants burned the estates of the landowners, destroying everything they got their hands on ... Almost never did the peasants steal, but with a bright flame burned magnificent manors, cattle-sheds, barns and granaries ... And many landowners fled, without even having time to look back at their beloved homes, on which former generations had lavished so much labour and love.

▲ From an eyewitness account of events in 1905.

Source C

Let those in power make no mistake about the temper of the people; let them not take outward indications of prosperity as an excuse for lulling themselves into security. Never were the Russian people so profoundly revolutionised by the actions of the government, for day by day faith in the government is waning and with it is a waning faith in the possibility of a peaceful issue of the crisis.

▲ From a speech made at the Octobrist Party Conference in 1913.

Source D

There has never been so much tension. People can be heard speaking of the government in the sharpest ... tones. Many say that the shooting of the Lena workers recalls the shooting of the workers at the Winter Palace of January 1905 ... there have been references in the Duma to the necessity of calling a Constituent Assembly and to overthrow the present system by the united strength of the proletariat.

▲ From a report by a Moscow Okhrana agent in 1912.

Source E

Date	Number of strikes
1910	222
1911	466
1912	2032
1913	2404

▲ Numbers of strikes in Russia; these figures were compiled by modern historians.

Source F

▲ A photograph of a demonstration against the government in 1913.

Study Source A

a What can you learn from Source A about the reasons why Nicholas II was unpopular in Russia? (4)

Study Sources A and B

b Does Source B support the evidence of Source A about the popularity of the government in Russia? Explain your answer by referring to both sources. (6)

Study Sources D and E

c How useful are Sources D and E as evidence about the opposition to the government in Russia? (8)

Study all of the sources

d 'The main reason for opposition to the Tsar in the period leading up to the First World War was the discontent of Russia's workers and peasants.' Use the sources and your own knowledge to explain whether you agree with this view. (12)

The impact of the First World War

Source A

General Ruzsky complained to me of a lack of ammunition and the poor equipment of the men ... The soldiers fought barefooted. The war hospitals were disorganised. They were short of bandages and such things.

The Grand Duke stated that he was obliged to stop fighting, temporarily, for lack of ammunition and boots.

There was plenty of material and labour in Russia. But as it stood then, one region had leather, another nails, another soles, and still another cheap labour.

▲ From a report to the Duma by Mikhail Rodzianko in 1916.

Source B

Soldiers from the neighbouring barracks, who were looking over a low fence into the street, knocked down the fence, beating up and driving out the police. Cossacks were called out to arrest the soldiers and workers. But the Cossacks decided not to act and they were withdrawn. The soldiers' behaviour caused consternation among the military hierarchy ... 130 men were arrested and threatened with court-martial.

▲ An eyewitness account of unrest in Petrograd in 1916.

Source C

There is a marked increase in hostile feelings among the peasants, not only against the government, but also against all other social groups. The proletariat of the capital is on the verge of despair. The mass of industrial workers are quite ready to let themselves go to the wildest excesses of a hunger riot ... the labour masses, led by the more advanced and already revolutionary-minded elements, assume an openly hostile attitude against the government.

▲ From an Okhrana report on events in Petrograd in January 1917.

Source D

Date	Index of prices
1914	100
1915	130
1916	141
1917	398

▲ An index of prices in Russia; the figures were compiled by modern historians.

Source E

Date	Bread ration
January 1916	1.25 kilograms
December 1916	1.0 kilograms
March 1917	0.8 kilograms

▲ Bread rations in Petrograd; these figures come from official Russian sources.

Source F

▲ A photograph of a demonstration in Petrograd in 1916.

Study Source A

a What can you learn from Source A about the effects of the First World War on the Russian Army? (4)

Study Sources A, B and C

b Does Source C support the evidence of Sources A and B? Explain your answer. (6)

Study Sources D and E

c How useful are these sources as evidence about the impact of the First World War on the people of Russia? (8)

Study all of the sources

d 'The most important effect of the war was to cut off food supplies to Petrograd.' Use the sources and your own knowledge to explain whether you agree with this view. (12)

1917: the reasons for collapse

Source A

It would be no exaggeration to say that Petrograd achieved the February Revolution. The rest of the country adhered to it. There was no struggle anywhere except in Petrograd. There was not to be found anywhere in the country any groups of the population ... or military units, which were ready to put up a fight for the old regime. Neither at the front nor at the rear was there a brigade or regiment prepared to do battle for Nicholas II.

▲ A description of the February Revolution written by Leon Trotsky.

Source B

The queues – well the queues haven't got smaller in the least; I think they're even bigger. You stand half the day, just as before ... They say 'It's all the same there's nothing to be had, the rich just keep fleecing the poor. The shopkeepers are the only ones making money.'

▲ An eyewitness describes queues in Petrograd in March 1917.

Source C

▲ A photograph of soldiers and workers fraternising in the streets of Petrograd in February 1917.

Source D

The Cossacks were firing on defenceless and unarmed crowds, striking people with whips, crushing the fallen with their horses. And then I saw a young girl trying to evade the galloping horse of a Cossack officer. She was too slow. A severe blow on the head brought her down under the horse's feet. She screamed. It was her inhuman, penetrating scream that caused something in me to snap. I jumped to the table and cried out wildly: 'Friends, friends! Long live the Revolution! To arms, to arms! They are killing innocent people, our brothers and sisters.'

They all joined me in the attack against the Cossacks and the police. We killed a few of them. The rest retreated.

▲ From a letter written by a sergeant in the Russian Army in March 1917, in which he describes how he persuaded his regiment to mutiny.

Source E

Date	Number of workers
6 February	20,000
7 February	30,000
10 February	250,000
12 February	350,000

▲ Estimates of the numbers of workers on strike in Petrograd in 1917; these figures were compiled in the 1980s.

Source F

Date	Number of members
1917 February	24,000
1917 April	100,000
1917 October	340,000

▲ Modern estimates of the numbers of members of the Bolshevik Party.

Study Source A

a What can you learn from Source A about why the Tsar was overthrown? (4)

Study Sources A, B and C

b Do Sources B and C support the evidence of Source A about why the Tsar was overthrown? In your answer refer to all three sources. (6)

Study Sources D and E

c How useful are these sources in helping you understand why the Tsar was overthrown? (8)

Study all of the sources

d 'The February Revolution succeeded because nobody was prepared to defend the monarchy.' Use the sources and your own knowledge to explain whether you agree with this view. (12)

The Bolshevik takeover

Source A

In the cavernous dark hallways where here and there flickered a pale electric light, thousands and thousands of soldiers, sailors and factory workers tramped in their heavy boots every day ... Smolni worked 24 hours a day. For weeks Trotsky never left the building. He ate and slept and worked in his office on the third floor and many people came to see him.

▲ A description of the Bolshevik headquarters, the Smolni Institute, in November 1917, written by a British woman who was living in Petrograd.

Source B

There can be no doubt about it – Lenin is an extraordinary phenomenon, a man of absolutely exceptional intellectual power ... he represents an unusually happy combination of theoretician and popular politician, who had the ability not only to seduce the masses, who have no other teaching but that of the Tsarist whip, but also the Bolshevik Party itself.

▲ A description of Lenin written in 1917.

Source C

The entire Praesidium headed by Lenin were standing up singing with excited, exalted faces and blazing eyes ... while the mass of delegates were permeated by the faith that all would go well in the future too. They were beginning to be persuaded of the Communist Peace, Land and Bread.

▲ An eyewitness account of a meeting of the Bolshevik Party on 7 November 1917.

Source D

Party	Number of seats
Socialist Revolutionaries	370
Bolsheviks	175
National groups	99
Left SRs	40
Kadets	17
Mensheviks	16

▲ The results of the General Election of November 1917.

Source E

The hall began to resemble a battlefield. Chairs and tables were overturned, pictures torn from the walls, in every row there were groups of soldiers trying to heckle speakers, their rifles cocked menacingly towards the platform. The sailors' faces were distorted with rage, they seemed almost inhuman. Their attitude was menacing; their impatient, feverish hands never left the trigger.

▲ A description of the opening of the Constituent Assembly on 18 January 1918, written by Olga Chernov, the wife of the leader of the Socialist Revolutionaries.

Source F

To hand over power to the Constituent Assembly would mean doing a deal with the bourgeoisie. The Russian Soviets place the interests of the toiling masses far above the interests of compromise ... Nothing in the world will induce us to surrender the Soviet power ... And by the will of the Soviet power, the Constituent Assembly, which has refused to recognise the power of the people, is dissolved. The Soviet Revolutionary Republic will triumph no matter what the cost.

▲ Lenin explains the closing of the Constituent Assembly.

Study Source A

a What can you learn from this source about the role of Trotsky in the Bolshevik seizure of power? (4)

Study Sources A, B and C

b Does the evidence of Source C support the evidence of Sources A and B about the role of Lenin in the Bolshevik seizure of power? Explain your answer. (6)

Study Sources D and E

c How useful are Sources D and E in helping you to understand the behaviour of the Bolsheviks at the opening of the Constituent Assembly in January 1918? (8)

Study all of the sources

d 'Lenin played a more significant part than Trotsky in the Bolshevik takeover of Russia.' Use the sources and your own knowledge to explain whether you agree with this view. (12)

Bolshevik rule and its impact / Civil War

Source A

Private ownership of all land shall be abolished forever; land shall not be sold, purchased, leased ... All land, whether state, crown, monastery, church, factory, private, public ... shall be confiscated without compensation and become the property of the whole people.

▲ From the Decree on Land, November 1917.

Source B

In order to provide planned regulation of the national economy, workers' control over the manufacture, purchase, sale and storage of produce and raw materials and over the financial activity of enterprise is introduced in all industrial, commercial, banking, agricultural co-operative and other enterprises, which employed hired labour.

▲ From the Decree on Workers' Control, November 1917.

Source C

Force is necessary for the transition from capitalism to socialism. The type of force is determined by the development of the revolutionary class and also by special circumstances. For example, the heritage of a long and reactionary war and the forms of resistance put up by the bourgeoisie. There is absolutely no contradiction between Soviet democracy and the exercise of dictatorial powers.

▲ From an article written by Lenin in 1918, in which he is explaining why force must be used in Russia.

Source D

Our revolution is in danger. Do not concern yourselves with the forms of revolutionary justice. We have no need for justice now. Now we have need of a battle to the death. I demand the use of the revolutionary sword, which will put an end to all counter-revolutionaries.

▲ From a directive issued in 1918 by Felix Dzerzhinsky, head of the Cheka from its formation.

Source E

В БОРЬБЕ С ЭКОНОМИЧЕСКОЙ РАЗРУХОЙ Мы НЕ ЗНАЕМ ОГРАНИЧЕНИЯ РАБОЧЕГО ВРЕМЕНИ

▲ A photograph of the Cheka in action.

Source F

The troops of the Army of the South blotted their reputation by pogroms against the Jews ... The pogroms brought suffering to the Russian people, but they also affected the morale of the troops, warped their minds and destroyed discipline.

▲ From the memoirs of General Denikin, the leader of the White Armies in Southern Russia, in which he is describing the White forces.

Study Source A

a What can you learn from Source A about the changes the Bolsheviks made in Russia? (4)

Study Sources A, B and C

b Do Sources B and C support the evidence of Source A about the way the Bolsheviks governed Russia? Explain your answer by referring to all three sources. (6)

Study Sources D and E

c How useful are these sources as evidence about the impact of Bolshevik rule on Russia? (8)

Study all of the sources

d 'The Bolsheviks succeeded because they used a mixture of terror and popular reforms.' Use the sources and your own knowledge to explain whether you agree with this view. (12)

Depression and the New Deal The USA: 1929~41

Essential Information

Introduction: the USA in the 1920s

After the First World War the USA became one of the richest countries in the world. The war had brought great economic benefits to the USA:

- European farmers could not produce the food needed for their armies. By 1918 American farmers were sending three times as much food to Europe as they had done in 1914.

- There was also a great demand for US manufactured goods to supply these armies.

- The USA loaned US$10.3 billion to the Allies during the war and 90 per cent of this money was used to buy US goods.

Between 1921 and 1933 the USA had three presidents, all from the Republican Party.

- Harding   1921–23
- Coolidge   1923–29
- Hoover   1929–33

Under Harding and Coolidge the USA prospered. The government had a **laissez-faire** policy. This meant interfering in the economic life of the country as little as possible. Businesses were left alone to make good profits and provide work for the people. There was, however, one significant piece of government interference. In 1922 the **Fordney-McCumber Tariff** put duties on foreign goods entering the USA. Since these foreign goods were now more expensive, people were more likely to buy US goods.

During the 1920s US businesses boomed and people's wages rose by an average of 8 per cent. This was enough for many of them to buy the new consumer goods, such as radios – or even cars.

An industrial revolution

One thing which helped people buy consumer goods was that they were cheap. Another was the spread of electricity. By 1927 the number of Americans living in houses powered by electricity had risen to 63 per cent (only 15 years before it had been 16 per cent). So the American people wanted irons, washing machines, radios and fridges for their homes.

The motor car

One product which had a major impact on the American way of life was the automobile (car). Henry Ford opened factories where mass production techniques (e.g. conveyer belts and workers specialising in one job, like attaching the steering wheel) meant cars could be produced quickly and cheaply. The number of cars produced each year rose from 1.9 million in 1920 to 4.5 million in 1929. The most famous of these was the **'Model T' Ford**. When it was first made it took over 12 hours to produce each car and cost US$850 to buy. By 1924 it took just over one hour and the cost was down to US$260!

The consumer boom

For those Americans in work in the 1920s, life was good. Wages increased and the cheaply produced consumer goods became available. By 1929 there were 26 million cars and 20 million telephones in the USA. There were also 10 million radios.

The car industry used enormous amounts of steel, glass, wood, petrol and leather. So around 5 million extra jobs were created in those industries too. On top of this came road building and the need for hotels and restaurants in places that before had been considered remote and out-of-the-way.

The car industry also changed how Americans bought things. People now used hire-purchase. They put down a deposit and paid off the balance in installments. This was how most consumer goods were purchased in the USA.

Poverty

But not everyone shared in the prosperity of the 1920s. Several groups actually lived in poverty, whilst others had 'never had it so good'.

- Unskilled workers in the big cities (usually immigrants) lived in **ghettos** and were paid very low wages. There were plenty of immigrants looking for unskilled work, so employers didn't need to pay high wages. These people were treated as second-class citizens, living in poor housing conditions and struggling to make ends meet.

- Farmers had prospered in the war. Many had taken on loans to extend their farms and grow more food.

However, problems were just around the corner for the farmers of the USA.

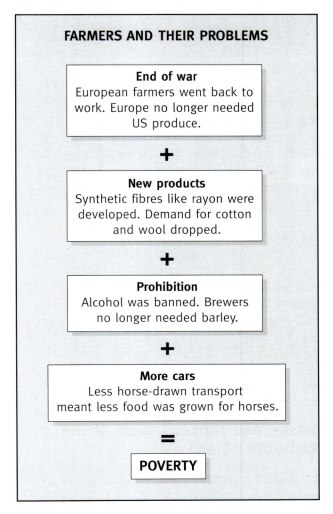

FARMERS AND THEIR PROBLEMS

End of war
European farmers went back to work. Europe no longer needed US produce.

+

New products
Synthetic fibres like rayon were developed. Demand for cotton and wool dropped.

+

Prohibition
Alcohol was banned. Brewers no longer needed barley.

+

More cars
Less horse-drawn transport meant less food was grown for horses.

=

POVERTY

So even in the most prosperous times, farmers earned only a fraction of what they had during the war. By 1924 600,000 farmers had become bankrupt.

As farmers were badly hit, so were their labourers. In the Southern states thousands of African-Americans lost their jobs and others saw their wages drop. In the North East states of the USA in 1929 the average wage was US$881 per year. In the Southern states it was only US$365.

Chapter 3 *Depression and the New Deal. The USA: 1929~41*

53

The share boom

During the 1920s the USA experienced a 'share boom'. Buying and selling shares became a national pastime. Because the economy was doing well, share prices in companies usually went up. So when people sold their shares they made a profit. This led to 'buying on the margin'. People would give their stockbroker (the person who did the actual buying on the New York Stock Exchange in Wall Street) a 10 or 20 per cent deposit. Then they would sell the shares, make a profit, pay off the 80 or 90 per cent they owed the stockbroker and keep the remainder. It seemed like an easy way to make money.

The danger

While share prices continued to rise, share dealing was an easy way to make money. So more and more people joined in – and the demand for shares helped push up prices even more. But what would happen if share prices began to fall? How would people buying on the margin pay their debts? But no-one worried. It wasn't going to happen...

Causes and consequences of the Wall Street Crash

But it did happen. By 1929 manufacturers were beginning to find it more difficult to sell their products. How many cars or radios did Americans need? So the manufacturers cut back on production. Profits started to fall and, as unemployment rose, people stopped spending as much.

Wall Street

Wall Street is the area of New York where stocks and shares are bought and sold daily.

Soon radios, telephones, refrigerators and other goods began to pile up in warehouses. It might have been possible to sell them abroad. But other countries were so angry about the duty added to any products that they tried to sell in the USA, they put duty on US goods coming into their countries, making these dearer.

Explain what was meant by the term *laissez-faire*.

How rich was the USA in the 1920s?

Explain why so many Americans bought shares in the 1920s.

So during the summer of 1929 share prices stopped rising and began to fall. Some shrewd investors decided it was time to sell up, but others thought the fall was just temporary. It wasn't. Soon real trouble began.

- During September selling increased and by mid-October there was a feeling of panic on Wall Street.

- On **'Black Thursday'**, 24 October, nearly 13 million shares were sold as prices fell sharply. Some investors held out, hoping that prices would rise.

- Then on 29 October, 16.4 million shares were sold. People were so scared of losing all their money, that they would take almost any price for their shares.

The dramatic fall in share prices in 1929 is known as the **Wall Street Crash**. It had a major impact on millions of Americans. The USA went into the worst economic decline in its history – the **Great Depression**.

The impact of the Depression on people's lives throughout US society

- Many shareholders lost all their money. They still owed stockbrokers for shares bought on the margin, so they had to sell their cars and even their homes to pay their debts.

- Obviously, many stockbrokers went bust because people could not repay their debts.

- Many banks suffered too. They had lent money to people to buy shares and some had invested huge sums in shares themselves. Most of this money was lost. Some banks had to close. Others called in loans made to companies to try to stay afloat.

- Companies were badly hit. Fewer people had money to buy their goods and the banks were demanding money back which they had borrowed to run their business. So they had to lay off workers to save money. This just increased the problem because now fewer people had money to go on buying goods!

The effects of the Wall Street Crash

Following the crash, about 20,000 companies went bankrupt in 1929. This increased to a peak of 30,000 in 1932. By the end of 1932, 12 million Americans were unemployed. The average family income dropped from US$2300 per year in early 1929 to US$1600 in 1932. In other words, Americans had about 30 per cent less money to spend.

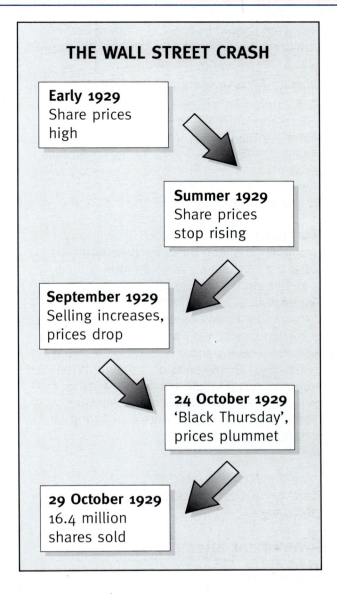

THE WALL STREET CRASH

Early 1929
Share prices high

Summer 1929
Share prices stop rising

September 1929
Selling increases, prices drop

24 October 1929
'Black Thursday', prices plummet

29 October 1929
16.4 million shares sold

From boom to bust

- By the end of 1931 there were 8 million unemployed in the USA (compared with 1.6 million in early 1929). More than 2.5 million people still in work had seen their wages cut.

- Many Americans found themselves queuing for bread and soup handed out by charity organisations (there was no 'dole' at the time).

- Others soon found themselves homeless, living on the edge of cities in shacks made from tin, cardboard and old crates. They called these cities **'Hoovervilles'** as an insult to President Hoover who they thought was not doing enough to help them.

- Another 1 million people (including 200,000 children) became **hoboes** (people drifting from city to city looking for work).

- Just to make things even worse, in 1930 there was a drought across the states in the West and South of the USA which reduced many farms to **dust bowls**. Around 7 million people suffered in the latest disaster to hit farming.

President Hoover

Hoover has been heavily criticised in US history as the man who did little to help people during the Great Depression. At the time people complained 'in Hoover we trusted and now we are busted'. They lived in Hoovervilles wrapped in 'Hoover blankets' (newspapers). But Hoover was saddened by the problems people faced. He thought, like many other Americans, that if the government helped it would stop people from being able to 'stand on their own two feet'.

Government attempts at recovery, 1929–33

President Hoover was in a very difficult position. He believed that government interference was wrong. Business had originally made the USA wealthy and business would help end the Great Depression. But as things got worse and charity organisations ran out of money, he was forced to act.

Hoover set up organisations to help people:

- The **Agricultural Marketing Act** gave aid to farmers.

- The **Reconstruction Finance Corporation** gave individual states money to pay unemployment relief.

- The **Federal Home Loan Bank** provided government money to help with home loans.

But Hoover was not popular and an event in 1932 made him even more popular. A group of First World War veterans were due to be paid a bonus in 1945. In 1932 they marched to Washington asking for the bonus to be paid early to help them through the Depression. They built a Hooverville and Hoover was so concerned that they were a threat to law and order that he called in the Army to clear them out. His treatment of the 'Bonus Marchers' seemed heartless to some Americans.

The nature of the New Deal: policies to deal with agriculture, industry, unemployment and welfare

The role of Roosevelt in recovery

Americans wanted a new president. In November 1932 they elected Franklin D. Roosevelt. He said that the only thing to fear in the USA was 'fear itself'. He promised Americans a '**New Deal**'. In radio broadcasts from the White House (they became known as 'Fireside Chats') he told the people what he intended to do.

Roosevelt's plans were new and dramatic. He said that the federal government (the government of all the USA, as opposed to the state governments of, for example, California or Florida) had to take responsibility for ending the Depression. Laissez-faire had to go. It was time for the government to spend money.

Source 1

▲ The Bonus Marcher's Hooverville.

Roosevelt and the banks

The Wall Street Crash had led to the closure of many banks. People had lost faith in them. So, on his first day in power, Roosevelt closed all the remaining banks. He only let them reopen once they had been checked and shown to be in sound condition. He also said that banks must not invest money on the stock exchange. People's faith in banks was restored and those who had money began putting it back into the banks.

Explain why the Wall Street Crash occurred in 1929.

What effect did the Depression have on the US people?

Alphabet agencies

As soon as Roosevelt took over in January 1933, he began three months of measures to end the Depression. People called this period the **'Hundred Days'**. Roosevelt asked Congress (the US parliament) to pass 15 separate measures. They agreed to all of them. The organisations they set up became known as 'Alphabet Agencies'.

- The **Civilian Conservation Corps** (CCC) was created to provide jobs. By mid-1933 there were over 1300 CCC camps in the countryside. They provided work for men aged 18–25 improving the countryside by tree-planting, road building etc. Eventually 2.5 million Americans went through this system.

- The **Federal Emergency Relief Act** (FERA) was set up to distribute US$500 million to states to create employment. Later this was replaced by the **Civil Works Administration** (CWA). By January 1934, 4 million Americans were employed.

- The **Tennessee Valley Authority** (TVA) carried out improvements across seven states beside the Tennessee River. Flood measures, soil improvement and installation of electric power helped farmers and created a tourist industry – and more jobs.

- The **Public Works Administration** (PWA) created jobs by setting up large-scale construction projects such as road building and constructing ports, hospitals and airports.

- To help factories recover, Roosevelt set up the **National Industry Recovery Act** (NIRA). Businesses who accepted standards for working conditions and wages were allowed to use the Blue Eagle logo, showing that they were trustworthy and were co-operating with the government in maintaining standards. These standards were set by the National Recovery Administration (NRA).

Chapter 3 *Depression and the New Deal. The USA: 1929~41*

57

Source 2

▲ President Roosevelt delivering his inaugural speech in March 1933.

- The **Agricultural Adjustment Act** (AAA) was very controversial. Farmers could not get good prices because of their overproduction of such produce as cotton, tobacco and dairy produce. So this Act paid farmers to leave fields empty or reduce the size of their dairy herds. Critics were horrified that farmers could be paid for agreeing not to produce, when thousands of people could not afford to eat properly. But the scheme worked. Farmer income rose and bankruptcies dropped.

What do you think Roosevelt meant when he said: 'The only thing we have to fear is fear itself'?

By the end of 1934 Roosevelt's New Deal was beginning to work. Unemployment had stopped going up and had begun to fall. The question was, would it work in the long term?

The Second New Deal

Roosevelt was determined that it must work and, in January 1935, he told Congress that it was time for the '**Second New Deal**'. To keep the people working, he introduced the **Works Progress Administration** (WPA). In the next nine years it spent US$11 billion on projects improving schools, airfields, hospitals, roads and playing fields. It even employed artists, actors and writers on community projects.

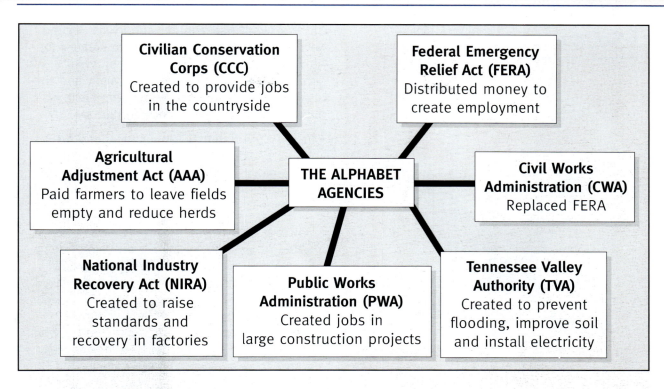

Civilian Conservation Corps (CCC)
Created to provide jobs in the countryside

Federal Emergency Relief Act (FERA)
Distributed money to create employment

Agricultural Adjustment Act (AAA)
Paid farmers to leave fields empty and reduce herds

THE ALPHABET AGENCIES

Civil Works Administration (CWA)
Replaced FERA

National Industry Recovery Act (NIRA)
Created to raise standards and recovery in factories

Public Works Administration (PWA)
Created jobs in large construction projects

Tennessee Valley Authority (TVA)
Created to prevent flooding, improve soil and install electricity

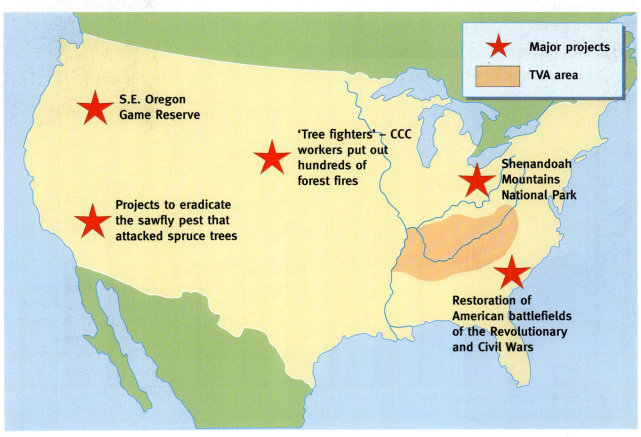

Major projects

TVA area

S.E. Oregon Game Reserve

'Tree fighters' – CCC workers put out hundreds of forest fires

Shenandoah Mountains National Park

Projects to eradicate the sawfly pest that attacked spruce trees

Restoration of American battlefields of the Revolutionary and Civil Wars

▲ New Deal Agencies – major projects.

▲ A poster promoting the NRA.

But Roosevelt had another aim in his Second New Deal. He did not just want to create jobs. He was particularly concerned to provide security for the unemployed, the aged and the disabled. He wanted to remove the fear that these people had about their future.

- In 1935 the **National Labour Relations Act** (sometimes called the Wagner Act) helped workers act against employers who used unfair practices, like sacking them for joining a union.

- However, the law that Roosevelt was most proud of was the Social Security Act of 1935. It provided pensions for those over 65, unemployment benefits and help for disabled people. It was paid for by contributions from workers, employers and the government. Roosevelt said that this Act summed up what the New Deal was all about – removing fear from people's lives.

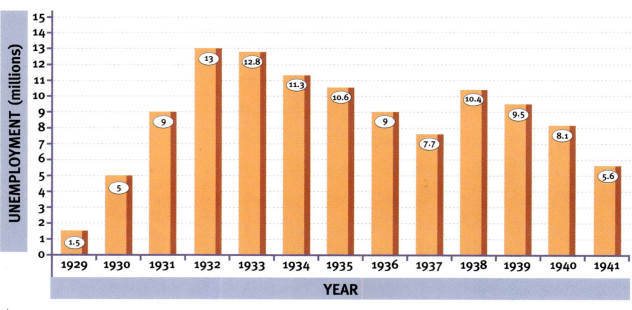

▲ Unemployment in the USA 1929–41

Opposition to Roosevelt and the New Deal

Roosevelt's measures were extremely popular with the voters. In the Presidential Election of 1936 he won over 60 per cent of the votes. This was much higher than usual. But there were still plenty of Americans who hated what he was doing.

- During the election campaign, Roosevelt had to put up with bitter attacks on both him and his family. Some critics claimed that he was a traitor to his class. He came from a rich background and he had raised the taxes of the rich to pay for the New Deal.

- Some Americans agreed with Roosevelt's Republican opponent that the New Deal was taking away the US people's initiative and self-reliance. On page 63 there is an example of the kind of vicious joke that opponents made of the New Deal.

- The New Deal didn't just lead to higher taxes, it meant more government interference. Not only did NIRA and the Wagner Act try to tell businesses what to do, but there was a huge growth in the number of civil servants. Between 1933 and 1938 the number rose from 500,000 to 850,000. The opponents also disliked the increase in government powers that the New Deal brought – particularly when Roosevelt tried to increase his influence by getting his supporters into the Supreme Court (see page 62).

The cartoon below is criticising Roosevelt's attempts to control the Supreme Court. Notice how Congress is horrified by what he is saying.

Describe the key features of the help that Roosevelt gave to the US unemployed in the 1930s.

Source 4

THAT COMPASS DOESN'T POINT THE WAY I WANT TO GO. CHANGE IT. NOW!

▲ **Roosevelt and the Supreme Court.**

Chapter 3 *Depression and the New Deal. The USA: 1929–41*

61

- The New Deal helped workers form unions. One result of this was that there were more strikes as unions tried to win better wages and conditions for their workers. Although it was illegal, many employers sacked workers who tried to start unions.

- The most famous of Roosevelt's opponents was Senator Huey Long of Louisiana. But he complained that Roosevelt was not doing enough, not that he was doing too much. Long set up his own 'Share our Wealth' movement campaigning for every American family to have an income of US$5000 a year. By 1935 he claimed to have 7.5 million people on his mailing list.

Roosevelt and the Supreme Court

One of the tasks of the Supreme Court in the USA is to check that no law is passed that goes against what is written in the American Constitution. In 1935 the Court said that NIRA was 'unconstitutional'. Roosevelt did not like this. He thought that the judges were out of touch with public opinion. What was needed were some new judges. In 1937 he proposed six new judges, saying that the workload of the court was so heavy that new judges were necessary.

His proposal upset not only some of his critics, but also some of his supporters. What he was really doing was making sure that the court had a majority of his own supporters, so that he would not have any more trouble. This was seen as a threat to how America made sure that it was governed properly. Roosevelt dropped the plan, but his actions had lost him support.

During the next four years, six judges retired and he replaced them with his own supporters.

The extent of recovery and success of the New Deal to 1941

At the very time that Roosevelt was having difficulties with the Supreme Court, the American economy took a turn for the worse.

- Industrial production fell.

- Large numbers of shares were sold.

- Unemployment jumped by 5 million people in one year.

Roosevelt had to go back to Congress and ask for US$3.8 million to help put these problems right. (The President does not have money to spend, unless Congress first agrees to let him have it.)

Why was there opposition to some of Roosevelt's measures to help the unemployed?

Why did Senator Long win the support of many US people?

What was the purpose of:

a) The Civilian Conservation Corps;

b) The Agricultural Adjustment Act;

c) The Social Security Act?

So had the New Deal worked or had it been a waste of time and money?

The people of the USA

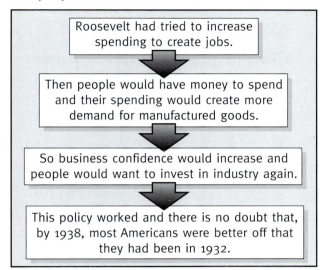

Roosevelt had tried to increase spending to create jobs.

⬇

Then people would have money to spend and their spending would create more demand for manufactured goods.

⬇

So business confidence would increase and people would want to invest in industry again.

⬇

This policy worked and there is no doubt that, by 1938, most Americans were better off that they had been in 1932.

A popular joke from the USA in the 1930s

Socialism: If you own two cows you give one to your neighbour.

Communism: You give both cows to the government and the government gives you back some milk.

Fascism: You keep the cows, but give the milk to the government, which sells it back to you.

New Dealism: You shoot both cows and milk the government.

This joke was attacking Roosevelt. The Americans didn't like Socialism, Communism or Fascism. In this joke they didn't like the New Deal either!

Other countries

It is also worth considering that in some other countries, the solution to the economic problems of the 1930s was to go to war (as Japan did) to choose an extreme leader (as happened in Germany). The USA had not resorted to either of these approaches. That is why some Americans were proud to say that the New Deal was a victory for democracy and the 'American way of life'.

The Second World War

But the New Deal was not a complete success. As mentioned above, things started to go wrong in 1937, and in 1941 there were still 6 million unemployed in the USA. What really finished the job for Roosevelt was the USA joining the Second World War in 1941. The spending needed to prepare the USA for war finally ended the Great Depression. The growth of the armed forces meant that more weapons were needed. So many jobs were created in factories supplying those weapons – and other supplies like food and clothing.

In what ways was the New Deal successful?

In what ways was the New Deal a failure?

Chapter 3 *Depression and the New Deal. The USA: 1929~41*

63

Causes and consequences of the Wall Street Crash

Source A

Company	31 August 1928	3 September 1929	29 October 1929
American and Foreign Power	$38.00	$167.75	$73.00
AT and T	$182.00	$304.00	$230.00
Hershey Chocolate	$53.25	$128.00	$108.00
IBM	$130.86	$241.75	–
People's Gas, Chicago	$182.86	$182.86	–
Detroit, Edison	$205.00	$350.00	–

▲ Selected share prices, Wall Street, 1928–29.

Source B

▲ From the *New York Times* report on the
Wall Street Crash, October 1929.

Source C

I knew something was terribly wrong because I heard everybody talking about the stock market. Six weeks before the Crash I wanted to sell shares which had been left to me by my father. My family adviser persuaded me to keep hold of the shares, even though I could have got $160,000. Four years later I sold them for $4000.

▲ From an interview in 1970 with an American who was in New York in October 1929.

Source D

We in America are nearer to the final triumph over poverty than ever before in the history of any land. The poorhouse is vanishing from among us.

▲ From a speech by Herbert Hoover in the autumn of 1928.

Source E

The Hoover administration encouraged overproduction through its false policies. It refused to recognise problems at home; moreover, it not only delayed reform but forgot reform.

▲ From a speech by Franklin Roosevelt during his first presidential campaign, 1932.

Source F

We've got more wheat, more corn, more food, more everything in the world than any nation ever had, yet we are starving to death. We are the first nation in the history of the world to go to the poorhouse in an automobile.

▲ Will Rogers, a US humourist, speaking in 1931.

Study Source A

a What can you learn from Source A about the American stock market in the late 1920s? (4)

Study Sources A, B and C

b Do Sources B and C support the evidence of Source A? Explain your answer by referring to all three sources. (6)

Study Sources D and E

c How useful are these sources in helping you to understand why there was a 'Crash' in 1929? (8)

Study all of the sources

d 'The Crash in stockmarket prices on 29 October 1929 took America completely by surprise.' Use the sources and your own knowledge to explain whether you agree with this view. (12)

Chapter 3 *Depression and the New Deal. The USA: 1929–41*

65

The impact of the Depression on people's lives throughout US society

Source A

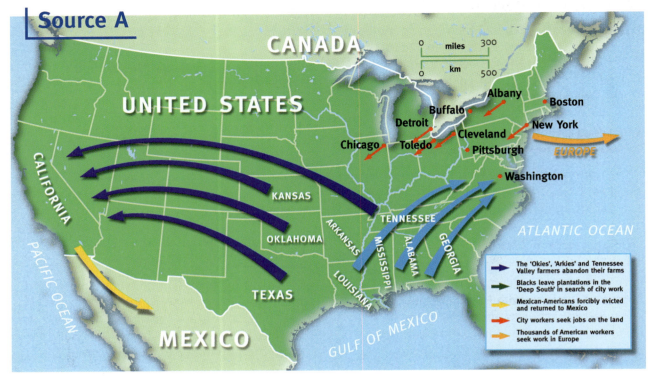

▲ The movement of population throughout the USA during the 1930s.

Source B

Year	Unemployed (approximate)
March 1930	3.5 million
March 1931	7.75 million
March 1932	11.75 million
March 1933	14.0 million

▲ Chart showing how unemployment increased from 1930 to 1933.

Source C

▲ Unemployed people in New York in 1931. The men are queuing for Christmas dinner. It is Christmas Day.

Source D

The average man won't really do a day's work unless he is caught and cannot get out of it. There is plenty of work to do, if people would do it.

▲ From a speech made in 1931 by Henry Ford, who ran a successful business manufacturing motor cars.

Source E

Here were all those people living in old, rusted-out car bodies. I mean that was their home. There were people living in shacks made of orange crates. One family with a whole lot of kids were living in a piano box. This wasn't just a little section, this was maybe 10 miles wide and 10 miles long. People living in whatever junk they could put together.

▲ From an interview with Peggy Terry in 1970. Peggy Terry had lived in a Hooverville in the 1930s.

Source F

People who were wealthy before the Depression had much greater chances of weathering the economic storm and coming out with minimal financial damage. A handful of people took advantage of the rock bottom prices brought on by the Depression in order to increase their wealth.

▲ From an American history textbook written in 1991.

Study Source A

a What can you learn from Source A about the impact of the Depression on the people of the USA? (4)

Study Sources A, B and C

b Do Sources B and C support the evidence of Source A? Explain your answer. (6)

Study Sources D and E

c How useful are these sources as evidence of the plight of the unemployed in the 1930s? Explain your answer. (8)

Study all of the sources

d 'The Depression affected only the working classes in the early 1930s.' Use the sources and your own knowledge to explain whether you agree with this view. (12)

Chapter 3 *Depression and the New Deal. The USA: 1929–41*

67

Government attempts at recovery, 1929–33

Source A

We have been passing through one of those great economic storms which periodically bring hardship and suffering on our people. I am convinced we have now passed the worst and we shall recover. There is one certainty in the future of a people such as ourselves and that is, prosperity.

▲ From a speech by President Hoover, May 1930.

Source B

	Failed businesses	Farm income in US$ billions	Average weekly earnings in manufacturing
1930	26,355	4.1	$24.77
1931	28,285	3.2	Not available
1932	31,822	1.9	$16.21

▲ Economic statistics from Hoover's presidency.

Source C

I see nothing in the present situation that is either menacing or pessimistic. I have every confidence there will be a revival of activity in the spring and that during the coming year the country will make steady progress.

▲ From a speech by Andrew Mellon, President Hoover's Secretary of the Treasury, January 1930.

Source D

Economic depression cannot be cured by simply making laws or intervention by the President. The economy can only be healed by the producers and consumers themselves.

▲ Adapted from a speech by President Hoover in 1930.

Source E

Hoover failed ... He first coldly assured the people that the Depression was an illusion which it was their patriotic duty to ignore. When economic collapse occurred in Europe, he denounced the Depression as something un-American from which we should isolate and insulate ourselves.

▲ From a book written in 1948 by Robert Sherwood. Sherwood was a speech writer for President Roosevelt.

Source F

Everybody wanted to have somebody to blame the Depression on. Hoover had the misfortune to be inaugurated in March 1929, just in time to get the blame for the Crash. When the collapse came, Hoover did not sit still – he brought business and union leaders to the White House where they promised to try to keep wages up and keep factories going. He actually cut his own presidential salary by one-fifth.

▲ From an American history textbook written in 1987 by D. Boorstin.

Study Source A

a What can you learn from Source A about President Hoover's attitude to the Depression? (4)

Study Sources A, B and C

b Do Sources B and C support the evidence of Source A? Explain your answer. (6)

Study Sources D and E

c How useful are these sources in helping you to understand the economic problems of the USA in the early 1930s? (8)

Study all of the sources

d 'President Hoover did not bring the USA out of the Depression because he did too little too late.' Use the sources and your own knowledge to explain whether you agree with this view. (12)

The nature of the New Deal: policies to deal with agriculture, industry, unemployment and welfare

Source A

Unemployed citizens face the grim problem of existence and an equally great number toil with little return. Our greatest … task is to put people to work. This is no unsolvable problem if we face it wisely and courageously. It can be accomplished by direct recruiting by the government itself, treating the task as we would treat the emergency of war, but at the same time, through this employment, accomplishing greatly needed projects. [We must] raise the values of agricultural products. There must be a strict supervision of all banking.

▲ From President Roosevelt's statement to Congress when he became President in 1933.

Source C

▲ Workers in the Civilian Conservation Corps with President Roosevelt in 1933.

Source B

There was a problem with the price of cotton. Prices were down to 4 cents a pound and the cost of producing was 10 cents. So the government set up a programme to plough up the cotton. A third of the crop was ploughed up. Cotton prices went up 10 cents, maybe 11.

▲ From an interview in 1970 with C. R. Baldwin. Baldwin had been the Assistant to the Secretary of Agriculture in the New Deal.

Source D

… the migrants streamed in on the highways and their hunger was in their eyes … When there was work for a man, ten men fought for it … if that fella'll work for 30 cents, I'll work for 25 … I'll do it for 20. No, me, I'm hungry. I'll work for 15 cents. I'll work for food … The kids … I'll work for a little piece of meat.

▲ From the novel *The Grapes of Wrath* by John Steinbeck, written in 1939.

Source E

Any jackass can spend the people's money. Any crackpot with money at his disposal can build himself a dictatorial crown. It is time for the American people to perform a sit-down strike – on politicians. The politicians are sitting down on you waiting for the Supreme Court to put its head on the chopping block.

▲ From a speech in 1937 by the radio priest, Father Charles Coughlin, an opponent to Roosevelt.

Source F

▲ The Tennessee Valley area and the states affected by the work of the TVA.

Study Source A

a What can you learn from Source A about the situation in the USA in 1933? (4)

Study Sources A, B and C

b Do Sources B and C support the evidence of Source A? Explain your answer. (6)

Study Sources D, E and F

c How useful are these sources in helping you to understand the work of President Roosevelt? (8)

Study all of the sources

d 'President Roosevelt's measures to improve agriculture were popular and effective.' Use the sources and your own knowledge to explain whether you agree with this view. (12)

Chapter 3 *Depression and the New Deal. The USA: 1929–41*

71

Opposition to Roosevelt and the New Deal

Source A

Roosevelt did not get everything his own way. In 1936 the Supreme Court ruled against the Agricultural Adjustment Act. Roosevelt was disturbed that this court could overrule laws which the elected President and Congress had passed. He thought this was because they were old men who lived in the past.

▲ From a British textbook, 1989.

Source B

Our President evidently has noted the apparent success of Adolf Hitler and is aiming at the same dominance.

▲ A US political commentator writing in 1937 about President Roosevelt's decision to reform the Supreme Court.

Source C

By bringing into the Supreme Court a steady stream of new and younger blood, I hope to make justice speedier and less costly. Also I intend to bring in younger men who have had personal experience and contact with today's circumstances and know how average men have to live and work.

▲ From a radio broadcast by President Roosevelt, 1937.

Source D

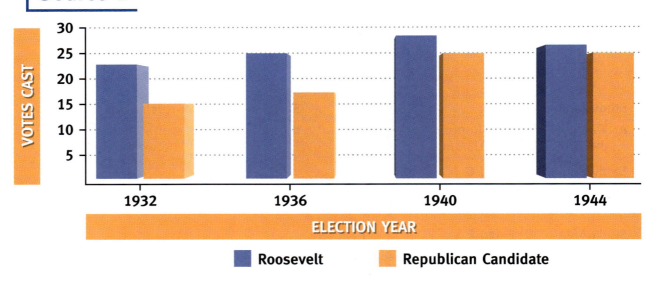

▲ This graph shows the number of votes, in millions, cast in the Presidential Elections between 1932 and 1944.

Source E

Roosevelt's proposals would not banish older judges from the courts. They would not reduce expense nor speed decisions. They would place the courts under the will of Congress and the President and would destroy the independence of the courts.

▲ From the Senate Judiciary Committee's rejection of President Roosevelt's proposals to bring in more judges, 1937.

Source F

Dear Mr President,

This is just to tell you everything is all right now. The man you sent found our house all right and we went down the bank with him and the mortgage can go a while longer. You remember I wrote you about losing the furniture too. Well, your man got it back for us. I never heard of a President like you, Mr Roosevelt. Mrs _____ and I are old folks and don't amount to much, but we are joined with those millions of others in praying for you every night. God bless you, Mr Roosevelt.

▲ A letter sent to President Roosevelt by a grateful voter in 1934.

Study Source A

a What can you learn from Source A about the conflict between Roosevelt and the Supreme Court? (4)

Study Sources A, B and C

b Do Sources B and C support the evidence of Source A? Explain your answer. (6)

Study Sources D and E

c How useful are these sources for showing the popularity of the changes Roosevelt wished to make to the Supreme Court? (8)

Study all of the sources

d 'Roosevelt's attempt to reform the Supreme Court was an unwise move which seriously undermined his popularity.' Use the sources and your own knowledge to explain whether you agree with this view. (12)

Chapter 3 *Depression and the New Deal. The USA: 1929–41*

73

The extent of recovery and success of the New Deal to 1941

Source A

Mrs Roosevelt,

I suppose from your point of view the work relief, old age pensions, slum clearance and all the rest seems like a perfect remedy for all the ills of this country, but I would like for you to see the results, as the other half see them. We have always had a shiftless, never-do-well class of people whose one and only aim in life is to live without work ... There has never been any necessity for anyone who is able to work, being on relief in this locality, but there have been many eating the bread of charity and they have lived better than ever before. I have had taxpayers tell me that their children come home from school and ask why they couldn't have nice lunches like the children on relief.

▲ A letter sent to President Roosevelt's wife, Eleanor.

Source B

The New Deal is encouraging the unfit to be more unfit. Even such a measure as old-age insurance removes one of the points of pressure which has kept many persons up to the strife and struggle of life.

▲ An extract from a pamphlet written by the American Liberty League in 1935.

Source C

I've been dealing with unemployed people for years and they want to 'get off' poor relief – but they can't – where can they turn to if they can't turn to their government?

▲ From a speech in 1933 by Harry Hopkins, a member of President Roosevelt's administration.

Source D

There were three reasons why Roosevelt wanted war. One: you had 10 million Americans unemployed after six years of the New Deal. Two: to be a war president because then you become a great man overnight. Three: he hoped to put through a United Nations, of which he would be the author and be like the uncrowned ruler of the world.

▲ From an interview in 1970 with a Republican Congressman.

Source E

Before Roosevelt became President, there was one person to take care of all the letters the White House received. Under Roosevelt, there are 50 and they handled the thousands of letters written to the President each week.

▲ **From an American history book about Roosevelt and the New Deal, written in 1963.**

Source F

My name is William Edwards, I live down Cove Creek way,
I'm working on a project they call the TVA.

The government began it when I was but a child,
But now they are in earnest and Tennessee's gone wild.

Oh, see them boys a-comin' – their government they trust;
Just hear their hammers ringin' – they'll build that dam or bust.

I meant to marry Sally, but work I could not find;
The TVA was started and surely eased my mind.

I'm writing her a letter, these words I'll surely say:
'The Government has saved us, just name our wedding day.'

Oh, things looked blue and lonely until this come along;
Now hear the crew a-singing and listen to their song.

'The Government employs us, short hours and certain pay;
Oh, things are up and comin', God bless the TVA.'

▲ **A popular song at the time of the New Deal.**

Study Source A

a What can you learn from Source A about attitudes to helping the needy under the New Deal? (4)

Study Sources A, B and C

b Do Sources B and C support the evidence of Source A? Explain your answer. (6)

Study Sources D, E and F

c How useful are Sources D, E and F in helping you to understand whether the New Deal was a success? (8)

Study all of the sources

d 'By 1941, Roosevelt got the USA working again and had given the people hope.' Use the sources and your own knowledge to explain whether you agree with this view. (12)

Nazi Germany: 1930~39

Hitler, Nazism and Nazi beliefs

Adolf Hitler was born in Austria in 1889. He was not a particularly good student at school and, after finishing, he failed to win a place at art school in Vienna. He was forced to make a living selling postcards and giving art lessons.

When the First Word War broke out in 1914, he volunteered for the German Army. He was a good soldier and won medals for bravery. He later said that this was the happiest time of his life.

In October 1918 he was temporarily blinded by gas and was in hospital when the war ended.

Source 1

▲ Hitler in the uniform of lance-corporal in a Bavarian volunteer regiment, November 1914.

Hitler was devastated to hear that Germany had surrendered and came to believe that the Army had been 'stabbed in the back' by the 'November Criminals' (the politicians who had surrendered in November).

After the War

After the war, Hitler joined the German Workers' Party. Its leader, Anton Drexler, hated Jews and blamed them for Germany's defeat in the war. The Party was very small and so Hitler was able to rise to be leader by 1921. The Party changed its name to the National Socialist German Workers' Party. It thought that 'National' would attract support from nationalists and 'Socialist' would attract support from workers. But in 1921 the 'Nazi' Party, as it became known, had very few supporters.

The Party grows

At first the Nazis were just one of a number of tiny opposition parties which existed in the **Weimar Republic**. They had very little support, but they did attract some Germans because they criticised the hated Treaty of Versailles. But Hitler had big plans for the Party.

The Treaty of Versailles

This made Germans very angry because of the harsh terms it imposed on them:

- Germany was forced to accept blame for starting the war – and pay **reparations**.
- Strict limits were placed on the size of Germany's armed forces.
- Germany lost 14 per cent of its land, including its colonies.

The Beer Hall Putsch

In 1923 Hitler tried to seize power in Munich. He lead a **putsch** (revolution) against the local government. By this time the Nazi Party had 35,000 members and he hoped he would be able to use this support to gain power. But the putsch did not succeed. Hitler was jailed, the Nazi newspaper was banned and so was the Party! But the putsch was not a total failure. It gave Hitler publicity across Germany – and he used his trial to put over his anti-Jewish views. Whilst in prison he wrote **Mein Kampf** (*My Struggle*), a book in which he set down all his ideas.

- All Germans must be prepared to sacrifice their own personal rights and freedoms for the good of Germany as a whole.

- Men and women had different roles to play in society; women as housewives and mothers, men as workers and soldiers.

- The Treaty of Versailles was an insult to Germany and should be overthrown.

- Communism was evil.

- The German people belonged to the Aryan race. It was a master race. All other races were inferior. At the bottom of the list were '**Untermenschen**' – Jews, black people, Slavs, gypsies. They should be removed from the German race.

Some of Hitler's views were too extreme and distasteful for the German people. But there were always those who were prepared to believe that their own problems were someone else's fault.

The Nazi rise to power

When Hitler was released from prison in December 1924 he set about trying to make the Nazis the largest Party in the **Reichstag** (the German equivalent of the British House of Commons). But the Germans were not interested in Hitler's views at this time. The Chancellor, Gustav Stresemann, had helped Germany solve many of its problems:

- The economic problems caused in 1923 by paying reparations and by inflation had been solved. Money had been borrowed from the USA and a new currency, the **Rentenmark**, was introduced into Germany.

- Germany had restored good relations with other countries. For example it had joined the **League of Nations** in 1926.

So, the German people were not interested in Hitler and his extreme views. The Nazis won only 12 seats (out of more than 400) in the 1928 elections to the Reichstag. But soon, all that was to change.

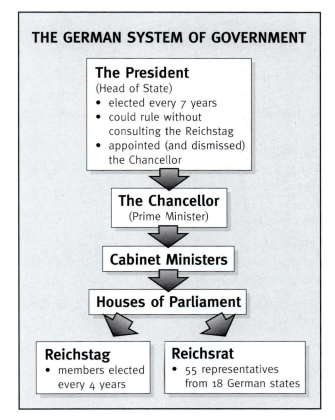

THE GERMAN SYSTEM OF GOVERNMENT

The President
(Head of State)
- elected every 7 years
- could rule without consulting the Reichstag
- appointed (and dismissed) the Chancellor

The Chancellor
(Prime Minister)

Cabinet Ministers

Houses of Parliament

Reichstag
- members elected every 4 years

Reichsrat
- 55 representatives from 18 German states

Source 2

▲ Unemployed people in Berlin, 1932, examining newspapers for job vacancies.

The Wall Street Crash, 1929

In October 1929 Stresemann died. A few weeks later there was a crash on the US Stock Exchange in Wall Street, New York. This had important effects in Germany:

- The USA had lent Germany large sums of money to pay reparations and invest in its businesses. Now it wanted it back.

- There would be no more loans to help in the future.

- The USA could not afford to buy goods produced in Germany any more.

The Weimar Republic

The Republic was founded after the Kaiser stood down in 1918:

- Germany was now a democracy.

- Members of the Reichstag were elected.

- The leader of the government was the Chancellor.

- There was to be a president who would be elected every seven years.

This meant that German businesses had to save money by cutting back on production and laying off workers. Within three years, unemployment had doubled to 6 million people.

This was just what Hitler wanted. As people became more desperate, they turned to political parties with more extreme ideas (like his). He flew around Germany making speeches and used newspapers and cinemas to spread his ideas. He told the German people two things:

1. That their problems were the result of actions by Communists and Jews.

2. That the Nazis would take action to restore Germany's economy.

Hitler was telling the people what they wanted to hear. He was not telling them exactly what he was going to do – just giving them someone to blame for their problems and promising to sort it out. It was a message which appealed to millions of Germans.

Proportional Representation
One of the problems that the Weimar governments had in the period 1924–29 was that members of the Reichstag were elected by proportional representation. If a party won 7 per cent of the total vote, then it got 7 per cent of the seats. This meant that there were a large number of parties and no one party had more seats than all the others put together.

So, unlike in the British system, no party could say, 'We are the government, there are more of us than you, this is what we want to do and we will use our votes to make sure it happens.' In Germany, several parties had to join together to form a government. That usually worked well, but if tough decisions had to be made (like cutting teachers' pay, because the country could not afford to pay them) then sometimes the parties could not agree and the government could not take action.

This is what happened in Germany in 1931.

The Nazis also told the German people that they were the party of discipline and order.

They even had their own Army, the Brownshirts (or **Stormtroopers**) who paraded through German towns. Led by Enrst Röhm, they created an impression of strength and order. (Sometimes they used violence to break up meetings of political opponents, but the Nazis did not publicise that sort of thing.)

Why was the Wall Street Crash so important in the rise of the Nazi Party to power in 1933?

The problems in Germany, the Nazi propaganda and the work of the Stormtroopers helped the Nazi Party to grow. In 1930 it won 107 seats in the Reichstag and in July 1932 it won 230 seats. It was now the largest party in Germany. But the Nazis were not asked to be the government by the President, Hindenburg. He hated Hitler's views on the Jews. He knew that thousands of them had fought bravely and died for Germany in the First World War.

During 1932, elections for the President were held. Hitler stood against Hindenburg. He lost, but he got 13 million votes, which showed how popular he was. There was another election to the Reichstag in November 1932. This time the Nazis won only 196 seats, but they still had plenty of support.

Hitler as Chancellor
In 1932 the Chancellor, von Papen, was replaced by von Schleicher. Von Papen persuaded Hindenburg that Hitler would make a better Chancellor – as long as he, von Papen, was made Vice-chancellor to keep an eye on him and stop him introducing too extreme measures. In January 1933 Hindenburg asked Hitler to be Chancellor. Hitler agreed to have von Papen as his Vice-chancellor and to have just three Nazis as Cabinet members. Von Papen expected to be able to control Hitler, but he was soon proved wrong.

Creation of the totalitarian state

Not only did Hitler soon have control of the government of Germany, but he also took steps to set up a **totalitarian** state in Germany. That is, a state in which the government controls all aspects of peoples' lives – their laws, their education, even their jobs.

The Reichstag Fire

Hitler immediately called a new election for 5 March 1933. Just six days before that election, on 27 February, the Reichstag building was burned down. The police arrested a Dutch Communist called Marinus van der Lubbe. There is no doubt that van der Lubbe was involved, but some historians believe that he had been persuaded to start the fire by the Nazis. Then they could claim that the Communists were starting a revolution and take steps against them. That would help the Nazis win more seats in the election.

How did the fire start?

Marinus van der Lubbe was a pathetic figure who suffered from mental illness. On the day that the Reichstag caught fire, he was found inside carrying matches. He had apparently set fire to the building using his shirt. He was put on trial, found guilty and executed. In later years, various Nazis were said to have been responsible for getting van der Lubbe to start the fire.

- Hermann Goering said that he had been responsible.

- Josef Goebbels was the most likely culprit.

- Karl Ernst may well have been ordered by Goebbels to carry out the deed.

Hitler used the burning down of the Reichstag to act against his opponents. Over 4000 Communists were arrested and Hindenburg agreed to issue an order banning them from holding public meetings. In the election the Nazis won 288 seats out of a total of 647. Hitler did not quite get the majority he wanted, but the 81 Communists elected were banned from taking their seats, so he was nearly there. But he intended to make sure he had full power.

The Enabling Act

Hitler wanted to change the German **Constitution** to give himself full powers. To make this special change, it was necessary to get a two-thirds majority in the vote in the Reichstag. To make sure he got his way, he stationed Stormtroopers around the building. They made Hitler's opponents aware that a vote against the Enabling Law would mean trouble. The Enabling Law was passed by 441 votes to 84.

In March 1933 the Reichstag passed the **Enabling Law**. This said that Hitler had the power to make laws in Germany without needing the Reichstag's approval for a period of four years.

The Reichstag had given up its powers. It met only 12 times and passed only four laws. The only speeches heard there were made by Hitler. He had become a **dictator** in Germany.

Hitler in action

Hitler immediately used his new powers to deal with any possible opposition:

- All political parties except the Nazis were banned.

- Concentration camps were set up and leading opponents imprisoned in them.

- Trade unions were banned and replaced with the government's own 'Labour Front'.

Why was Hitler appointed Chancellor in January 1933?

How did Hitler try to take advantage of the Reichstag Fire?

- The German secret police, the **Gestapo**, was used to arrest suspected opponents. Often they were tried and sentenced in secret.

- Judges had to be loyal Nazis and impose sentences the way the Nazis wanted. Between 1930 and 1932 only eight people were executed in Germany. Between 1934 and 1939 534 people were executed. Another 167,734 were under 'protective arrest'.

- In every village or district there were Nazi spies. Each block of flats had a Nazi 'warden' to keep an eye on visitors.

The Night of the Long Knives

One problem which Hitler faced came from within his own party. The leader of the Stormtroopers, Ernst Röhm wanted the Party to do more to help the workers. He also wanted to be leader of the Army. Hitler needed the support of the Army generals, and knew that they hated Röhm and the Stormtroopers.

So on 29 June 1934, Röhm and around 400 other Stormtroopers were arrested and put to death. Many of them were loyal Nazis, but Hitler was determined to take no chances.

Five weeks later, Hindenburg died. Hitler did not hold an election for a new president.

Instead, he combined the offices of Chancellor and President. Germany would now have a **Führer** – Hitler.

The Nazi State

Between 1933 and 1938 the Nazis took control of every aspect of life in Germany.

- All forms of entertainment were controlled. Radio, film, books and newspapers were censored.

- In schools, teachers had to be members of the Nazi Party and textbooks had to contain the Nazi message. So History was about Nazi heroes and new subjects, such as 'Race Studies', appeared. Girls were educated to be mothers (lots of PE, biology and domestic science). Boys were educated to be soldiers (PE, science and mathematics were emphasised).

- Sport was emphasised in Germany and used as a chance to show the superiority of the Aryan race. The 1936 Olympics were held in Berlin. Germany won more medals than any other country, but the greatest athlete at the games was the American Jessie Owens. He was black!

- Young people were expected to join youth movements set up especially for them. For boys these were: Pimfen at the age of five, German Youth at 10, and Hitler Youth at 14. For girls there was the League of German Maidens fron 10 to 21 years old.

The 1936 Olympic Games

Hitler was pleased that the Germans won so many medals at the Berlin Olympics. But he wasn't pleased about Jesse Owens. Owens won gold medals in the 100 yards, 200 yards, long jump and 4 x 100 yards relay. As a black man, Hitler thought Owens was inferior! He refused to shake Owen's hand and present his medals.

Source 3

▲ A class run according to Nazi philosophy in a German school – the children are having a lesson on the strategy of new military road-building.

The youth movements were part of Hitler's plan to have the whole of Germany supporting Nazi ideas. He knew that if he could get children to accept his ideas, then they would probably still believe in them when they became adults. So it was very important to Hitler to control education and to control the organisations that young people attended. That way he could make sure they received the right 'message'.

The youth movements were places where 'fun' was combined with learning about Nazi ideas. There were camps and games at the weekend which had an emphasis on healthy outdoor pursuits. All the time, however, the Nazi values of loyalty to the Führer and putting the good of the country above personal needs were emphasised. German children were left in no doubt about what their country expected from them.

The youth movements were very popular with many young Germans, and by 1939 there were more than 8 million members.

Hitler also wanted to control the beliefs of adults. He was very worried about the influence that religion had upon the German people. He knew that people with strong religious beliefs were more likely to do what their priest or pastor said than obey their Nazi leaders. So he was determined to get the Churches on his side.

▲ **In Reich churches, swasticas were displayed on the altar.**

- Hitler liked to say that he was a Roman Catholic and in 1933 he signed the **Concordat** with the Pope. The Church promised not to intefere in politics if Hitler did not interfere in religion. Hitler did not keep his promise and the two sides fell out. In 1941 a letter from the Pope criticising the Nazis was read out in pulpits all over Germany. Hitler responded by sending priests and nuns to labour camps.

- Relations with the Protestant Churches also worsened. 800 Protestant churchmen were sent to labour camps. Some, like Pastor Martin Bonhoeffer died for their beliefs. In 1943 he was arrested and executed for working with the resistance movement.

In education and in religion Hitler tried to stop people thinking for themselves. If he could control the information people received, his ideas would be accepted without question. Most people accepted the Nazi control of their lives. It was easier than complaining. However, many artists, musicians and scientists left the country rather than submit to Nazi ideas.

Source 5

▲ Children's school textbooks contained anti-Semitic material.

Racism and the treatment of minorities

The Nazis wanted a pure German race. They said that the Aryan race (to which the Germans belonged) was superior – but that it was in danger of being polluted by mixing with other 'inferior' races.

The Jews

This nonsense was just an excuse to attack the Jews. The Nazis claimed, wrongly, that the Jews were weakening the natural superiority of the German race. But what Hitler was really doing was using the age-old tactic of giving people someone to pick on. Many Jews looked different from other Germans, and Jewish people often lived or worked together. They were an easy target. By ignoring the vast achievements of Jewish people in art, music, literature, business, architecture – in fact, in almost every area – the Nazis were able to persuade many Germans that the Jews should be treated differently from other citizens.

Persecution of the Jews

- The persecution of Jews began almost as soon as Hitler was in power. In 1933 the Nazis ordered a boycott of Jewish shops. Jews were also banned from some professions, such as medicine and law.

- The **anti-semitic** (anti-Jewish) views of the Nazis were taught in schools. Schoolchildren were taught to hate Jews and Jewish children were picked on at school. Sometimes maths problems involved working out how much it would cost to bomb cities with a high Jewish population.

- In 1935 the Nazis introduced the **Nuremberg Laws**. Anyone who had a Jewish grandmother was declared to be Jewish. Jews were not allowed to marry non-Jews, and their right to vote was taken away.

- In the same year Jews were banned from public places such as swimming pools, restaurants and parks.

- In 1938 a Jewish student shot dead a German diplomat in Paris. So the Nazis ordered a widespread attack on Jewish property in Germany. On **Kristallnacht** (the Night of Broken Glass) houses, property and 300 synagogues were attacked. Then a fine of 1 million marks was imposed on the Jewish population.

- Large numbers of Jews fled Germany during the 1930s (which was what the Nazis wanted). But they had to leave most of their property and savings behind.

THE NAZIS AND THE JEWS

Hitler was anti-Semitic

Jewish shops were boycotted

Schoolchildren were taught to hate Jews

Nuremberg Laws took away Jewish rights

Jewish property was attacked on Kristallnacht

Large numbers of Jews fled Germany

Opposition to Nazi rule

Most Germans accepted Nazi rule. This was partly because, until 1939, the worst things that the Nazis did were not known about. The Nazis had restored law and order, improved the economy and given the German nation its pride back. (Remember that the dreadful massacre of the Jews and gypsies in the **Holocaust** did not begin until 1942.) But there was still some opposition.

- As you read earlier, some of the members of the Catholic Church refused to follow Nazi policies and were punished for it.

- Most opposition, however, came from young people, particularly after membership of the Nazi youth movements was made compulsory in 1939 – and when persecution of the Jews became more intense.

- There were a number of student groups which distributed leaflets and organised meetings to oppose the Nazis. One such group was the 'White Rose', based at Munich University. Its leaders were executed in 1944.

- Some youngsters objected to the restrictions placed on them. They wanted to dance to American and English songs, and listen to Jazz music. The Nazis said that these 'swing groups' were degenerate.

- Some groups, like the Edelweiss Pirates and Navajos Gang, hated the Hitler Youth and even went as far as beating up some of its members.

Rivalry within the Party
In 1934 Hitler had dealt with Röhm, partly because he saw him as a possible rival. Hitler encouraged rivalry between senior Party members so that no outright rival to him emerged.

The social impact of Nazism

For ordinary Germans Nazi rule brought about some important changes in their everyday lives:

- Women were expected to give up work when they got married. If they had four or more children they were given a special medal. They were encouraged not to wear make-up and to wear traditional dress. However, some of the Nazi leaders' wives, like Magda Goebbels, refused point blank to follow this advice.

- Keeping women at home was one way to reduce unemployment. Another was the Labour Service. At the age of 18, people were given six month's work at very low pay. They carried out tasks like building Autobahns (motorways). This was done with hand tools, because it gave more people work to do.

- In 1935 conscription was introduced. After Labour Service, most men went into the Army. When Hitler started re-arming his forces, jobs were created in munition factories.

These measures helped reduce unemployment from 6 million in 1933 to 500,000 in 1938 (according to the Nazis). At one point Hitler claimed to be reducing unemployment by 126,000 a week.

Although many of the jobs were temporary (how many Autobahns could be built?), the high level of unemployment had been brought down. The Depression had had been defeated in Germany.

The Nazis and the Arts

The Nazis controlled all forms of art in Germany. Films were made about great events in German history, but anti-war art, such as the novel *All Quiet on the Western Front* were banned. Non-German art forms, like jazz, were forbidden. So were the works of Jewish composers artists and painters.

The Nazis didn't like impressionist or post-impressionist painting. Hitler liked paintings to be realistic. It was even better if they carried a message supporting Nazi beliefs and values.

In what ways did the treatment of Jews change from 1933 to 1939?

In what ways were the lives of ordinary women changed in Nazi Germany?

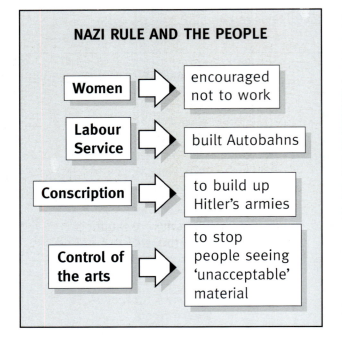

NAZI RULE AND THE PEOPLE

Women ⇨	encouraged not to work
Labour Service ⇨	built Autobahns
Conscription ⇨	to build up Hitler's armies
Control of the arts ⇨	to stop people seeing 'unacceptable' material

Source 6

▲ A painting from the school of Realism which supported Nazi beliefs.
This painting shows the ideal Nazi family in their ideal roles.

Why do you think the Nazis were so
concerned about controlling the Arts?

Chapter 4 *Nazi Germany: 1930~39*

Hitler, Nazism and Nazi beliefs

Source A

I knew all was lost. Only fools, liars and criminals could hope on the mercy of the enemy. In the nights hatred grew inside me, hatred for those responsible for this deed. In the days that followed, my own fate became known to me. I decided to go into politics.

▲ From an article written by Hitler describing the moment he heard about the Armistice in November 1918.

Source B

It is ridiculous to attempt to liberate ourselves from the chains of Versailles unless we take our destiny in our own hands and unless we work ... at our science of war. For there can be no doubt for anyone – between our present misery and our future happiness, there is war. This is why everybody, man, woman and child must know what war is.

▲ From the *Science of Military Defence*, a book written by a Nazi, Leipzig, 1932.

Source C

It is necessary, then, for better or for worse, to resort to war if one wishes seriously to arrive at pacifism. The pacifist idea will perhaps work on that day when the man superior to all others will have conquered the world and become the sole master of the Earth. First, then, the battle, and afterwards – perhaps – pacifism.

▲ From *Mein Kampf*, written by Adolf Hitler in 1924.

Source D

Germany has a right to greater living space [*Lebensraum*] than other nations. Our foreign policy is to unfold, enlarge and protect the entire German racial community, no matter where Germans might live in other countries. Space is paramount. Britain and France are both inspired by hate and will oppose Germany. They will have to be fought.

▲ From a speech made by Hitler in November 1937.

Source E

▲ A poster published by the Nazi Party in the 1930s.

Source F

Hitler invaded Austria in 1938 to complete the Anschluss, or union with Germany. Although this was a deliberate breach of the Treaty of Versailles there were many who were prepared to accept Hitler's claim that he was simply righting a serious wrong. If the Treaty of Versailles had recognised the right of other people of the same nationality and language to rule themselves, then, said Hitler, it was only proper that this right should also apply to Germans.

▲ A comment on support for Hitler's policy of reversing Versailles in a modern school textbook.

Study Source A

a What can you learn from Source A about Hitler's aims? (4)

Study Sources A, B and C

b Do Sources B and C support the evidence of Source A about the aims of the Nazis? Explain your answer by referring to all three sources. (6)

Study Sources D and E

c How useful are these sources in helping you to understand the beliefs of the Nazis? (8)

Study all of the sources

d 'Nazi beliefs meant that war was inevitable.' Use the sources and your own knowledge to explain whether you agree with this view. (12)

The Nazi rise to power

Source A

Hitler himself spoke at sixteen major rallies. Columns of SS troops shouting slogans marched through the villages and towns from morning till night. In every market square an SA band or Nazi minstrels played marches for hours on end.

▲ From an eyewitness account of the part played by Hitler in election campaigns in February 1933.

Source B

Here it seemed to me was hope. Here were new ideals ... The perils of communism ... could be checked. Hitler persuaded us, that instead of hopeless unemployment, Germany could move towards economic recovery. He had mentioned the Jewish problem only in passing. But his remarks did not worry me ... It was during these months that my mother saw an SA parade in the streets of Heidelberg. The sight of discipline in a time of chaos ... seems to have won her over.

▲ From *Inside the Third Reich,* by Albert Speer, a German architect and former Nazi minister during the Second World War, in which he describes a meeting that Hitler addressed in 1931.

Source C

▲ A photograph of an SA rally at Nuremberg in 1933.

Source D

There stood Hitler in a simple black coat and looked over the crowd, waiting – a forest of black swastika pennants swished up, the jubilation of the moment was given vent in a roaring salute. His main theme – out of parties shall grow a nation, the German nation. He laid into the system – 'I want to know what there is left to be ruined by this state!' When the speech was over, there was roaring enthusiasm and applause.

▲ **An eyewitness account of a speech made by Hitler at a Nazi Party rally in 1932.**

Source E

What had Hitler provided to persuade the Germans to give up their freedom so happily? Well, there was something for everyone in his political stewpot. Work for the unemployed, an army for the generals, a phoney religion for the gullible, a strident manner in foreign affairs for those who still smarted under the indignity of a lost war. Hitler knew he needed the support of the middle class, so he threw up a smoke screen of respectability around everything he did.

▲ **Christabel Bielenberg, a British woman living in Germany, describes events in 1934.**

Source F

They call me a stateless corporal and a housepainter. Is there anything improper in earning one's daily bread by manual labour? ... the day of reckoning is not far off. An increasing number of industrialists, financiers, intellectuals and Army officers are now looking for a man who will at last bring some order into affairs at home, who will draw the farmers, the workers and the officials into the German community once more.

▲ **From an interview with Hitler in a German daily newspaper in May 1931.**

Study Source A

a What can you learn from Source A about the methods used by the Nazis in election campaigns? (4)

Study Sources A, B and C

b Does the evidence of Source C support the evidence of Sources A and B? Explain your answer. (6)

Study Sources D and E

c How useful are Sources D and E as evidence about the appeal of Hitler and the Nazis? (8)

Study all of the sources

d 'It was solely the brilliance of Hitler's leadership which brought the Nazis to power.' Use the sources and your own knowledge to explain whether you agree with this view. (12)

Creation of the totalitarian state

Source A

Adolf is a swine. He will give us all away. He's getting matey with the generals – they are his cronies now ... the generals are a lot of old fogeys. They've never had a new idea ... I'm the nucleus of a new army don't you see that? Don't you understand that what's coming must be new, fresh and unused? You only get the opportunity once to make something new and big that will help lift the world off its hinges.

▲ From a reported conversation between Ernst Röhm and other members of the SA.

Source B

▲ A photograph of leading members of the Nazi Party, taken on 31 January 1933.

Source C

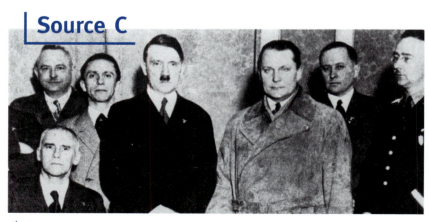

▲ The same photograph as published in late 1934. The missing figure is Ernst Röhm.

Source D

Rearmament is too serious a business to be carried out by swindlers, drunkards and homosexuals.

◄ A comment made by General Walther von Brauchitsch, the Commander in Chief of the German Army in 1934.

Source E

The Führer with soldierly decision and exemplary courage has himself attacked and crushed the traitors and murderers. The Army as the bearer of arms of the entire people, far removed from the conflicts of domestic politics, will show its gratitude through devotion and loyalty.

▲ A statement made by the German Defence Minister, General von Blomberg, in July 1934, after 'The Night of the Long Knives'.

Source F

I swear by God this holy oath, that I will render to Adolf Hitler, Führer of the German Reich and people, Supreme Commander of the armed forces, unconditional obedience, and I am ready, as a brave soldier, to risk my life at any time for this oath.

▲ The oath sworn by members of the German armed forces after the death of President von Hindenburg in August 1934.

Study Source A

a What can you learn from Source A about relations between Hitler and Ernst Röhm in 1934? (4)

Study Sources A, B and C

b Does the evidence of Source C support the evidence of Sources A and B about the relationship between Hitler and Röhm? Explain your answer. (6)

Study Sources D and E

c How useful are these sources in helping you to understand why 'The Night of the Long Knives' took place? (8)

Study all of the sources

d 'The Night of the Long Knives gave Hitler complete control of Germany.' Use the sources and your own knowledge to explain whether you agree with this view. (12)

The Nazi state

Source A

What puffs and patters?

What clicks and clatters?

I know what, oh what fun

It's a lovely Gatling gun.

▲ A Nazi nursery rhyme.

Source B

This Archangel is leading the column of comrades, a column formed by warriors of the Reich. They have only one enemy – the opponents of the Reich and its rulers. We do not want to speak the warm words of peace here. Our words are dictated by the terrible appeal of war. Young people, raise your hands and swear an oath before this monument, which is dedicated to bloodshed.

▲ From a speech made by a Hitler Youth leader on 31 October 1933 at the unveiling of a monument to the Archangel Michael.

Source C

So stand the Storm Battalions,

Ready for the racial fight.

Only when Jews lie bleeding

Can we be really free.

▲ A verse from the National Socialist *Little Song Book*.

Source D

Adolf Hitler gave us back our faith. He showed us the true meaning of religion. He came to take us from the faith of our fathers? No, he has come to renew for us the faith of our fathers and to make us new and better things ...

Just as Christ made his 12 disciples into a band faithful to the martyr's death whose faith shook the Roman Empire, so now we witness the same spectacle again: Adolf Hitler is the true Holy Ghost.

▲ From a speech made by the Reich Minister for Church Affairs in 1935.

Source E

Adolf Hitler to thee alone we are bound. In this hour we would renew our solemn vow; in this world we believe in Adolf Hitler alone. We believe that National Socialism is the sole faith to make our people blessed. We believe that there is Lord God in heaven, who has made us, who, leads us, who guides us and who visibly blesses us. And we believe that the Lord God has sent us Adolf Hitler that Germany might be established for all eternity.

▲ A prayer published by the Nazis for use in Reich churches.

Source F

KOMM ZU UNS!

DEUTSCHES JUNGVOLK IN DER HITLER-JUGEND

▲ A poster advertising the Nazi Youth movement.

Study Source A

a What can you learn from Source A about Nazis' attitudes to education? (4)

Study Sources A, B and C

b Do Sources B and C support the evidence of Source A about Nazi policies towards the young? Explain your answer by referring to all three sources. (6)

Study Sources D and E

c How useful are these sources as evidence about Nazi policies towards religion? (8)

Study all of the sources

d 'The Nazis believed that they could use young children to control their parents.' Use the sources and your own knowledge to explain whether you agree with this view. (12)

Racism and the treatment of minorities / Opposition to Nazi rule

Source A

On the evening of 9 November 1938, Dr Goebbels told the Party leaders that there had been anti-Jewish riots during which shops and synagogues had been set on fire. The Führer had decided that such actions were not to be prepared or organised by the Party, but neither were they to be discouraged. The Reich propaganda director said that the Party should not appear in public to have started the disturbances, but that in reality it should organise them and carry them out in secret.

▲ From a secret report of the Nazi Supreme Court on the events of Kristallnacht.

Source B

In one of the Jewish sections an 18-year-old boy was hurled from a three-storey window to land with both legs broken on a street of broken glass littered with burning beds. The main streets of the city were a positive litter of shattered glass. All of the synagogues were completely gutted by fire. One of the largest clothing stores was destroyed. The fire brigade made no attempt to put out the fire. It is very difficult to believe, but the owners of the clothing store were actually charged with setting fire to their own store, and were dragged from their beds at 6 a.m. and thrown into prison. Many male Jews have been sent to concentration camps.

▲ From a report on the events of Kristallnacht, 9 November 1938. This was written by the American Consul in Leipzig on 21 November 1938.

Source C

▲ A photograph of the damage caused by Kristallnacht. This is the interior of a synagogue in Munich.

Source D

Two SS men came to my house to fetch me. When about 20 people had been collected we were put into a lorry and taken to police headquarters. On the way I saw Jewish shops which had been destroyed. The big synagogue was in flames.

At the police station we were lined up in the yard. There were already hundreds there. Some had been there since early morning. About six o'clock we were formed into a procession of about 2000 and began to march to the railway station. Crowds lined the streets, some shouted abuse, but the majority remained silent.

▲ From a letter written by a Jew in February 1939. This was smuggled out of Germany and published by the German Freedom Party.

Source E

▲ A poster encouraging anti-Semitism in 1939. It suggests that Jewish butchers used rats to make sausages.

Source F

All damage to Jewish businesses or dwellings on 8, 9 and 10 November 1938 must be repaired by the Jewish occupant or by Jewish businessmen.

A fine of 1000 million Reich marks has been imposed on the Jews of German nationality.

From 1 January 1939, a Jew cannot be a businessman any longer. If any Jews are leading employees in businesses, they will be dismissed after six months' notice.

Jews are not permitted to employ female citizens of German blood under 45 years of age as domestic help.

▲ Decrees issued by Hermann Goering, 12 November 1938.

Study Source A

a What can you learn from Source A about the effects of Kristallnacht? (4)

Study Sources A, B and C

b Does the evidence of Source C support the evidence of Sources A and B about the effects of Kristallnacht? Explain your answer with reference to all three sources. (6)

Study Sources D and E

c How useful are these sources as evidence of Nazi policies towards the Jews? (8)

Study all of the sources

d 'Kristallnacht was organised and planned by the Nazis.' Use the sources and your knowledge to explain whether you agree with this view. (12)

The social impact of Nazism

Source A

Every Aryan hero must marry a blonde Aryan woman with blue, wide open eyes, a long oval face, a pink and white skin, a narrow nose and who is under all circumstances a virgin. The Aryan hero must only marry his equal Aryan woman, but not one who goes out too much or likes theatres, entertainment or sport, or who cares to be seen outside her house.

▲ From *The Knowledge of the Nation,* a book published in Germany in 1934.

Source B

We want our women tried and true
Not as decorated toys
The German wife and mother too
Bears riches no foreign woman enjoys.

The German woman is noble wine
She loves and enriches the earth.
The German woman is bright sunshine
To home and hearth.

Worthy of respect she must always be seen;
Not of strange races the passion and game
The Volk must remain pure and clean.
That is the Führer's highest aim.

▲ From *The ABC of National Socialism,* a book published in Germany in the 1930s.

Source C

Fifty-two-year-old pure Aryan doctor, veteran of the Battle of Tannenberg, who intends to settle on the land, desires male progeny through a registry-office marriage with a healthy Aryan, virginal, young, unassuming, economy-minded woman, adapted to hard work, broad-hipped, flat-heeled and earring-less.

▲ An advert that appeared in a German newspaper in the 1930s.

Source D

A German woman does not use make up!
A German woman does not smoke!
A German woman has a duty to keep herself fit and healthy!

▲ From the rule book of the League of German Maidens.

Source E

There is no room for political women in the world of National Socialism. All that this movement has ever said and thought on the subject goes against political women. Woman is relegated to her ordained family circles and to her business as a wife. The German revolution is an event made by, and supremely concerned with, the male.

▲ **From an article published in Germany in 1933.**

Source F

▲ **A poster published in Germany in the 1930s showing the ideal Nazi family.**

Study Source A

a What can you learn from Source A about Nazi beliefs about the role of women? (4)

Study Sources A, B and C

b In what ways do Sources B and C support the evidence of Source A about Nazi attitudes towards women? (6)

Study Sources D and E

c How useful are these sources as evidence of the ways that women were treated in Nazi Germany? (8)

Study all of the sources

d 'The Nazis believed that the role of women was to serve men.' Use the sources and your own knowledge to explain whether you agree with this view. (12)

CHAPTER 5

The world at war: 1938~45

Appeasement, Chamberlain and the outbreak of war

Neville Chamberlain

From 1937 Neville Chamberlain was Prime Minister of Britain. It was Chamberlain who had to deal with the problems caused by Hitler.

- In 1938 Hitler joined Austria and Germany together as one country (**Anschluss**). This was against the Treaty of Versailles. Chamberlain protested, but there was little he could do.

- Chamberlain also knew that Britain was not strong enough to help Czechoslovakia if Hitler attacked it. So he came up with a policy called **appeasement**. He would agree to Hitler's demands for Czechoslovakia (as long as they seemed reasonable). Hitler would be satisfied and war would be avoided.

There were many people in Britain who agreed with this plan. They had good reason to:

- They remembered the horrors of the First World War and did not want another war.

- Hitler was anti-communist and could be used to oppose the threat of the Soviet Union.

- Hitler was seen as doing a good job restoring Germany to its rightful place as a major power.

- The Treaty of Versailles had been very harsh on Germany. If Hitler broke it sometimes, did it really matter?

Chamberlain did not see his policy as giving in to Hitler (though some of his critics, like Winston Churchill, did). Chamberlain knew that the British armed forces were not strong. Appeasement would give him time to rebuild those forces, especially the RAF. Then he could negotiate with Hitler from a position of strength.

Source 1

▲ Mussolini, Hitler and Chamberlain at Munich. Mussolini (left) is shaking hands with Edouard Daladier (French Prime Minister 1938–40).

Appeasement tested – Czechoslovakia 1938

But Hitler didn't see things that way. Hitler thought Chamberlain was weak and intended to bully Britain into agreeing to his demands. On 15 September he announced that he thought the German-speaking inhabitants of Western Czechoslovakia should be able to govern themselves. (They lived in an area called the Sudetenland, which had been given to Czechoslovakia in 1918.) This seemed reasonable, so Chamberlain and the French leader, Daladier, agreed. The Czech government was forced to agree. But when Chamberlain told Hitler the news, the German leader told him that he thought the Sudetenland should actually be handed over to Germany.

Chamberlain was horrified by Hitler's views. He couldn't see how a handover could be managed. So Britain and France would probably have to try to stop Hitler. War looked inevitable.

The Munich Conference 1938

Britain now prepared for war. Children were evacuated from cities (to protect them from bombs) and air raid shelters were built. But war did not come. Instead, the Italian leader, Mussolini, proposed a conference to try to avoid war. At the conference were:

- Hitler of Germany

- Chamberlain of Britain

- Mussolini of Italy

- Daladier of France

The four leaders agreed that Hitler should have the Sudetenland. In return he promised to make no more demands for land in Czechoslovakia, and that Germany and Britain would never go to war again. This was the **Munich Agreement**. Chamberlain returned to Britain saying that he had brought 'peace in our time'. He was given a hero's welcome and appeared on the balcony of Buckingham Palace between the King and Queen. He was the man who had saved Britain from war.

The end of appeasement

The problem with Chamberlain was that he believed what Hitler told him. But Hitler had no intention of keeping his promises. He thought that Chamberlain was weak and would give in under pressure. So, during 1939, he carried out a series of actions showing how little he cared for the Munich Agreement.

- In March 1939 he occupied the rest of Czechoslovakia. Chamberlain knew that appeasement had failed and stepped up the re-arming of his forces.

- In August 1939 the world was shocked to hear that Hitler and Stalin of the Soviet Union had signed an agreement called the **Nazi-Soviet Pact**. They were supposed to hate each other! They did, but an agreement at this time suited both of them. Hitler could invade Poland (which he had always wanted). He could take Western Poland and the Soviets could take Eastern Poland (which had previously been Soviet territory).

- Britain and France had been expecting the Soviet Union to block any German attack on Poland. They both had agreements to protect Poland. So if Hitler attacked Poland, that meant war.

Sure enough, Hitler invaded Poland on 1 September 1939. Britain and France then declared war. The Second World War had begun.

Reasons for early German success

- The German attack on Poland was a complete success. The British and French had declared war, but there was little they could do to help Poland. Within three weeks Poland was defeated.

- For the next six months little happened and the British people started talking about 'the Phoney War'. The only fighting was in Denmark and Norway, which Hitler easily captured.

- But in May 1940 things changed. Hitler invaded Belgium, Holland and France. Soon the **British Expeditionary Force**, which had been sent to resist the Germans, had retreated until it was trapped on the French beaches at Dunkirk.

- In the first two weeks of June 310,000 troops were rescued from Dunkirk. The newspapers called this 'the miracle of Dunkirk' and the Daily Mirror had the headline 'BLOODY MARVELLOUS'. But Dunkirk had been a serious defeat – 68,000 men were killed, 120,000 vehicles, 90,000 rifles and 2300 heavy guns were left behind in France.

Source 2

▲ A formation of 'Stuka' dive-bombers.

Reasons for the German success

- Germany had rebuilt its armed forces so that it had huge resources. Poland, Denmark, Holland and Norway all had tiny armed forces.

- The Germans used a tactic called **Blitzkrieg** (lightning war). It involved sudden and rapid attacks by dive bombers, tanks and paratroops. They had practiced it in the Spanish Civil War (1936–39). Now it had worked in Poland and France.

- France had pinned all its hopes on a line of fortifications along its border called the **Maginot Line**. The French believed that it would be impossible for the Germans to break through it. However, the Germans just went round it. The French had not extended the Maginot Line to the sea. This was because they did not want their allies, the Belgians, to be on the wrong side of the line.

- So, the Germans invaded France from Belgium, where there was no Maginot Line. The French thought that the Germans would not be able to get their tanks through the Belgian forests. But they did.

- The French were so shocked that some of their generals lost heart. Once the Germans had got round the Maginot Line and reached the English Channel, the French couldn't see how they could avoid defeat.

Why do you think the British government was so keen to describe Dunkirk as a great event for the British?

What was Blitzkrieg?

What was the Maginot Line?

Falls and survivals

The fall of France
On 22 June 1940 the French surrendered. The Germans took over Northern and Western France. But they allowed the French to govern the rest of their country. Marshall Petain was put in charge of a government based in Vichy. Of course it had to do what the Germans told it. Then in 1942 the Germans occupied all of France.

Britain next
Once France had been defeated, Hitler turned his attention to Britain. It is likely that Hitler did not want to invade Britain. What he hoped was that, once Britain was left to fight Germany on its own (as it was after France was defeated), it would make peace with Germany. When the new Prime Minister, Winston Churchill (who took over when Chamberlain stood down), made it clear that Britain would not make peace, Hitler began to prepare for battle with Britain.

- At first shipping in the English Channel and English ports was attacked.

- Then bombing raids were carried out on RAF bases. This was the '**Battle of Britain**'. Hitler knew that he could not send forces across the Channel safely until the RAF had been defeated. In the summer of 1940 the German Luftwaffe came very close to defeating the RAF, but didn't realise just how close.

- In September 1940 Hitler tried a new tactic. He would bomb British cities until the British people were so disheartened they would force their government to give in to Hitler. So Hitler launched '**the Blitz**'. From September 1940 to May 1941 German bombers attacked British cities almost every day. They killed over 40,000 people and made another 2 million homeless.

- London was a major target, but so were other industrial towns or ports. Coventry was hit by a very heavy raid in November 1940. Nearly 500 people were killed in one night.

- The Germans used special bombs called **incendiaries**, which started fires when they exploded. But they also used huge, explosive bombs. Some of these weighed 1000 pounds (2200 kilograms).

- The attacks were supposed to break the morale of the British people. The official government line at the time was that the British could take it and were carrying on as normal. There is plenty of evidence, however, which showed that many people were stretched to breaking point by the terror of the attacks.

Fortunately, the British held out until the spring of 1941. At that point Hitler turned his attention away from Britain. It was time to deal with the Soviet Union.

Invasion of the Soviet Union

In June 1941 Hitler launched his invasion of the Soviet Union. He had signed an agreement with Stalin in 1939 (see page 101), but everyone knew that one day he would attack the Soviet Union.

German troops swept into the Soviet Union in huge numbers. They made a three-pronged attack towards Leningrad, Stalingrad and Moscow. The Soviet Army retreated in the face of such strength. As they did so, they carried out a **scorched-earth** policy. This meant that they destroyed anything which might be of use to the Germans. In November 1941 the Germans reached the outskirts of Moscow. But they never got any further. They were short of supplies and the Soviet winter caused illness and frostbite to their soldiers. They had some success in Leningrad and Stalingrad, but the heroic resistance of the Soviet Army and people inflicted heavy losses on the Germans.

Operation Barbarossa

This was the name given to Hitler's invasion of the Soviet Union. The Germans advanced for thousands of kilometres, but they could not defeat the Soviet weather! In December 1941 the temperatures fell to minus 40°C. The fuel in the German tanks and lorries froze, and the German soldiers had very little winter clothing. They had thought they would win by the time the weather became really cold.

The long way home

The **Eastern Front** proved to be a disaster for the Germans. In February 1943, the German Sixth Army was surrounded at Stalingrad and forced to surrender. It was the first major defeat of the German armed forces in the war. It was also the beginning of the end for the Germans in the Soviet Union. Soviet forces slowly drove them west back into Germany. The advance of the Soviet Red Army did not stop until it reached Berlin in 1945.

Reasons for the German defeat

The attack had come too late in the year. Hitler had originally planned an attack for April. That would have given time for a German victory before winter.

Hitler underestimated the resistance of the Soviets. Around 20 million Soviet civilians died in what the Soviet Union called 'The Great Patriotic War'.

The Soviet weather was too much for the Germans. They did not have winter supplies and the Soviet scorched-earth policy prevented them using captured supplies.

German advances

Furthest extent of German advances, December 1942

FINLAND

Leningrad

Smolensk

POLAND

Stalingrad

Kiev

HUNGARY

ROMANIA

Black Sea

BULGARIA

N   0   400 km
     0   250 miles

▲ Map of the Eastern Front.

- The Japanese had already taken over large areas of land by 1941. It had captured Manchuria in China in 1931 and, by 1937, was threatening to take over large parts of the rest of China. It wanted to build what it called the 'Greater East Asia Co-prosperity Sphere', which was another name for a Japanese Empire.

- The USA did not want this as it would harm US trade. The USA had already shown its disapproval of what the Japanese were doing. In early 1941 it cut off supplies of oil to Japan in protest against Japan's actions in China. The USA was Japan's main supplier, so this was very bad news. The Japanese began to think that they would have to fight the USA eventually, so it was better to strike whilst the Americans were unprepared.

The causes of the war in the Pacific

On 7 June 1941 the Japanese launched a surprise attack on the US Navy base at Pearl Harbor, Hawaii. The following day President Roosevelt declared war on Japan. Why had the Japanese done this?

- In the 1920s and 1930s Japan was a country with a growing population. It had no raw materials of its own to supply its industries. The Japanese leaders decided that they should conquer other lands to get space for Japanese settlers and to source raw materials. So Japan wanted to build an Empire in the Far East.

Advances by Japan

Territory held by Japan in December 1941

Territory captured by Japan from December 1941 to July 1942

JAPAN

MANCHURIA

Tokyo

Hiroshima

Nagasaki

CHINA

Okinawa

BURMA

Hong Kong

CAMBODIA

PHILIPPINES

MALAYA

Singapore

BORNEO

SUMATRA

DUTCH EAST INDIES

JAVA

NEW GUINEA

AUSTRALIA

2100 miles north east of Wake

Pearl Harbor

HAWAII

Wake

Guam

Guadalcanal

0   miles   600
0   km   1000

▲ Map of Asia showing Japanese advances.

- The Japanese attack came at 8 am and took Pearl Harbor completely by surprise. The attack killed 2400 Americans, sank eight battleships and damaged or destroyed 350 planes.

- But the effects of the attack could have been worse. The three American aircraft carriers were at sea at the time and so escaped unharmed. Eventually, the US would rebuild its forces and take revenge.

- But during 1942 the Japanese had almost total success. The Americans had been weakened, France and Holland were occupied by the Germans. Britain was fighting for its survival. None of the powers that owned land in the Far East could stop the Japanese.

- By the end of the year the Japanese had captured Indo-China, Malaya, Indonesia, the Philippines, Burma and the great British naval base at Singapore. Even India and Australia seemed under threat.

What effects did the Blitz have on Britain?

Why did Operation Barbarossa fail?

Why did the Japanese attack Pearl Harbor?

Reasons for German defeat in the Second World War

In early 1941 it looked like the Germans would have an easy victory. But by 1943 that victory was slipping away. Hitler's errors were partly to blame for this.

- In 1940 he had told the generals not to attack the British forces on the beach at Dunkirk.

- He had also ordered the switch from attacking the RAF to bombing British cities in 1941.

- He had ordered the attack on the Soviet Union in June 1941.

- He had held back production of submarines in 1939 so that, in 1941, Germany had only 37 submarines (although those submarines did sink hundreds of merchant ships – it was only when long-range flying boats began to escort convoys that the Allies won the 'Battle of the Atlantic').

Another reason for the defeat of the Germans was the determination of the British people.

- Britain stood alone between June 1940 and June 1941. The people's courage at that time was an example to the rest of the world.

- Prime Minister Churchill also played a major part. He maintained British morale with his rousing speeches and refusal to consider peace.

The USA also contributed in a major way to the defeat of the Germans.

- In 1940 the USA gave the British US destroyers in return for islands in the Caribbean.

- In 1941 Roosevelt agreed to 'Lend-Lease' equipment to Britain. It would not have to pay for it until later.

- Once the USA joined the war, its military and economic might was a key factor in the Allies' victory. American bombers played a major role in raids on Germany, using as many as 1000 planes at a time. The Allies were trying to destroy German industry, but even as late as 1945, 90 per cent of German industry was still working at full production. It was a different story when it came to German cities. In just one raid on Dresden in February 1945 2600 tonnes of bombs were dropped. About 70 per cent of the buildings were destroyed and 150,000 people were killed.

Source 3

▲ A large convoy of ships seen from a US Navy flying boat patrolling the Atlantic.

- Overconfidence was another reason for the German defeat. Hitler asked his armed forces to do too much. For example, in 1941 he sent troops to Africa to help the Italians. At first they were very successful, but eventually they were defeated. Then the Germans had to send troops to Italy to try to stop the Allies occupying it.

- But perhaps the major reason for Germany's defeat was the decision to invade the Soviet Union. Almost 90 per cent of all Germany's casualties in the whole war came in the Soviet Union. There were huge losses in equipment too. For example at the Battle of Kursk in July 1943, the Soviet army destroyed 1500 German tanks. There was no way that the Germans could win in the Soviet Union after this.

- The Soviet policy of destroying everything they could not carry away left the German forces without adequate supplies of food. Hitler also made mistakes in the way that he treated some of the racial minorities in the Soviet Union. People like the Ukranians and the Tartars hated the Soviet Union and had been treated very badly by Stalin. They welcomed the Germans as people who would free them from Soviet rule. If Hitler had treated these people well, he would have won their support. Instead he treated them as sub-humans. Thousands were sent back to Germany as slave labour – or were shot. So the Soviet campaign dragged on and eventually the huge Soviet Red Army overpowered the Germans.

REASONS FOR THE DEFEAT OF GERMANY

Hitler's errors in 1939-41
not enough submarines
not defeating the British at Dunkirk
not defeating the RAF

The determination of the British
standing alone 1940-1
Churchill's inspiring leadership

The American entry into the war
providing the British with supplies
bringing huge resources into the war
playing major part in fighting after 1941

German over-confidence
stretching the army too far
invading the Soviet Union

The determination of the Soviet Union
brave resistance by Soviet people
'scorched earth' policy
huge losses for the German army

By 1945 Germany was running out of soldiers and equipment. The people were losing their desire to carry on with the war.

D-Day

In the West, the British, US and Canadians landed troops in Normandy in North West France. They landed at five beaches with code names Sword, Juno, Gold, Omaha and Utah.

This massive operation had taken great planning. The largest ever fleet of ships was put together and 10,000 aircraft provided air cover. Gliders took paratroops to important positions which they attacked before the main force arrived. The Allies even took their own harbour to land equipment once the beaches had been captured.

The Germans expected the Allied landing to be near Calais and they were taken by surprise. Even so, there was fierce fighting and some of the beaches were only taken after very heavy fighting and very high loss of life.

The Germans fought desperately to stop the Allied forces reaching Germany. The Allies were held up for only a month by the Germans, and were soon on their way. They liberated Paris within six weeks and, by September 1944, were approaching Germany.

At the time Germany had been bombed almost non-stop and an Allied **blockade** meant the people were starving. When the Allies got to Germany they found that some of the enemy soldiers were old men, or young boys. The Germans were short of soldiers too.

For the last two years of the war the Allies had far more men and supplies. They had simply ground down the Germans. On 8 May 1945 the Germans surrendered. By then, Hitler had already committed suicide in his bunker in Berlin.

Germany in 1945

Although many German factories were still working in 1945, the Allied blockade of Germany was very successful. There was a shortage of food, fuel and raw materials. By the end of the war, many Germans had lost the will to fight on.

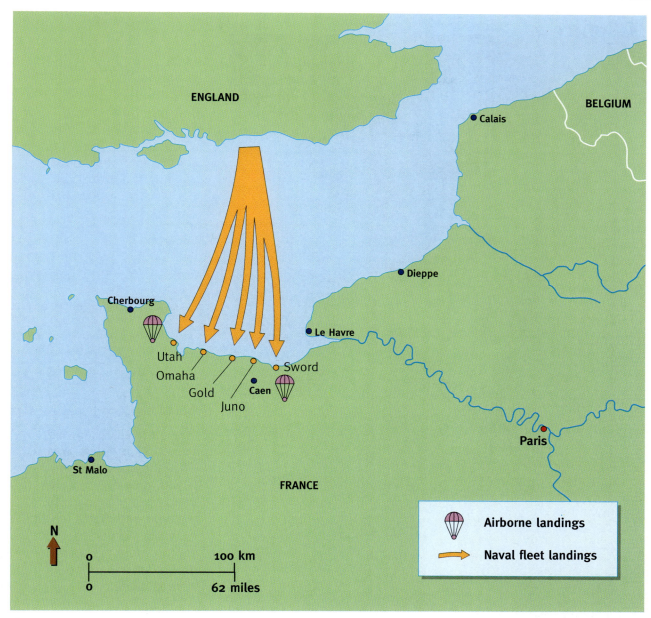

▲ **The D-Day landings in Normandy.**

Map labels:
ENGLAND
BELGIUM
Calais
Dieppe
Cherbourg
Le Havre
Utah
Omaha
Sword
Gold
Caen
Juno
St Malo
Paris
FRANCE

Legend:
Airborne landings
Naval fleet landings

N
0   100 km
0   62 miles

The Defeat of Japan

The war with Germany was over, but the war with Japan continued for another three months before it too surrendered. Why did Japan fail to win the war, when in early 1942 its forces had swept all before them?

- Some Japanese commanders thought that the war was lost right at the start. They had not destroyed the three US aircraft carriers which would normally have been at Pearl Harbor.

So the American fleet would take less time to rebuild.

- This could be seen as early as June 1942 when, at the Battle of Midway Island, the Americans sank four Japanese aircraft carriers. These were so important to Japan that even some of their own leaders now expected them to lose. They knew that American manpower, oil and rapid production of weapons would eventually prove too much for them.

Source 4

▲ A painting of a Japanese aircraft carrier under fire at Midway Island.

Island hopping

The US forces used this approach to defeat Japan. Once they captured an island, they built an airbase, then moved on to the next one. Some which were too difficult to capture were left alone. So the Japanese forces were isolated.

- But there was a long way to go before the war in the Pacific ended. The Japanese had won control of huge areas in the Pacific and were determined to keep them. Their soldiers refused to surrender – even if the situation was hopeless.

- So at Leyte in the Philippines almost 80,000 of them died trying to stop the USA recapturing the island. Obviously, such resistance also brought high casualties amongst the American soldiers.

- The US forces decided to use a policy called **'island-hopping'**. In this way they got nearer and nearer Japan. Finally, they captured Iwo Jima and Okinawa (though it cost the lives of 28,000 US marines). These two islands were close enough to Japan for US bombers to make regular raids. Soon much of Japan had been devastated by US bombers. But still the Japanese did not surrender.

Reasons for the defeat of Japan

In mainland South East Asia the Japanese advance had finally been halted in 1944. Japanese forces were soon forced out of Burma and those in India also began to retreat in August 1944. So, by the end of 1944, the Japanese were losing to the British in Burma and India, and the US forces were recapturing the lands that were occupied by the Japanese in the Pacific.

The Atomic bomb
By the summer of 1945 the Japanese conquests had been recaptured and the Allies were ready to invade Japan itself. But the US President, Harry S. Truman, was concerned about what the casualties would be. The Japanese had died in their thousands defending lands they had captured. They would be even more determined to protect their homeland. Truman's military advisers told him that an attack on Japan would probably cost the Allies half a million men. There had to be a way to persuade the Japanese to surrender.

Scientists in the USA had developed the **atomic bomb**, which could destroy huge areas on its own. Truman considered dropping such a bomb on an uninhabited island to show the Japanese what it could do. But he thought this would not be enough to persuade them.

So on 6 August 1945 a US plane, the *Enola Gay*, dropped an atomic bomb on the Japanese city of Hiroshima, killing 80,000 people. Three days later a second bomb was dropped on Nagasaki killing another 40,000. At this point, the Japanish Emperor told his forces to surrender.

But it might not have been the atomic bomb which ended the war. The Japanese had hoped that the Soviet Union would help them get better terms if they surrendered. However, on 9 August the Soviet Union joined the war against Japan. There was no choice left. The Japanese had to surrender. The war was over.

The effects of the atomic bomb

When the USA dropped the first bomb on Hiroshima, the heat at the centre of the explosion was so great that all solids were turned into gas. There was also a wind of 750 miles (1200 km) an hour that tore people apart. Then came radiation. It caused flesh to melt and hang down in strips. Years later it was still causing babies to be born with deformities.

What was 'island-hopping'?

Why did the Americans drop the atomic bomb on Japan?

Why did Japan lose the Second World War?

Appeasement, Chamberlain and the outbreak of war

Source A

We are in no position to enter into a war with such a formidable power as Germany, much less if Germany were aided by Italian attacks on our Mediterranean bases. Therefore, until we have rearmed we must adjust our foreign policy to our circumstances. I do not myself take too pessimistic a view of the situation. The dictators (Hitler and Mussolini) are too often regarded as though they were inhuman.

▲ From a letter written by Neville Chamberlain to a friend in the USA on 16 January 1938.

Source B

You only have to look at the map to see that nothing that France or we could do could possibly save Czechoslovakia from being overrun by the Germans if they wanted to do it. The Austrian frontier is practically open; the great Skoda munition works are within easy bombing distance of the German aerodromes, the railways all pass through German territory. Therefore we could not help Czechoslovakia, it would simply be an excuse for going to war with Germany. I have therefore abandoned any idea of giving guarantees to Czechoslovakia.

▲ From Neville Chamberlain's diary, 20 March 1938.

Source C

I had established a certain confidence, which was my aim. In spite of the hardness and ruthlessness I thought I saw in his face, I got the impression that here was a man who could be relied upon when he had given his word.

▲ From a letter written by Neville Chamberlain to his sister after meeting Hitler at Berchtesgaden in September 1938.

Source D

▲ Photograph of Neville Chamberlain who was greeted by cheering crowds after he had returned from Munich on 30 September 1938.

Source E

Be Glad in your hearts. Give thanks to your God.

The wings of peace settle about us and the peoples of Europe. People of Britain your children are safe. Your husbands and your sons will not march to battle.

If we must have a victor, let us choose Chamberlain. For the Prime Minister's conquests are mighty and enduring – millions of happy homes and hearts relieved of their burden. To him the laurels.

▲ From the *Daily Express*, 30 September 1938.

Source F

In 1938 Czechoslovakia was the one country ready for war. The Czechoslovak Army of 35 divisions faced a German Army which was slightly larger, but the Czechs were better equipped than the Germans in a number of ways, notably artillery. In military terms, Hitler's aggression was lunacy, as his generals knew. The avoidance of war in 1938 was not only a shameful act, but a foolish one.

▲ A comment on Chamberlain's policy of appeasement from a modern history book.

Study Source A

a What can you learn from Source A about Neville Chamberlain's policy towards Hitler in early 1938? (4)

Study Sources A, B and C

b Do Sources B and C support the evidence of Source A about Chamberlain's policy? Explain your answer by referring to both sources. (6)

Study Sources D and E

c How useful are these sources in helping you to understand the reaction to the Munich Agreement in Britain? (8)

Study all of the sources

d The writer of Source F described Chamberlain's actions in September 1938 as 'shameful' and 'foolish'. Use the sources and your own knowledge to explain whether you agree with this view. (12)

Reasons for early German success

Source A

Our strength lies in our quickness and brutality. I have given the command and I will shoot everyone who utters one word of criticism. The aim in war is not to reach a certain point, but of completely destroying the enemy. I met those poor worms Daladier and Chamberlain in Munich. They will be too cowardly to attack. I shall attack France and England at the most favourable and earliest moment. Breaking the neutrality of Belgium and Holland is of no importance. No one will question what we have done.

▲ From speeches made by Hitler to his generals in late 1939.

Source C

Three months before the collapse, I made a tour of the French front. When we reached the ill-fated section of Sedan, the French commander had taken us to the River Meuse and shown us the wooded banks and rushing waters. 'Look at the terrain,' he had said to us. 'No German Army can get through here.'

▲ From the memoirs of a British politician, written after the Second World War.

Source B

In 1940 the Germans devised a plan to cut off British and French Armies in northern France. First they invaded Belgium and Holland, intending to draw British and French Armies to help those countries. Then from 12 May, they struck in the area of Sedan, at the top of the Maginot Line. Fierce strokes launched by tanks and Stuka dive-bombers soon cracked a way through the defences. By using fast-moving Panzer divisions the Germans advanced swiftly.

▲ From a modern history textbook.

Source D

▲ German attacks in 1940.

Source E

On we went at a steady speed. Every so often a quick glance at the map by a shaded light and a short wireless message to Divisional Headquarters to report the position and this was the success of the 25th Panzer division. We were through the Maginot Line! It was hardly believable. Twenty-two years before we had stood for four and a half years before this self-same enemy.

▲ From a description of the German advance in 1940 written by General Rommel.

Source F

▲ Germans troops advancing in the Ardennes in May 1940.

Study Source A

a What can you learn from Source A about Hitler's plans for war? (4)

Study Sources A, B and C

b Does Source C support the evidence of Sources A and B about Hitler's military strategy? Explain your answer referring to all three of the sources. (6)

Study Sources D and E

c How useful are these sources in helping you to understand the successes of the German army in May 1940? (8)

Study all of the sources

d 'The main reason for the defeat of the Allies in 1940 was the French belief that the Maginot Line would stop the German advance.' Use the sources and your own knowledge to explain whether you agree with this view. (12)

Falls and survivals / Invasion of the Soviet Union

Source A

Conflicting orders started coming in to erect barriers or lay mines or so on. Then another order would cancel this and then another order would arrive saying that it had to be done at once. I personally received an order from the Chief of Staff on the evening of 22 June telling me to withdraw my troops from the border. I could sense the nervousness and lack of agreement. The troops and the staff were below strength, and they had inadequate communications and transport. They were not ready for battle.

▲ From the memoirs of the Commander of the Soviet Eighth Army, describing the events of 22 June 1941.

Source C

The enemy is cruel and implacable. He is out to seize our lands, which have been watered by the sweat of our brows, to seize our grain and oil, which have been obtained by the labour of our hands. He is out to restore the rule of landlords, to restore Tsarism, to destroy the national culture and national existence as states of the Russians, Ukrainians, Belorussians, Lithuanians, Latvians, Estonians, Uzbeks, Tartars, Moldavians, Georgians, Armenians, Azerbaijanians and the other free peoples of the Soviet Union. The enemy wants to Germanise them and convert them into slaves.

▲ From the first speech made by Stalin after the German invasion, made on 3 July 1941.

Source B

The Germans were vastly outnumbered by Soviet forces. But they had the priceless advantage of excellent organisation and of surprise. The Soviet master spy Richard Sorge, a German newspaper correspondent working in Tokyo, had warned Stalin in April of the German plan. But Stalin simply did not expect the Führer to turn East when he had not yet defeated Britain.

▲ From a modern history textbook.

Source D

Those Arctic blasts that had taken us by surprise in our protected positions cut through our attacking troops. In a couple of days there were 100,000 casualties from frostbite alone. A few days later our winter clothing arrived. There was just enough for each company to be issued with four heavy fur-lined greatcoats and four pairs of felt-lined boots. Four sets of winter clothing for each company. Sixteen greatcoats and sixteen pairs of winter boots to be shared among a battalion of 800 men.

▲ From the diary of a German soldier in the USSR written in late 1941.

Source E

▲ A photograph of Soviet troops in December 1941.

Source F

German attacks on the Soviet Union in 1941.

Study Source A

a What can you learn from Source A about the reasons for the successes of the German Army at the beginning of Operation Barbarossa? (4)

Study Sources A and B

b Does Source B support the evidence of Source A about the reasons for German successes in 1941? Explain your answer by referring to both sources. (6)

Study Sources D and E

c How useful are these sources in helping you to understand German successes in 1940? (8)

Study all of the sources

d 'The weather was the main reason for the failure of Operation Barbarossa in 1941.' Use the sources and your own knowledge to explain whether you agree with this view. (12)

The causes of war in the Pacific

Source A

If the Japanese government takes any further steps in pursuance of its policy of military domination by force or threat of force of neighbouring countries, the government of the United States will be compelled to take immediately any steps which it may consider necessary to safeguard the security of the United States.

▲ From a note sent by the US government to the Japanese government on 17 August 1941.

Source B

In the first few months of war it is very likely that we would achieve total victory. I am convinced that we should take advantage of this opportunity. We should use the high morale of the Japanese people and their determination to overcome the crisis facing our country, even at the risk of losing their lives. It would be better to attack now than to sit and wait while the enemy puts more and more pressure upon us.

▲ From a speech made at a meeting of the Japanese government and the Japanese military commanders on 5 November 1941.

Source C

I lunched with the President today at his desk in the Oval Office. We were talking about things far removed from war when at about 1.40 the Secretary of the Navy Knox called and said that they had picked up a radio call from Honolulu advising that an air raid attack was on and that it was 'no drill'.

I said that there must be some mistake. The President thought the report was probably true and thought it was just the kind of unexpected thing the Japanese would do.

▲ From the diary of Harry Hopkins, one of Roosevelt's advisers, 7 December 1941.

Source D

	Destroyed or damaged
Battleships	8
Cruisers and other warships	11
Aircraft	188
Casualties	dead or missing 3219 wounded 1272

▲ The damage inflicted by the Japanese attack on Pearl Harbor.

Source E

▲ A photograph of US warships being attacked at Pearl Harbor.

Source F

Yesterday, December 7 1941 – a date which will live in infamy – the United States of America was suddenly and deliberately attacked by naval and air forces of the Empire of Japan. The United States was at peace with that nation and was still in conversation with its government and its Emperor, looking forward to the maintenance of peace in the Pacific.

▲ From a speech made by President Roosevelt on 8 December 1941.

Study Source A

a What can you learn from Source A about relations between the USA and Japan in 1941? (4)

Study Sources A, B and C

b Does the evidence of Source C support the evidence of Sources A and B? Explain your answer. (6)

Study Sources D and E

c How useful are Sources D and E as evidence about the effects of the attack on Pearl Harbor? (8)

Study all of the sources

d 'The attack on Pearl Harbor was a failure.' Use the sources and your own knowledge to explain whether you agree with this view. (12)

Reasons for German defeat

Source A

On 24 May the German Air Force reported no sudden concentration of shipping in the ports of Dover, Folkestone and along the Thames. On 2 June it became obvious that the weather along the Channel was going to worsen. Rommel, who had expected an attack in early June, if the reports that Allied training had been taking place during low tide were true, chose now to go and see Hitler. His wife's birthday was on 6 June, so he could combine business with pleasure.

▲ From a modern history textbook referring to events in 1944.

Source B

If I know the British, they'll go to church next Sunday one last time and then sail on Monday. Army group B says they are not going to come yet and when they do it'll be at Calais. So I think that we'll be welcoming them on Tuesday, right here.

▲ From a reported conversation between General Erich Marcks and another German officer on 1 June 1944.

Source C

For various reasons, almost all of the senior commanders of the German forces were absent from their stations during the early morning of 6 June. General Friedrich Dollman, commanding the German Seventh Army, was on his way to Rennes in Brittany, with most of the divisional commanders. The German High Command had studied earlier Allied landings in the Mediterranean, all of which had taken place in fine, calm weather. The Germans therefore saw this period as a respite, during which they could stage exercises.

▲ From a modern history textbook referring to events in 1944.

Source D

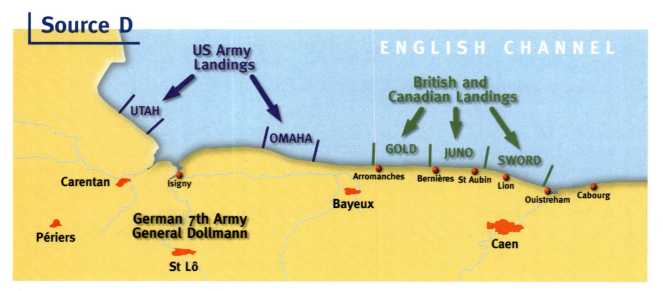

▲ The D-Day landings, 6 June 1944.

Source E

▲ A photograph of the D-Day landings at Omaha beach in June 1944.

Source F

There was often disagreement between Hitler and his generals, as he was always suspicious of them. He refused to delegate authority to them and preferred to play off one against the other. There was little agreement between the generals themselves and Hitler preferred to keep it that way. Despite Rommel's pleas, Hitler refused to hand over control of the crack Panzer divisions in Normandy.

▲ From a modern history textbook.

Study Source A

a What can you learn from Source A about German preparations for D-Day? (4)

Study Sources A, B and C

b Do Sources B and C support the evidence of Source A about German preparations for D-Day? Explain your answer by referring to all three sources. (6)

Study Sources D and E

c How useful are Sources D and E in helping you to understand why the D-Day landings succeeded? (8)

Study all of the sources

d 'The main reason for the success of the D-Day landings was the careful planning of the Allies.' Use the sources and your own knowledge to explain whether you agree with this view. (12)

Reasons for the defeat of Japan

Source A

The total strength of the Japanese Army was estimated at about 5 million men. The Air Force Kamikaze attacks had already inflicted serious damage on our seagoing forces. There was a very strong possibility that the Japanese government might decide upon resistance to the end. We estimated that the major fighting would not end until the latter part of 1946 at the earliest.

▲ From an article written by Henry Stimson, the US Secretary for War in 1945.

Source B

I was a 21-year-old lieutenant leading a rifle platoon. When the bombs dropped and news began to circulate that the invasion of Japan would not take place, after all, that we would not be obliged to run up the beaches near Tokyo assault-firing while we were shelled and mortared, we cried with relief and joy. We were going to live. We were going to grow up to manhood after all.

▲ From an interview with a US Army officer.

Source C

It was my reaction that the scientists and others wanted to make this test because of the vast sums that had been spent on the project. My own feeling was that in being the first to use it we had adopted the ethical standards common to barbarians in the Dark Ages. I was not taught to make war in that fashion.

The use of this barbarous weapon at Hiroshima and Nagasaki was of no material assistance in our war against Japan. The Japanese were already defeated and were ready to surrender because of the effective sea blockade and the successful bombing with conventional weapons.

▲ From the memoirs of Admiral William Leahy, the US Chief of Staff in 1945.

Source D

The war situation has developed not to Japan's advantage. Moreover the enemy has begun to employ a new and most cruel bomb, the power of which to do damage is incalculable, taking the toll of many innocent lives. We have resolved to pave the way for a grand peace for all generations.

▲ From the radio broadcast made by the Emperor of Japan announcing the surrender.

Source E

The Americans dropped atom bombs on the Japanese cities of Hiroshima and Nagasaki killing hundreds of thousands of civilians. Officially Washington 'claimed' that the bombings were aimed at bringing the end of the war nearer and avoiding unnecessary casualties. But they had entirely different objectives. Neither strategy nor tactics required the use of the atom bomb. The purpose of the bombings was to intimidate other countries, above all the Soviet Union.

▲ From a history book published in the Soviet Union in 1984.

Source F

We feared that, if the Japanese were told that the bomb would be used on a given locality, they might bring our boys who were prisoners of war to that area. Also if we were to warn the Japanese and if the bomb then failed to explode, we would have given aid and comfort to the Japanese military.

▲ From evidence given to a committee by the US Secretary of State; the committee was discussing the possibility of warning the Japanese about the use of the bomb.

Study Source A

a What can you learn from Source A about the use of the atom bomb in August 1945? (4)

Study Sources A, B and C

b Does the evidence of Source C support the evidence of Sources A and B? Explain your answer. (6)

Study Sources D and E

c How useful are Sources D and E as evidence about the effects of the atomic bomb? (8)

Study all of the sources

d The writer of Source F believed that there was no alternative to dropping the atom bomb on a Japanese city. Use the sources and your own knowledge to explain whether you agree with this view. (12)

CHAPTER 6

Conflict in Vietnam: c.1963~75

Essential Information

In the early 1960s the Americans fought a war in Vietnam which proved to be a great humiliation for them. Even though the USA was one of the two world superpowers, it was unable to defeat a communist **guerilla** force operating against the government of South Vietnam. How had the USA become involved in this war?

Reasons for US involvement in Vietnam

- During the Second World War, Japan had conquered the French colony of Indo-China (Laos, Cambodia and Vietnam). After the Japanese defeat it was decided that Indo-China should be returned to France.

- However, many Vietnamese people wanted to be free from rule by Europeans. They formed the League for Vietnamese Independence (Vietminh). The communist leader of the Vietminh, **Ho Chi Minh**, declared Vietnam to be independent on 2 September 1945.

- The French wanted to keep their colony and war broke out. By 1952 the French had lost 92,000 men and spent several hundred million francs on the war. They asked the USA for help.

- President Truman did not want Vietnam to become communist (remember this was the time of the **Cold War**), so he gave the French financial help. Despite this, the French did not win the war. They suffered an embarrassing defeat at Dien Bien Phu in May 1954. They decided to leave Indo-China.

- A conference was held in Geneva where it was decided that:

1. Laos and Cambodia would be independent countries.

Source 1

▲ Ho Chi Minh.

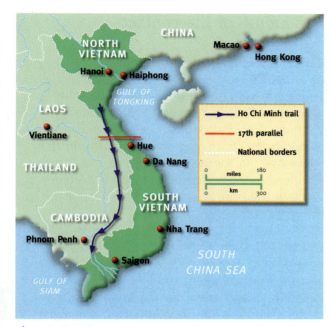

▲ The division of Vietnam.

The Domino Theory?

In the years after the Second World War, the Americans tried desperately to stop the spread of communism. They feared that if Vietnam became communist, then the other countries of South East Asia would follow one at a time. This was called the '**Domino Theory**', because each country would fall to communism like one domino after another. So, President Eisenhower was determined to stop the spread of communism in Vietnam.

Helping South Vietnam

The USA decided that the best way to stop communism was to help President Diem in South Vietnam. From 1954–61 the USA gave over US $1 billion to South Vietnam. Much of it was spent on building up the South Vietnamese Army. But some of it found its way into the pockets of Diem and his advisors. Diem was a corrupt leader who behaved like a dictator and threw any opponents into prison. This included not only communists, but also religious leaders, trade unionists and journalists.

2. Vietnam would be divided in two. The North would be controlled by the communist Ho Chi Minh; the South would be controlled by the anti-communist Ngo Dinh Diem.

3. In 1956 Vietnam would be united into one country and elections would be held to choose a government.

• However, things did not work out quite like this – largely because the Americans were so concerned that the re-united Vietnam might be a communist country.

Diem treated the people of South Vietnam so badly that some of them formed the **National Liberation Front** (NLF) to get rid of him. Ho Chi Minh in the North sent military supplies to help the NLF in the South. Soon the NLF controlled parts of the countryside in South Vietnam and was popular with many of the South Vietnamese. This was because:

1. The NLF promised to bring about changes in the economy and land ownership.

2. It said that it represented all classes and religions.

3. It promised to re-unite Vietnam.

But Diem had the support of the USA which sent out 'advisers' to help him combat the NLF.

The Kennedy Years

In 1960 John F. Kennedy became President of the USA. He took a strong stand against communism and sent 16,000 American advisers to train the South Vietnamese Army (ARVN) in their fight against the **Vietcong** (as the Americans called the NLF).

Strategic villages

The Americans had a plan to prevent the Vietcong influencing the population of South Vietnam. Vietnamese peasants were moved to special villages surrounded by barbed wire. The Vietcong could not get in. But the Vietnamese people did not like having to move to these villages and became even more anti-Diem. Some joined the Vietcong in retaliation!

Pressure on Diem

Diem had been very tough on the Buddhist religion (he was a Catholic even though 70 per cent of the Vietnamese were Buddhist). So Buddhist monks campaigned against him. Some actually set fire to themselves to make their discontent public. President Kennedy became so worried that he threatened to withdraw aid if Diem did not improve. Then, in November 1963, Diem was overthrown in a coup supported by the American President.

Lyndon Johnson

The overthrow of Diem did not lead to the defeat of the communist Vietcong. Kennedy's successor, Lyndon Johnson, wanted to send troops to Vietnam or at least to bomb North Vietnam. But officially, the USA was not at war with North Vietnam. So Johnson doubted that the US Congress would approve of such warlike actions (or agree to pay for them).

Then in August 1964 came a fortunate event for Johnson. North Vietnamese gunboats were accused of attacking the *USS Maddox*, an American surveillance ship, in Gulf of Tonkin. President Johnson asked Congress to agree to him taking 'all necessary measures to repel armed attack against the forces of the USA'. It agreed and the USA was now ready to fight a war against the Vietcong and North Vietnam.

The nature of the conflict

United States and South Vietnam

On 8 March 1965, 3500 US marines arrived in South Vietnam. The USA also launched **'Operation Rolling Thunder'** against North Vietnam. President Johnson said he was going to bomb the North Vietnamese 'back into the Stone Age'. In the next three years the Americans dropped more bombs on North Vietnam than the Allies dropped on Germany in the whole of the Second World War.

The Ho Chi Minh Trail

What the US troops were aiming to do was to prevent North Vietnam sending supplies to the Vietcong. These came down a series of jungle tracks called the **Ho Chi Minh Trail**. But the US bombing did not destroy the trail and did not starve the Vietcong of supplies. The USA was still certain of victory, however. After all, it was a superpower with the latest military technology. If the USA increased its manpower, it was bound to win. By the end of 1965 there were 180,000 troops in Vietnam, but still there was no victory. Perhaps new tactics were needed.

- The first change in tactics came when the US forces introduced 'search and destroy' tactics. They went into the jungle looking for the Vietcong. But the Americans were not skilled at jungle warfare. Even when they found Vietnamese in the jungle, there was no way of telling who were Vietcong and who were innocent villagers. This was especially so because most villagers were anti-American and would not say who the Vietcong were.

- So the Americans tried to win the 'hearts and minds' of the Vietnamese people. They set up special development projects giving assistance in farming, or better medical facilities. But, whatever they did, the Americans could not shed the image that most Vietnamese people had of them. They were unwelcome invaders telling the Vietnamese how to run their own country.

- It seemed the only way to win the war was by brute force. If the Vietcong hid in the jungle, then the jungle would have to be destroyed. This was done in a variety of ways. A chemical called 'Agent Orange' stripped the leaves from the trees. **Napalm** set fire to large areas of jungle. Unfortunately, Agent Orange also caused illness in anyone breathing it and napalm burned anything it came into contact with – including people.

THE NEW TACTICS OF THE US FORCES

Search and destroy
- warfare in the jungle
- to find and kill the Vietcong

BUT

- US forces unskilled at jungle warfare
- Vietcong or not?

Hearts and minds
- development projects set up
- farming and medical assistance

BUT

- Vietnamese people still did not welcome the Americans

Destroy the jungle
- to stop the Vietcong hiding
- jungle destroyed by Agent Orange and napalm

BUT

- Agent Orange caused ill-health
- napalm caused terrible burns

Why did the Americans become involved in Vietnam?

What were the aims of the NLF?

Why was President Diem so unpopular in South Vietnam?

North Vietnam and the War

The North Vietnamese were keen to support the Vietcong in the South. Both of them were communist and anti-American. The North Vietnamese hoped that the Vietcong could win the South Vietnamese people over to communism. Since the South Vietnamese government was so unpopular, this was not hard. Sometimes, however, the Vietcong threatened to murder peasants or burn their villages down if they did not support them.

In North Vietnam the US bombing caused the death of over 100,000 civilians. But instead of causing North Vietnam to give in, it just made them more determined to resist.

The Vietcong got supplies along the Ho Chi Minh Trail. They were sent not only by North Vietnam, but also other communist countries like the Soviet Union and China. The US troops found it very hard to stop the supply chain. The Vietcong set booby traps for US soldiers in the jungle and many died painful deaths. The Vietcong also had a very complicated set of tunnels in the jungle. They hid in these when US soldiers came into the area.

The Tet Offensive

Although the Vietcong used mostly guerilla tactics, there were times when they launched full-scale attacks on the Americans. One of these came in the 'Tet Offensive' of January 1968. Almost 60,000 Vietcong drove deep into South Vietnam and even reached the US embassy in the capital, Saigon. The Vietcong attack was eventually turned back, but it had a major psychological effect on the USA back home. The Vietcong were an enemy which was supposed to be vastly inferior to the US troops. So why was the US embassy under attack?

Time to leave?

The Tet Offensive helped persuade the USA that the Vietnam War was becoming unwinnable. US casualties had risen from 1130 in 1965 to 12,588 in 1968. When the Commander-in-Chief, General Westmoreland asked President Johnson for another 200,000 troops, Johnson sent just 30,000. The President was thinking of leaving Vietnam, not sending even more troops. He began to have 'talks about peace talks' with the North Vietnamese.

Why did the Americans not win the Vietnam War?

Although they had much stronger forces, the Americans failed to win in Vietnam. There were several reasons for this.

1. Tactics

   The Americans had better weapons, but the Vietcong used **guerrilla tactics**, avoiding major battles where the American weapons could be used.

2. Lack of support

   The Americans were hated by the local people, many of whom gave their support to the Vietcong.

3. Lack of support at home

   As the war dragged on, the American people became sickened by what was happening and by the enormous cost. Demonstrations against the war played a major part in persuading Nixon to introduce Vietnamisation.

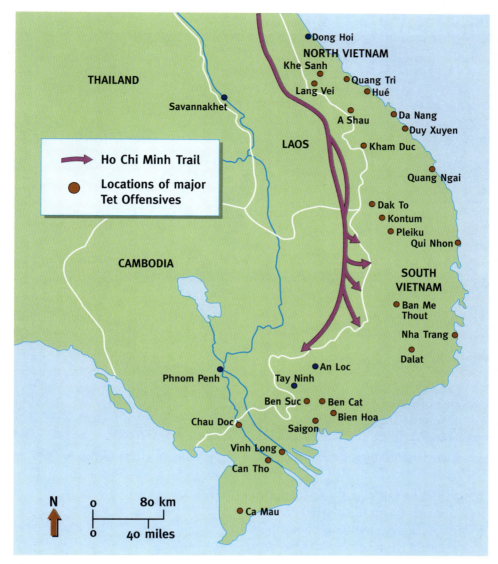

Map legend:
➤ **Ho Chi Minh Trail**
● **Locations of major Tet Offensives**

THAILAND

Savannakhet

●Dong Hoi
NORTH VIETNAM
Khe Sanh
Lang Vei ●Quang Tri
●Hué
LAOS
A Shau ●Da Nang
●Duy Xuyen
●Kham Duc

Quang Ngai

●Dak To
●Kontum
●Pleiku
Qui Nhon●

SOUTH VIETNAM

●Ban Me Thout

CAMBODIA

Nha Trang●
●Dalat

●An Loc
Phnom Penh
Tay Ninh
Ben Suc● ●Ben Cat
●Bien Hoa
Chau Doc●
Saigon
Vinh Long●
Can Tho

N
0   80 km
0   40 miles

●Ca Mau

▲ **The map shows what happened during the Tet Offensive.**

Vietnamisation

By 1968 the US people had turned against the war in Vietnam. They wanted their troops out. But the USA could not just leave because for years it had been saying that the war was in its interests. So the US government introduced 'Vietnamisation'. That is, turning the war over to South Vietnam to fight.

Nixon and Vietnamisation

In 1968 Nixon was elected President. He soon decided that US troops should leave Vietnam.

- The war was costing US$500 million and 300 casualties each week – and yet the USA did not seem to be getting any nearer to victory.

- Nixon said that he was going to 'Vietnamise' the war. That meant ensuring South Vietnam could fight it on its own. Then the US soldiers could leave.

▲ A Vietcong poster showing how the communist forces used guerrilla tactics to fight the US forces.

- Nixon began peace talks and also stepping up other measures to persuade North Vietnam to agree to peace. Heavy bombing of North Vietnam increased. Bombers were also sent into Laos and Cambodia to bomb Vietcong bases there. In 1969 US troops began missions into those countries.

- At home, there was widespread opposition to the war, especially from students. Nixon had promised to reduce US involvement in Vietnam and, in the period 1969–71, almost half a million troops were sent home. By the end of 1971 there were just 140,000 left.

Guerrilla warfare

The Vietcong knew that they were not as strong as the US troops. So instead of fighting large battles, they used guerilla tactics. This involved using booby traps, ambushes and sabotage. Since they had the support of the Vietnamese people, after an attack they could slip back into the jungle and mix with the locals. So the Americans could not catch them.

- What Nixon needed was a peace agreement so that he could justify removing US troops. He thought it would also help him win the 1972 Presidential Election! In October 1972 he announced that 'peace is at hand'. President Thieu of South Vietnam called the peace a betrayal. But it did not matter. The USA was determined to leave.

- A ceasefire was agreed on 23 January 1973. American troops would withdraw and the Vietcong would remain in the positions they held at that moment. This agreement was signed on 27 January. The two men who negotiated the agreement, Henry Kissinger of the USA and Le Duc Tho of North Vietnam, were later awarded the Nobel Peace prize.

- To help the South Vietnamese, the Americans promised them US$1 billion worth of military equipment. This would help them fight the war against the Vietcong.

Henry Kissinger

Henry Kissinger was one of President Nixon's most trusted advisors. Nixon put him in charge of trying to bring about a peace treaty to end the war. After many difficulties he was finally successful and was rewarded with the Nobel Peace Prize in 1973. (He shared it with the North Vietnamese diplomat Le Duc Tho.) In August 1973 President Nixon appointed Kissinger as Secretary of State. This was a great honour as Kissinger was the first foreign-born citizen of the USA to be given this job (he was born in Germany).

What tactics did the Americans use in Vietnam?

What tactics did the Vietcong use?

The impact of the war on the peoples of Vietnam and the USA during the 1960s and 1970s

The USA

The Vietnam War was the most important issue in US political life in the 1960s and 1970s. It was even more important as an issue in the 1968 and 1972 Presidential Elections than improving civil rights for African Americans.

American soldiers were drafted (conscripted) into the Army for one year. The ordinary soldiers (GIs) averaged just nineteen years of age. Although African Americans made up just one tenth of the population of the USA, they made up 20 per cent of the Army.

What are we fighting for?

- As the war continued, many young men found ways to avoid having to go to Vietnam. These 'draft-dodgers' fled to Canada or went to prison instead of fighting.

- In Vietnam many of the soldiers wondered what they were fighting for. They were told they were fighting for freedom, but the Vietnamese did not want them there. Drug abuse became a serious problem. In 1970 it was estimated that 58 per cent of US soldiers smoked marijuana and 22 per cent used heroin. In 1971, 5000 troops needed treatment for wounds, but more than 20,000 needed treatment for serious drug abuse.

- There were even cases of officers shot in the back for risking their troops. 'Fragging' (throwing a fragmentation grenade into officers' tents) killed 83 officers between 1969 and 1971. More than 500,000 of the 10 million US soldiers deserted between 1960 and 1973.

Opposition at home

Although protests against the war began in 1964, at that time most US citizens were still in favour of the war. As soldiers came home in body bags and the cost of fighting soared, so did opposition to the war. Surely there was a better way to spend US$25 billion a year?

Vietnam was the first 'televised' war. Millions of Americans saw the action from their living rooms – and they were shocked by what they saw. In 1967 there were major protests against the war across the USA. In 1967 the US government put up taxes to pay for the war. This made the US people even more angry. Many civil rights leaders felt that the money should be spent on improving the welfare system at home in the USA.

Many historians think that the pictures of the US embassy being attacked as part of the Tet Offensive hardened US opinion against the war. In a matter of weeks, the number of people who said they thought President Johnson was doing a good job fell from 48 per cent to 36 per cent. When news came through of the My Lai massacre, even more Americans wanted their troops to come home.

Student opposition

Much of the opposition to the war came from students. There were widespread demonstrations in universities and colleges across the USA throughout the war. These protests increased when the government decided that students should be drafted into the Army in the same way as other people. Until then students had been exempt. It was thought better to let them finish their studies.

Sometimes student demonstrations got out of control and the police had to be called in to keep order. In 1968–69, 4000 students were arrested. In May 1970 there was a peaceful anti-war demonstration at Kent State University in Ohio. The Governor called in the National Guard to disperse the students. Matters got out of hand and, in the confusion, four students were shot dead. They were not even part of the demonstration, just by-standers. The US public was shocked and anti-war feeling increased even more.

My Lai

My Lai was a South Vietnamese village which the Americans thought was hiding Vietcong. Forces led by Lt. William Calley entered the village in March 1968. They found no Vietcong, but killed 347 unarmed men, women and children. Calley was later imprisoned for life, but was released after just three years.

The people of Vietnam

- The people of North Vietnam suffered from bombing raids which were amongst the heaviest in the history of warfare. These caused terrible damage and led to shortages of basic necessities. Like in the USA, North Vietnamese men were also conscripted into their army. Since there were fewer people in North Vietnam, being conscripted was much more likely.

- Of course, the war had an even greater impact in the South. In South Vietnam the South's own Army was fighting, but there were also Vietcong guerillas and armies from North Vietnam and the USA. Often the local people were terrorised by both sides. The US troops destroyed villages as they tried to find the Vietcong. The Vietcong destroyed villages to show how they were more powerful than the USA.

- More than 8 million tonnes of bombs were dropped, together with millions of tonnes of chemicals which were used to destroy the jungles. These chemicals caused a large number of casualties at the time, but have caused even more since. Many children have been born with deformities as the chemicals found their way into the water and food chain. There are also land mines which continue to kill and maim today.

Why did the Americans lose the war in Vietnam?

▲ A civilian in Hanoi in an air-raid shelter.

The reunification of Vietnam

After the **Paris Peace Agreement** in 1973, the USA hoped that South Vietnam would be able to hold out against the Vietcong and North Vietnamese. South Vietnam had an army of over 1 million men and the promise of financial help from the USA. But in 1974 President Nixon became involved in the **Watergate Scandal** (see page 231). He was in such difficulty that he could not persuade Congress to give large sums to help South Vietnam. After Nixon's resignation President Ford asked Congress for US$1500 million, but was given only US$700 million.

Then, in December 1974, the North Vietnamese launched an attack on the South. By 1975 they had captured the South Vietnamese capital, Saigon (including the US embassy). In 1976 Vietnam was reunited under the control of a Communist government in the North.

The consequences of the war

- Out of a total population of 32 million, 2.5 million Vietnamese soldiers and civilians were killed and a further 1.5 million were wounded.

- The USA lost 58,000 men in the war. However, the horrors of the war had such a lasting impact on the soldiers that almost twice that number have committed suicide since the end of the war.

- After reunification, the North Vietnamese forced a communist system on South Vietnam. Hundreds of thousands of South Vietnamese were forced into 're-education centres'. Many people in the South did not want to live under a communist regime and more than a million of them fled the country in the period 1969–90. Most of these became '**boat-people**', escaping on almost anything which floated. At least 50,000 of them drowned, but almost a million settled in the West, mostly in the USA. Amongst those settling in the USA were 50,000 'American-Asian' children of US soldiers and Vietnamese women. Many of these have found that they are not really accepted by either society.

The war had a major impact on the USA.

1. The USA's image as the world's strongest power was seriously damaged by its failure to win the war. The USA also had to face the disgrace of being accused of war crimes as a result of the use of chemicals.

2. The enormous cost of the war prevented President Johnson from introducing many of the changes he wanted to make to build his 'Great Society'.

3. The war also changed the attitude of many US citizens to their government. They saw their government carrying out tough measures against protestors, and the Army performing acts of atrocity, such as at My Lai. Television brought home terrible pictures of war. Perhaps the USA wasn't such a great country after all?

4. Many of the returning soldiers found it very difficult to fit back into US society. The war had been lost and some people saw them as failures. They also had the problem of trying to forget the terrible things they had seen. Marriages broke down and the divorce rate soared.

5. To try to come to terms with the war, there have been thousands of books written about Vietnam. Musicians have composed songs and Hollywood has made numerous films. *Full Metal Jacket*, *The Deer Hunter* and *Good Morning Vietnam* all help the USA to understand how it lost a war it thought it couldn't lose.

Numbers of soldiers killed during the Vietnam War	
58,000	US soldiers
137,000	South Vietnamese soldiers
approx. 700,000	North Vietnamese soldiers
approx. 1 million	Vietcong

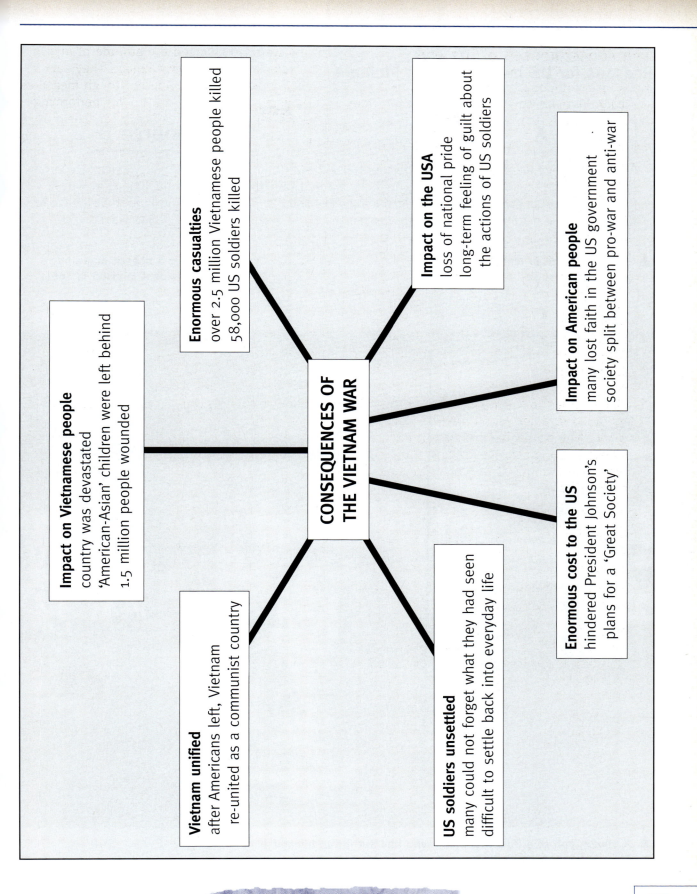

CONSEQUENCES OF THE VIETNAM WAR

Enormous casualties
over 2.5 million Vietnamese people killed
58,000 US soldiers killed

Impact on the USA
loss of national pride
long-term feeling of guilt about the actions of US soldiers

Impact on American people
many lost faith in the US government
society split between pro-war and anti-war

Impact on Vietnamese people
country was devastated
'American-Asian' children were left behind
1.5 million people wounded

Enormous cost to the US
hindered President Johnson's plans for a 'Great Society'

Vietnam unified
after Americans left, Vietnam re-united as a communist country

US soldiers unsettled
many could not forget what they had seen
difficult to settle back into everyday life

Reasons for US involvement in Vietnam

Source A

President Kennedy saw Vietnam as President Eisenhower had – part of the fight against communism. Kennedy wanted to help the South Vietnamese army with US technology. He also wanted to give economic aid to South Vietnam.

▲ From an American textbook published in 1991.

Source B

If we quit Vietnam, tomorrow we'll be fighting in Hawaii and next week we'll have to fight in San Francisco.

▲ From a speech made by President Johnson in 1964.

Source C

▲ A photograph of a Buddhist monk who had set fire to himself. The photograph was taken in 1963.

Source D

We seek an independent, non-communist South Vietnam. We do not require South Vietnam to serve as a western base or become a member of the western alliance. South Vietnam must be free to accept outside assistance in order to maintain its security.

▲ From a report written in 1964, by Robert McNamara, the US Secretary of Defence.

Source E

I have dedicated my life to serving the revolution and I am proud to see the growth of international communism. My ultimate wish is that the Communist Party and my people will stay together for the building of a peaceful, united and independent Vietnam.

▲ An excerpt from Ho Chi Minh's will, read in May 1969.

Source F

Let every nation know, whether it wishes us well or ill, that we shall pay any price, bear any burden, meet any hardship, support any friend, oppose any foe to assure the survival and success of liberty.

▲ From President Kennedy's inaugural speech in 1961.

Study Source A

a What can you learn from Source A about why the USA became involved in Vietnam? (4)

Study Sources A, B and C

b Do Sources B and C support the evidence of Source A about US involvement in Vietnam? Explain your answer. (6)

Study Sources D and E

c How useful are these sources in helping you to understand the reasons for US involvement in Vietnam? (8)

Study all of the sources

d 'The USA sent combat troops to Vietnam solely to protect its advisers and the South Vietnamese government from attacks by Vietcong and North Vietnam forces.' Use the sources and your own knowledge to explain whether you agree with this view. (12)

The nature of the conflict

Source A

It was explained to us that anything alive in that area was supposed to be dead. We were told that if we saw a 'gook' (slang for Vietnamese person) or thought we saw one, no matter how big or small, shoot first. No need for permission to fire. It was just a turkey shoot – men, women and children, no matter what their ages, all went into the body count. This was a regular 'search and destroy' mission in which we destroyed everything we found.

▲ **Sergeant James Weeks, a US soldier fighting in Vietnam, describes the orders he was given in 1967.**

Source B

▲ **A photograph of dead civilians, massacred at My Lai by US soldiers in 1968.**

Source C

We didn't look at the Vietnamese as human beings. They were sub-human. To kill them would be easy for you. If you continued this process you didn't have any bad feelings about it because they were a sub-human species. We used terms like 'gooks' and 'zipperheads' and we had to kill different insects every day and they would say, 'There's a gook, step on it and squash it.'

▲ **A US marine speaking about his training in the 1960s.**

Source D

A question posed to the Americans surveyed was:

In view of the developments since we entered the fighting in Vietnam, do you think the United States made a mistake sending troops to fight in Vietnam?

The results were:

Yes	52%
No	39%
No opinion	9%

▲ An opinion poll conducted by Gallup in January 1969.

Source F

The Vietcong adopted the military tactics of Mao Zedong, the Chinese Communist leader. Mao said, 'The enemy advances, we retreat, the enemy camps, we harass, the enemy tires, we attack, the enemy retreats, we pursue.'

▲ A description of Vietcong military tactics, from a British school textbook published in 1996.

Source E

WE WILL FIGHT AND FIGHT FROM THIS GENERATION TO THE NEXT

▲ A North Vietnamese woodcut from the 1960s.

Study Source A

a What can you learn from Source A about US methods of warfare in Vietnam? (4)

Study Sources A, B and C

b Do Sources B and C support the evidence of Source A? Explain your answer. (6)

Study Sources D and E

c How useful are these sources as evidence of American and Vietcong attitudes to the war? (8)

Study all of the sources

d 'The USA lost the war because American public opinion forced the politicians to withdraw from South Vietnam.' Use the sources and your own knowledge to explain whether you agree with this view. (12)

The impact of the war on the peoples of Vietnam and the USA during the 1960s and 1970s

Source A

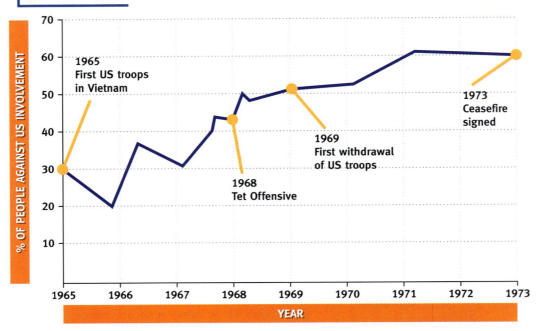

▲ A graph showing the US public's opposition to the Vietnam War, 1965–73. It is taken from a high school textbook published in the USA.

Source B

In 1967, tens of thousands of Americans protested across America. Congressmen put more pressure on President Johnson. The churches and black civil rights leader Martin Luther King led the opposition. Black Americans resented the high number of black casualties in the war.

▲ From a study of the Vietnam conflict by a British historian, written in 1998.

Source C

▲ Pro-war demonstrators in Florida in 1967.

Source D

We huddled the villagers up. We made them squat down. I fired about four clips-worth of bullets into the group ... The mothers were hugging their children. Well, we kept on firing.

▲ Paul Meadlo, a soldier at My Lai in 1968, giving evidence at the trial of Lieutenant William Calley.

Source E

Officer: When you go into My Lai you assume the worst ... you assume they're all VC.

Soldier: But sir, the law says killing civilians is wrong. We're taught that, even by the army.

Officer: Of course killing civilians is wrong. But these so-called civilians are killers. Female warriors out in the rice fields spying.

Soldier: But how do you know that this peasant or that peasant is VC? They look alike ...

▲ From *If I Die in a Combat Zone*, by Tim O'Brien. O'Brien was an American soldier who served two years in Vietnam and won seven medals.

Source F

By 1971, the morale of the American army had plummeted. In that year, President Nixon warned the new graduates of the West Point Military Academy that they would be leading troops guilty of drug abuse and insubordination.

▲ From a study of the Vietnam War written in 1998 by a British historian.

Study Source A

a What can you learn from Source A about opposition to the Vietnam War in America? (4)

Study Sources A, B and C

b Do Sources B and C support the evidence of Source A? Explain your answer. (6)

Study Sources D and E

c How useful are these sources in helping you to understand why some Americans opposed involvement in the war? (8)

Study all of the sources

d 'The US government withdrew from the war because it could not rely on its soldiers.' Use the sources and your own knowledge to explain whether you agree with this view. (12)

Reasons for the US defeat

Source A

▲ A Vietcong patrol in South Vietnam in 1966.

Source B

On the evening of 31 January 1968, about 70,000 Vietcong troops launched surprise attacks on more than 100 cities and towns in Vietnam. The boldest stroke was an attack on the US embassy in Saigon.

▲ From a study of the Vietnam War written in 1992 by a British historian.

Source C

If we spread out too thin and our soldiers moved out of the village we pacified, the Vietcong came right back in again. The guy who might have been your cook during the day, that night he put on his black pyjamas and took out his AK47 from under his mattress and went out to your camp to shoot at you.

▲ From an interview in 1980 with Dan Pitzer, an American soldier who was a prisoner of the Vietcong for four years.

Source D

The US can go on increasing aid to South Vietnam. It can increase its own army. But it will do no good. I hate to see the war go on and intensify. Yet our people are determined to struggle. It is impossible for westerners to understand the force of the people's will to resist and to continue.

▲ Pham Van Dong, a leading North Vietnamese politician, speaking in 1964.

Source E

In sending US troops to South Vietnam, the US invaders and land grabbers have met a people's war. The people's war has succeeded in gathering all the people to fight their attackers in all ways and with all kinds of weapons.

 Vo Nguyen Giap, a North Vietnamese Army general speaking in 1967.

Source F

▲ **South Vietnam's police chief executing a member of the Vietcong in the Tet Offensive in 1968.**

Study Source A

a What can you learn from Source A about Vietcong methods of warfare in South Vietnam? (4)

Study Sources A, B and C

b Do Sources B and C support the evidence of Source A about Vietcong methods of warfare? Explain your answer. (6)

Study Sources D and E

c How useful are Sources D and E as evidence of growing support for the Vietcong and North Vietnam in the late 1960s? (8)

Study all of the sources

d 'The Vietcong and North Vietnamese forces were successful because they used guerrilla tactics.' Use the sources and your own knowledge to explain whether you agree with this view. (12)

The reunification of Vietnam

Source A

In October 1972, peace talks re-opened in Paris. For the first time in nearly ten years of war, peace seemed within reach. The US offered concessions – the Vietcong would play a part in the final negotiations. With the 1972 presidential election approaching, the White House was eager to reach a firm agreement of peace.

▲ From an American history textbook written in 1990.

Source B

When we read the drafts of the agreement – what we were prepared to give as concessions to the North Vietnamese – it was clear that there was no way the government of South Vietnam was going to be able to withstand Vietcong infiltration and propaganda before the election. Once I saw the concessions, I knew that we were prepared to sell South Vietnam down the river.

▲ Edward Brady, a US intelligence adviser, who was present at the Paris Peace talks, speaking in 1978.

Source C

Rather than explore the differences that existed between the US and North Vietnam, President Nixon gave the signal for a new operation – Linebacker Two. Starting on 18 December 1972, B-52 bombers and other aircraft flew nearly 3000 missions over Hanoi and Haiphong. They dropped 40,000 tons of bombs in eleven days.

▲ From a book about the Vietnam conflict written in 1983 by an American journalist.

Source D

In 1973, President Nixon secretly promised to intervene, if need be, to protect South Vietnam. Is an American's word reliable these days?

▲ President Thieu of South Vietnam, in his resignation speech of April 1975.

Source E

It was clear that the South Vietnamese forces were spread pretty thin in the Central Highlands. The South Vietnamese complained of a lack of hand grenades and ammunition. They were not operating aggressively ... One company of troops had been hit hard by a North Vietnamese regiment. The South Vietnamese forces had not been properly equipped to defend the camp.

▲ From an interview in 1980 with K. Moorefield, special adviser to the US Ambassador to South Vietnam in 1975.

Source F

The army of South Vietnam was beginning to fall apart and morale was very poor. An American investigation in the summer of 1974 reported that 90 per cent of the South Vietnamese troops were not being paid enough to support their families. Corrupt government officials were stealing the soldiers' pay.

▲ From a British history textbook about Vietnam written in 1997.

Study Source A

a What can you learn from Source A about the Paris Peace talks? (4)

Study Sources A, B and C

b Do Sources B and C support the evidence of Source A? (6)

Study Sources D and E

c How useful are these sources for understanding the military problems faced by South Vietnam after 1973? (8)

Study all of the sources

d 'Vietnam was reunited because the USA had given too many concessions to the North Vietnamese at Paris.' Use the sources and your own knowledge to explain whether you agree with this view. (12)

Consequences for the USA of its failure in Vietnam

Source A

On returning home, American soldiers did not expect to be treated as criminals or child murderers as they sometimes were. Many veterans found it difficult to get jobs or get their own jobs back. More American veterans have committed suicide since the war than were killed in the war itself. They felt betrayed by a country which was embarrassed by them.

▲ From a British history textbook about Vietnam written in 1995.

Source B

Source C

'How do you feel about killing all of those innocent people?' The woman asked me. I didn't know what to say. The bartender got a little uptight.

'Excuse me,' I called the bartender over. 'Could I buy these people a drink?' I felt guilty. I did kill. I tried to make up for it somehow.

'We don't accept any drinks from killers,' the girl said to me.

▲ A former soldier describing his return to the USA. He was in an airport bar, speaking to people of his own age (19).

▲ Photograph of the Vietnam War Memorial Wall in Washington DC. The wall was paid for by subscriptions from Vietnam veterans.

Source D

He called it the madman theory. He said: 'I want the North Vietnamese to believe I've reached the point where I might do anything to stop the war. We'll just slip them the word that I'm obsessed about communism. Tell them that I can't be restrained and that I've got my hand on the nuclear button. If we do that Ho Chi Minh himself will be in Paris in two days begging for peace.'

▲ From *The Ends of Power* by H. R. (Bob) Haldeman, 1978, one of President Nixon's closest advisers during the Vietnam War. Haldeman is explaining Nixon's decision to extend the bombing campaign.

Source E

However we got into Vietnam, whatever the judgement of our actions, ending the war honourably was essential for the peace of the world. We could not simply walk away from an enterprise as if we were switching a TV channel. As the leader of democratic alliances we had to remember that scores of countries and millions of people relied for their security on the US' willingness to stand by allies.

▲ Henry Kissinger, National Security Adviser, speaking after the end of the Vietnam War.

Source F

The USA was certainly weakened by the Vietnam War. At home, it prevented President Johnson building his Great Society. But more importantly, the USA became unwilling to involve itself in any international conflict until the Gulf War in 1991. When the Gulf War was over, Bush said: 'By God, we've kicked the Vietnam syndrome once and for all.'

▲ From a British history textbook written in 1998.

Study Source A

a What can you learn from Source A about the impact of the war on US soldiers? (4)

Study Sources A, B and C

b Do Sources B and C support the evidence of Source A? Explain your answer. (6)

Study Sources D and E

c How useful are these sources in helping us to understand US policies in Vietnam? (8)

Study all of the sources

d Source F suggests that the most important effect of the war on the USA was its unwillingness to become involved in world conflicts. Use the sources and your own knowledge to say whether you agree that this was the most important effect of the war on the USA. (12)

CHAPTER 7

The end of apartheid in South Africa: 1982~94

Essential Information

The National Party and the nature of its rule

- The **National Party** was set up in South Africa in 1914. Its aim was to protect the interests of the **Afrikaners** in the country. When Jan Hertzog became Prime Minister in 1924, he made Afrikaans the official language. He also said that non-white people should not be able to have skilled jobs in mines.

- In 1918 the Afrikaners set up the Broederbond (brotherhood). It was totally committed to maintaining white supremacy in South Africa.

- In 1948 the National Party won the General Election in South Africa. The Prime Minister, Daniel Malan, appointed a cabinet made up totally of Afrikaners. He also began introducing the system of '**apartheid**'.

Who are Afrikaners?
They are white people in South Africa who are descended from Dutch and German settlers. They speak a language called Afrikaans and have a history of rivalry with descendants of British settlers. They went on a 'Great Trek' in 1836 and set up their own states in Transvaal and the Orange Free State. They also fought the Boer War against the British in 1899–1902.

Acts relating to apartheid

The Population Registration Act 1950 This categorised all South Africans as either white, native (black African) or coloured.

The Group Areas Act 1950 This divided up South Africa into areas in which each of the three groups lived. Anyone in the 'wrong area' had to move.

The Promotion of Bantu Self-government Act 1959 This set up Bantustans, homelands where black South Africans ruled themselves. Of course, any decisions which the government didn't like were changed.

The Bantu Education Act 1953 This set out the level of education to be given to black children. They received a lower level of education than white children. This stopped them gaining skilled jobs and kept them 'in their place'.

The Pass Book Act 1952 This made all black South Africans carry a pass (identity book). Permission had to be given to be out after 9 pm or to be in white areas. This was shown in the pass book, which was regularly checked by police.

The Separate Amenities Act 1953 This set up apartheid in restaurants, beaches, cinemas and theatres.

Other laws These took away the right to vote for non-whites and banned mixed marriages. Even sexual intercourse between whites and non-whites was banned.

The system of apartheid, and its economic and social consequences

Apartheid means 'apartness'. The National Party believed that the different racial groups in South Africa should be kept apart. The white people, the black people, the Asians and the coloured people (those of mixed race) should live apart and have 'separate development'. What this really meant was white supremacy, and control of the country by white people.

Before 1948 there were already some laws keeping the races apart, but the new government extended this and made it more formal. Malan and his successors (Hendrik Verwoed and John Vorster) also made sure the rules were strictly enforced.

By introducing these laws, the National Party ensured white control in South Africa. It also ensured that it maintained itself in power. This was quite an achievement because only 12 per cent of the population were Afrikaners.

Increasingly, black South Africans became second-class citizens in their own country. Many of them lived in '**townships**' on the edge of major towns. The most famous of these was the South West Township of Johannesburg, known as **Soweto**. A million black South Africans lived here in very poor conditions. They travelled into Johannesburg every day to work. These townships soon became centres for groups opposing apartheid, such as the **African National Congress** (ANC) and the **Pan African Congress** (PAC)

The Power of the Police
To make sure that apartheid laws were followed, the government increased police powers. From 1965 they were allowed to detain anyone suspected of breaking the apartheid laws for up to 180 days without charge. Stories of torture during detention were common. Recently these stories have been shown to be true.

Keeping control
As well as increasing the powers of the police, other measures were taken:

- A secret police force, the **Bureau of State Security** (BOSS), was set up.

- In 1972, the **State Security Council** was set up. This gave BOSS and the military more say in how the country was run.

- In the 1980s the **Civil Co-operation Bureau** (CCB) was set up. It carried out attacks on opponents of apartheid. In 1988 it assassinated Dulcie September, a member of the ANC.

▲ All black people had to carry a pass book.

- Black South Africans were forbidden to stay in white areas for more than three days.

- Banning orders were issued regularly by the government. These were used to stop journalists writing critical articles about the government, and to prevent opponents of apartheid attending meetings or even leaving their homes.

- Huge numbers of South Africans were employed by the government to keep control. Police numbers almost doubled in the 1970s and white South Africans were asked to volunteer for the 'Active Citizen Force'. Spending on the Army increased fourfold.

All these measures cost money. South Africa was rich in diamonds and gold and could afford it, but the government was worried that the cost of apartheid was running out of control. This was a time too when Western countries were starting to boycott South African goods as a protest against apartheid.

However, the apartheid system was having another damaging effect on the economy. Black South Africans had a very low level of education. To succeed against world competition, South African businesses wanted well-educated workers. The days when all that was needed were agricultural labourers and miners were gone. So the government had a problem. How could it provide better education without increasing demands for better treatment?

Support for, and opposition to, apartheid in South Africa

Support

Support for apartheid was restricted to Afrikaners. It was not just keeping the black South Africans in second place, but it was an attempt to protect the Afrikaner culture from British influence as well. So, many white South Africans of British descent opposed apartheid.

In the 1980s people accused the Afrikaners of behaving like their ancestors on the Great Trek. When attacked they drew their wagons into a protective circle or 'laager'. Critics said that apartheid showed the laager mentality of the Afrikaners – especially when they used insulting terms such as 'Kaffir' to describe black South Africans.

Some white English-speakers accepted apartheid but their political party, the Liberal Party, opposed it. One of its most influential critics was the MP Helen Suzman. But the National Party won every election from 1948 to 1994, so there was little the Liberals could do.

Opposition

Not surprisingly, apart from the Liberal Party, there was plenty of opposition to apartheid.

- The most important opposition was the African National Congress. This had originally been set up in 1912 to campaign for the rights of black South Africans. In 1949 Walter Sisulu became its Secretary-General. He decided to make the organisation more active by starting a Programme of Action. This included strikes and demonstrations.

- Another more violent organisation was the Pan African Congress. This was set up in 1959. You can tell what its views were from its slogan 'One settler, one bullet'.

- A third organisation was set up by Chief Mangosutho Buthelezi in 1975. He was the Prime Minister of Kwazulu, one of the homelands set up by the South African government. He set up a movement called **Inkatha**, which aimed to have independence

Source 2

▲ Anti-apartheid demonstrators picketing Barclays Bank in London 1978. They wanted to encourage people to close their accounts as Barclays was involved in raising huge loans for South Africa.

for the Zulu nation. The ANC and Inkatha were often in conflict. The South African secret services used this to their advantage by arranging massacres of one side's supporters, knowing that the attacks would be blamed on the other. Then the two sides would attack each other.

The ANC in action

By the 1970s, the ANC had decided that there was a need for more violent opposition to apartheid. There were several reasons for this:

- Across Africa countries like Angola and Mozambique were becoming independent. Black South Africans wanted to control their country too.

- Government forces had carried out several controversial acts which angered the ANC.

Their leaders (including Nelson Mandela) had been imprisoned, demonstrations had been brutally broken up (with loss of life) and some leading ANC activists had been murdered by government forces.

Now was the time to take action.

- In 1980 the ANC began a series of attacks. It blew up an oil refinery and a nuclear reactor. It was supported by Angola and Mozambique. The South African government took measures against these countries to stop their support.

- So, the ANC decided to change tactics. It would make the townships ungovernable. In 1985 there were protests in many of the townships. They began at Crossroads in Capetown. The police and black settlers took part in fighting which caused more than 1000 deaths.

Source 3

▲ **Helen Suzman, South African opposition MP and anti-apartheid campaigner, pictured in 1999.**

- Violence spread to other townships and black South Africans organised strikes and boycotts. The government came close to losing control and introduced a **State of Emergency**. Over the next two years there were more than 2000 deaths as the police took violent measures to keep the situation under control.

- There was also fighting between the ANC and Inkatha. The ANC did not like the way Chief Buthelezi tried to govern Kwazulu as an independent country. They accused him of working with the government against the interests of all black South Africans

President Botha was forced to declare a State of Emergency in 1986 and 1987. This was what the ANC hoped for. They wanted to show the government that South Africa could not operate without their support.

In 1988, Botha decided to have talks with the ANC. He met with Nelson Mandela but, before any progress could be made, he had a stroke and was forced to resign. Now it was up to the new president, F. W. de Klerk.

Commonwealth and world reactions to apartheid

The rest of the world hated apartheid.

- When it was first introduced many nations protested to the South African government.

- In 1952 the United Nations condemned South Africa and said that there should be trade **sanctions** (restrictions) placed on the country.

- South Africa left the Commonwealth in 1961 before the other countries voted to expel it.

- In 1963 the **Organisation for African Unity** (that is, all the black African states) made ending apartheid one of its main aims.

- In 1974 South Africa was expelled from the United Nations.

It looked like strong action was being taken against South Africa. But this was not really so. Ways around bans and sanctions were usually found and trade with South Africa continued.

Why was this?

- African governments depended on South Africa to keep their economies going. When Kenya broke off trading with South Africa, other African countries just stepped in. Zambia and Zimbabwe had no coastline and had to use South African ports for imports and exports. Roughly 2 million citizens of Malawi and Mozambique lived and worked in South Africa.

- Margaret Thatcher of Britain, like many other western leaders, didn't want to impose sanctions because she thought that the people who would be most hurt if the South African economy was damaged were black Africans. She was probably right, but the ANC did ask Britain not to trade with South Africa.

- When sanctions were applied, there was usually a way around them. A ban on arms sales was agreed by the West. So the South Africans bought weapons from the Soviet Union, which wanted foreign currency.

- South Africa was rich in diamonds and gold. Its wealth meant that it could usually find someone willing to supply what it needed.

Action taken

Despite the reservations that some countries had, some did take measures to show their opposition to apartheid.

- In the 1980s a number of companies responded to protests in their own countries about their role in South Africa. Some 277 of them withdrew from the country. These included Pepsi and IBM.

- In 1969 the England cricket team was due to tour South Africa. Basil D'Oliveira, a coloured player, was picked for the team. The South Africans refused to accept D'Oliveira and the tour was cancelled. In protest, Britain and most other Commonwealth countries stopped sending sports teams to South Africa. This was a blow to a country which loved its sport. Genuine efforts were made in South Africa to have more coloured and black South Africans in their sporting teams – though these players could not mix with white South African players in restaurants after a game!

Source 4

▲ Civil unrest in many townships often led to violence between inhabitants and the security forces.

▲ Map of southern and central Africa.

BASIL D'OLIVEIRA – NOT GOOD ENOUGH OR NOT WANTED?

Smashing the Aussies

In August 1968 Basil D'Oliveira became a hero in the eyes of cricket lovers in Britain. In the last international game of the season he scored 158 runs against Australia – the greatest cricketing rival of the English team. This was a particularly good time for D'Oliveira to do so well. In a few months the English cricket team was going on tour to South Africa.

The players to go on that tour were due to be selected just one week after D'Oliveira had scored so many runs. As he had done so well he was bound to be amongst those chosen. That would be great news for him. He had been born in South Africa and would be delighted to play in the country of his birth.

The Shocking News

On 28 August the English cricket selectors announced who would be going on tour. D'Oliveira was not on the list. The selectors said that he had not been picked because he had not done well in the earlier games in the summer.

Many people had another idea. D'Oliveira was coloured and the South African government had made it clear that they did not want their team to play against a coloured player. (At this time all the other players in the English team were white.) Had the team been picked just to keep the South Africans happy?

Going After All!

Just three weeks later things took a dramatic turn. One of the English players dropped out because he was injured. The selectors chose D'Oliveira as his replacement. So he was going to South Africa after all. But it wasn't as simple as that. The South African Prime Minister was angry at the change. He said that England was sending 'a team of troublemakers' who would make people criticise apartheid. So he cancelled the tour, telling the English team that it was not welcome.

It was almost thirty years before England sent another cricket team to South Africa. By then apartheid was gone.

What does 'apartheid' mean?

What steps did the South African government take to make sure apartheid was carried out?

Changes to apartheid in the 1980s

Although the South African government was fighting hard to maintain apartheid, it was clear by the end of the 1970s that apartheid was not working.

- The idea that a large percentage of the population could be poorly educated and kept in low-skill jobs was not appropriate in a modern economy. South Africa needed skilled workers.

- Apartheid was causing terrible problems within the country. Huge sums were being spent to enforce the system and to put down opposition by black protest groups.

- Apartheid had destroyed South Africa's image abroad. The system, and the terrible measures taken to enforce it, had made South Africa the most hated nation on Earth.

In 1979, P. W. Botha became Prime Minister of South Africa. He was a strong supporter of apartheid, but felt that changes had to be made to adapt it to modern needs. He was concerned that South Africa was the target for communist countries such as the Soviet Union, China and Cuba. It could not resist this pressure if, at the same time, there were demonstrations and riots within the country. What was needed was a **'total strategy'** to deal with South Africa's problems.

▲ P. W. Botha, with other South African parliamentarians, after becoming Prime Minister in 1979.

The Total Strategy

- Part of Botha's plan involved increasing the power of South Africa's armed forces and attacking countries like Angola, which allowed the ANC to have bases in them.

- Tough measures were taken against opponents of apartheid. It was whilst Botha was Prime Minister that up to 300 ANC activists were murdered by South African agents.

- But Botha's major work came in trying to save apartheid by making changes. He wanted to win the support of better-off black South Africans. Then they would not support the ANC, and opposition to apartheid would be weakened.

Botha's measures

- Blacks could now buy property in white areas.

- There was a massive increase in spending on education for black South Africans. Hopefully this would help provide the skilled workforce that business wanted.

- **Segregation** in theatres, restaurants and hotels was no longer enforced.

- Mixed marriages were no longer illegal.

- From 1986 black South Africans no longer had to carry a pass book.

- In 1984 South Africa introduced a new Constitution (way of governing itself). Coloured people and Indians were now able to elect their own MPs (but the whites still made the decisions on what laws were passed).

▲ **Black and white South Africans dining in the same room in a restaurant after the end of 'Petty Apartheid'.**

Botha attacked

P. W. Botha hoped that his changes would save apartheid. But he was wrong. Not only did he fail to win the support of the black community, he also lost the backing of many of his own supporters.

- Black South Africans did not think that the changes went far enough. Those who co-operated with the government were attacked by other black South Africans. The ANC stepped up its opposition and South Africa went into a period when law and order almost broke down.

- Botha's changes also made him very unpopular with some white South Africans. Many of them left the National Party to join the Conservative Party, which opposed changes to apartheid.

- More extreme whites joined the **Afrikaner Resistance Movement** led by Eugene Terre Blanche. This group wore military uniforms and saw itself as fighting to save the Afrikaner way of life.

In 1983 opponents of apartheid combined to form the **United Democratic Front** (UDF). This organisation contained members from all South Africa's racial groups and showed that opposition to apartheid was uniting South Africans (although Inkatha did not join).

When elections under the new constitution were held in 1983 and 1984, the UDF campaigned for non-white South Africans not to vote. Less than one-fifth of those eligible to vote did so. This was a clear sign that Botha's reforms were not going to be supported.

Black South Africans not only failed to support Botha's reforms, they also took active measures to oppose them. Between 1984 and 1988, 3350 people died in disturbances.

The end of apartheid: the roles of Nelson Mandela, the ANC and De Klerk

Botha had met with Nelson Mandela in August 1989. At this meeting Mandela asked Botha to release all political prisoners. He was told that this was impossible. When ill-health forced Botha to resign, his successor, F. W. de Klerk, began to make important changes.

- In February 1990 the ANC, the PAC and the South African Communist Party were all legalised.

- All political prisoners were released and the death sentence was abolished.

- Nelson Mandela was released from prison. He had been in prison for 27 years.

A change of course
De Klerk's measures took everyone by surprise.

- Many of his own Party left in protest to join the Conservative Party.

- The Afrikaner Resistance Movement also grew in strength and, by 1993, had 20,000 members.

Although de Klerk had made important changes, he had no intention of handing over power to black South Africans. In 1989 the National Party struggled to win the General Election and the country was facing economic chaos. Something had to be done.

Nelson Mandela

Mandela became involved in politics in 1947. He was accused of treason in 1961, but found not guilty. He then lead Umkhonto we Sizwu (Spear of the Nation) which organised attacks on public buildings. He was arrested in 1962 and sentenced to life imprisonment in solitary confinement. He was not released until 1990.

What de Klerk hoped was that he could save apartheid by making some changes. Perhaps the rivalry between the ANC and Inkatha would help him. Perhaps Nelson Mandela would look less of a hero when he was involved in making real political decisions.

Unfortunately for de Klerk, Mandela proved to be a very talented negotiator. His calmness and moderate behaviour impressed many South Africans. The white South Africans could not believe that this was the dangerous terrorist Communist that they had been told to fear.

De Klerk also discovered that black South Africans were not going to be bought off with 'half-measures'. They wanted their political freedom.

Source 7

▲ Nelson Mandela.

Black majority rule

- Negotiations to introduce a new constitution began in 1991. The government was still not prepared to allow a constitution which gave black South Africans control of the government, so the talks broke down.

- Then the ANC suggested sharing power for five years. De Klerk agreed and an election was called for April 1994.

- One month before the election, the Afrikaner Freedom Movement invaded Bophuthatsawna, one of the tribal homelands. It hoped that this show of force would win it support.

- But the opposite was true. South Africans were horrified to see an armed uprising. The leaders were quickly arrested. Some died in a shoot out with police.

- The election was a great victory for the ANC. Nelson Mandela became the first President of a South Africa governed by majority rule. In a spirit of forgiveness and reconciliation, he appointed de Klerk as one of the Deputy Presidents and Chief Buthelezi was given a job as a Cabinet Minister.

In September 1994, Nelson Mandela and F. W. de Klerk were awarded the Nobel Peace Price for their part in ending apartheid.

The National Party and the nature of its rule

Source A

In 1976, all outdoor meetings were banned except for sports events and funerals. The Internal Security Act allowed the government to ban any organisation, individual or newspaper. In effect the Minister of Justice now decided what was a crime and what was not. Suspects were held without trial. But South Africa was a police state long before this happened.

▲ **From an American textbook published in 1991.**

Source B

The revolutionaries and radicals in our country never abolished their aim for South Africa to become a communist state. This is, of course, totally unacceptable to the majority of South Africans and the South African government is equally not prepared to accept that at any stage. Therefore it was necessary to curb the actions of certain persons and organisations.

▲ **From the announcement of the State of Emergency in 1988 by the Minister for Law and Order.**

Source C

Before the morning I was taken from the cell to the place where I was tortured the day before. I was handcuffed below the knees and my arms, and an iron bar was forced between my arms and my legs. I was left hanging between two tables. I was told to tell the truth. They put a rubber tube on my face and I was left bleeding from the nose. Somebody was stabbing me with a sharp instrument in my private parts. This went on for about four to five hours.

▲ **From a description of the treatment received in prison by a detainee.**

Source D

Botha needed the support of those Blacks who had achieved a degree of success under apartheid by acquiring skilled jobs and obtaining a higher standard of living. He therefore decided to water down apartheid. As he said, White South Africa had to 'adapt or die'.

Botha's reforms allowed some Blacks to buy property in white areas. These were the Blacks who had previously been allowed into those areas to work. The government also relaxed restrictions on trade unions, so that many black Africans were now able to join unions and improve their wages and working conditions. There was a massive increase in spending on education for black Africans, so that they would be better able to provide a skilled workforce suited to modern industry.

▲ **A comment on the South African government's policies in the 1980s, from a modern school textbook.**

Source E

▲ Armoured personnel carriers moving into Soweto in the 1980s.

Source F

On Tuesday 6 September 1977, a friend of mine named Stephen Biko was taken by South African political police to Room 619 of the Sanlam Building in Strand Street, Port Elizabeth, Cape Province. He was handcuffed, put into leg irons, chained to a grille and subjected to 22 hours of interrogation, in the course of which he was tortured and beaten. He sustained several blows to the head that damaged his brain causing him to fall into a coma and die six days later.

▲ From the book *Biko*, by Donald Woods.

Study Source A

a What can you learn from Source A about the methods used by the government in South Africa? (4)

Study Sources A, B and C

b Do Sources B and C support the evidence of Source A about the methods used by the government of South Africa? Explain your answer. (6)

Study Sources D and E

c How useful are these sources as evidence about the policies of the South African government? (8)

Study all of the sources

d 'During the 1980s, the South African government relied more and more on force to keep black people under control.' Use the sources and your own knowledge to explain whether you agree with this view. (12)

The system of apartheid, and its economic and social consequences

Source A

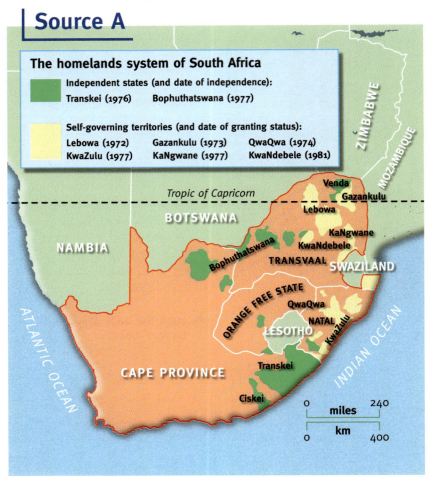

The homelands system of South Africa

Independent states (and date of independence):
Transkei (1976)   Bophuthatswana (1977)

Self-governing territories (and date of granting status):
Lebowa (1972)   Gazankulu (1973)   QwaQwa (1974)
KwaZulu (1977)   KaNgwane (1977)   KwaNdebele (1981)

▲ A map showing the Bantustans, or tribal homelands, set up by the South African government.

Source B

Between 1951 and 1986 at least 4,000,000 people were forced to move from white areas to Bantustans and black townships on the edge of white towns. Black people who had lived in Kenton-on-Sea for 25 years were given just 11 days' notice of their removal to the Ciskei Bantustan.

In these Bantustans black people would have their own government, but they would not be completely independent. The white South African government would still control defence and foreign policy.

It followed from this policy that blacks in white areas were now just visitors with no rights.

▲ From a modern school textbook.

Source C

It came so suddenly. They came with guns and police and all sorts of things. We had no choice. The guns were behind us. They did not say anything, they just threw our belongings in and off they went. There is nothing you can say or they will shoot you in the head. Soldiers and everything were there. We did not know, we still do not know, this place. When we came here they just dumped our things. What can we do now? We can do nothing.

▲ A description of a forced removal to a Bantustan.

Source D

White	68
Indian	61
Black	55
Coloured	51

▲ The life expectancy of people in South Africa in the 1980s.

Source E

▲ A policeman checking the pass books of black South Africans.

Source F

We should get away from the idea that these homelands could be regarded as dumping grounds for people whom we do not want in white South Africa. However, at the same time, it must be realised that the white areas should not be regarded as the dumping grounds for the surplus labour, which comes from the Bantu homelands.

▲ From a statement by a representative of the National Party.

Study Source A

a What can you learn from Source A about the treatment of black people in South Africa? (4)

Study Sources A, B and C

b Do Sources B and C support the evidence of Source A about the treatment of black South Africans? Explain your answer. (6)

Study Sources D and E

c How useful are these sources as evidence about the effects of apartheid on black South Africans? (8)

Study all of the sources

d The writer of Source F suggested that the black and white areas of South Africa received similar treatment. Use the sources and your own knowledge to explain whether you agree with this view of apartheid. (12)

Support for, and opposition to, apartheid in South Africa

Source A

I don't know any blacks of my age and have never spoken to any. I don't think it is a good idea that black and white should know each other. I would just hate to live with them. I don't like anything about them. I don't know if our black maid has any children. I never speak to her. I have never been into a Bantu location and don't want to.

▲ From a statement by a 17 year-old Afrikaner.

Source B

White South Africans had one of the highest standards of living in the world. Many white homes were huge by British standards, with big gardens and a swimming pool. There would often be living quarters for a maid or a nanny. Well-off white families employed between one and four black servants.

White areas had properly made roads, not dust tracks; there was good street lighting, too. White areas had libraries, museums, public gardens and so on. The whites who ran them could decide when, and if, other races could use them.

▲ From a modern school textbook.

Source C

It was never intended that if you give something to one group that equal provision should be made in every respect for other groups. In our country we have civilised people, we have semi-civilised people and we have uncivilised people. The government of the country gives each section facilities according to the needs of each.

▲ From a statement by the South African Minister for Justice in the early 1970s.

Source D

Let me remind you of three little words. The first is 'all'. We want all our rights. The second word is 'here'. We want our rights here in a united, undivided South Africa. We do not want them in impoverished homelands. The third word is the word 'now'. We want all our rights, we want them here and we want them now. We have been jailed, exiled, killed for too long. Now is the time.

▲ From a speech by the Reverend Allan Boesak in 1983.

Source E

We want a country that is united, democratic and non-racial. It must belong to all who live in it, in which all enjoy equal rights and in which the right to rule will rest with the people as a whole. Power must not rest with a collection of Bantustans and tribal groups, which are organised to maintain power for the minority.

▲ From a speech made by Oliver Tambo, the president of the ANC.

Source F

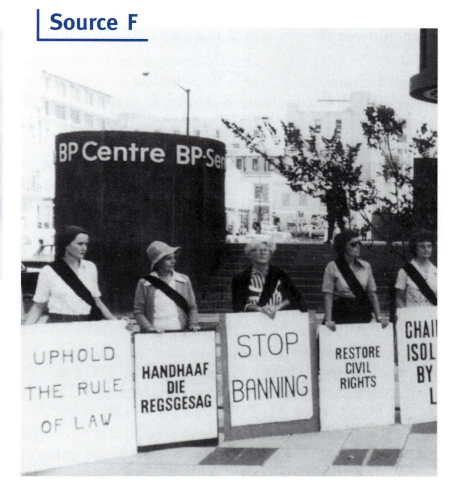

▲ Members of the Black Sash, an anti-apartheid movement, protesting in Johannesburg.

Study Source A

a What can you learn from Source A about relations between white people and black people in South Africa? (4)

Study Sources A, B and C

b Does the evidence of Source C support the evidence of Sources A and B? Explain your answer. (6)

Study Sources D and E

c How useful are these sources as evidence about the aims of black South Africans? (8)

Study all of the sources

d 'Apartheid was so deep-rooted that it would be almost impossible to overturn it by peaceful means.' Use the sources and your own knowledge to explain whether you agree with this view. (12)

Commonwealth and world reactions to apartheid

Source A

There is no case in history that I know where punitive general economic sanctions have been effective in bringing about internal changes.

▲ From a speech by Margaret Thatcher in 1986.

Source B

Sanctions will help to convince white South Africans that it is in their own interests to dismantle apartheid and enter negotiations to establish a non-racial and representative government. The white minority must see that apartheid is no longer a real option because the economic and political cost is too high. Sanctions will undermine the power of the apartheid regime and weaken its determination to resist change.

▲ From a study on sanctions by the Commonwealth, published in 1989.

Source C

Sustained international pressure and economic sanctions played a very important role in ensuring that it became impossible to continue with apartheid.

▲ From a speech by Nelson Mandela in 1994.

Source D

	South Africa	The rest of Africa
Industrial production	38%	62%
Minerals	45%	55%
Motor vehicles	49%	51%
Railways	50%	50%

▲ Percentage figures showing the production of goods and raw materials in the South African economy and for the rest of Africa combined in the late 1970s.

Source E

The foreign action that did South Africa the most damage occurred in 1985 when western banks refused to make any new loans and called in existing ones. South Africa was forced to repay US$13,000,000,000 by December 1985. As a result, the rand, the South African currency, lost 35 per cent of its value in thirteen days.

From 1989 to 1992 South Africa went through a serious recession, which saw its national income fall by 3 per cent every year.

▲ **From a modern school textbook.**

Source F

Breaking the Afrikaners' will by rising economic pressure abroad will not work. The government sees black rule as a mortal threat to language, to property, to identity and to physical security. It is pointless to think that fears such as these can be overcome by threats to the economy.

▲ **From an article in the newspaper *Johannesburg Business Day* in 1986.**

Study Source A

a What can you learn from Source A about the impact of sanctions upon South Africa? (4)

Study Sources A, B and C

b Does Source C support the view of sanctions given in Source A or Source B? Explain your answer. (6)

Study Sources D and E

c How useful are these sources as evidence about the impact of sanctions on the South African economy? (8)

Study all of the sources

d The writer of Source F believed that sanctions would have no effect on the South African government. Use the sources and your own knowledge to explain whether you agree with this view. (12)

Changes to apartheid in the 1980s

Source A

The world does not remain the same, and if we as a government want to act in the best interest of the country in a changing world, then we have to be prepared to adapt our policy to those things that make adjustment necessary, otherwise we die.

▲ From a speech made by P. W. Botha to a conference of the National Party in 1979.

Source B

While the National Party respects the multicultural nature of South Africa's population, it rejects any system that amounts to one nation or group in our country dominating the others. If Mr Mandela gives a commitment that he will not instigate or commit acts of violence, I will, in principle, be prepared to consider his release. My government and I are determined to press ahead with our reform programme. I believe that from today there can be no turning back.

▲ From a speech made by President Botha to a conference of the National Party in August 1985.

Source C

One of Botha's first moves was to recognise blacks as permanent residents of white cities, and grant them the right to own houses and property in the townships. He got rid of some of the more unpleasant apartheid laws and offered a vote of sorts to the coloureds and Indians. He started pouring money into black education and easing restrictions on black enterprise, hoping to create a black middle class as protection against revolution. To pay for this he taxed white South Africans. To whites who complained, P. W. had this to say: 'Adapt or die.'

▲ From a book written by an Afrikaner.

Source D

	Whites	Blacks
1970	33.3	15.9
1985	40.0	32.1
2000	44.2	53.6

▲ Population statistics shown in an advertisement published by the South African government in the 1980s.

Source E

▲ Protas and Susan Madlala, who were married in 1985.

Source F

I have no hope of real change from this government unless they are forced. We face a catastrophe in this land and only the action of the international community by applying pressure can save us. I call upon the international community to apply punitive sanctions against this government to help us establish a new South Africa – non-racial, democratic and just.

▲ From a news conference given by Archbishop Desmond Tutu in 1986.

Study Source A

a What can you learn from Source A about the policies of P. W. Botha? (4)

Study Sources A, B and C

b Does the evidence of Source C support the evidence of Sources A and B about Botha's policies? Explain your answer. (6)

Study Sources D and E

c How useful are these sources as evidence of the relationships between black and white South Africans in the 1980s? (8)

Study all of the sources

d 'P. W. Botha tried to change South Africa because he believed that black people should be treated as the equals of white people.' Use the sources and your own knowledge to explain whether you agree with this view of Botha's policies. (12)

The end of apartheid: the roles of Nelson Mandela, the ANC and de Klerk

Source A

It is time for us to break out of the cycle of violence and break through to peace and reconciliation. We will offer a new democratic constitution, universal franchise, equality before the law, better education, health services, housing and social conditions for all. The time for talking has arrived.

▲ From a speech made by President de Klerk in the South African parliament on 2 February 1990.

Source B

We reject black majority rule. We stand for power-sharing and group rights. We are not selling out to anyone. We are going to make it safer for our descendants to live in South Africa.

▲ From a speech made by President de Klerk in the Transvaal on 18 October 1990.

Source C

▲ A photograph of de Klerk, Mandela and Buthelezi in April 1994.

Source D

I told de Klerk that the ANC had not struggled against apartheid for 75 years only to yield to a disguised form of it. If it was his intention to preserve apartheid through group rights, then he did not truly believe in ending apartheid.

I saw my mission as one of preaching reconciliation, of binding the wounds of the country. I knew that many people, particularly the minorities, whites, coloureds and Indians, would be feeling anxious about the future, and I wanted them to feel secure.

▲ From Nelson Mandela's book *Long Walk to Freedom*, published in 1994.

Source E

Overseas investment is growing all the time. Tourism has more than trebled. The government has three priorities right now, Health, Education and Housing. Starter homes are being provided, funded by the government and building societies. An important factor in the whole process is lack of bitterness and desire for revenge. Mandela provides an excellent role model of forgiveness in his efforts to 'nation-build'.

▲ From comments by a South African businessman in January 1996.

Source F

▲ A cartoon published in a British daily newspaper in 1993. The figures are de Klerk and Mandela.

Study Source A

a What can you learn from Source A about the aims of President de Klerk? (4)

Study Sources A, B and C

b Does the evidence of Source C support the evidence of Sources A and B about the aims of de Klerk? Explain your answer. (6)

Study Sources D and E

c How useful are these sources as evidence about the role of Nelson Mandela in bringing about a peaceful solution to the problems facing South Africa? (8)

Study all of the sources

d The cartoonist in Source F suggested that de Klerk and Mandela played equal parts in ending apartheid in South Africa. Use the sources and your own knowledge to explain whether you agree with this view. (12)

CHAPTER 8

Nationalism and independence in India: c.1900~49

Introduction

In 1851, Britain held the Great Exhibition in London. Amongst the most popular stands at the exhibition were those containing items from India. The silks, jewels, silver and gold work (and the stuffed elephant) made people think of India as an exotic and mysterious place. The Prime Minister, Disraeli, called India 'the brightest jewel in the British crown'. In 1876, Queen Victoria was delighted to take the title 'Empress of India'.

India c.1900~49

British rule in India in the early twentieth century

The British in India

The British had forced control of parts of India by setting up a trading company called the East India Company. It had its own army and civil servants. In 1858, the British government took over control from the East India Company. Large numbers of British people went to India to work as civil servants, policemen or soldiers. Some of them went as private individuals to try to make their fortunes as merchants or owners of estates.

The Viceroys of India

1898–1905 Lord Curzon

1905–10 Lord Minto

1910–16 Lord Hardinge

1916–21 Lord Chelmsford

1921–26 Lord Reading

1926–31 Lord Irwin

1931–36 Lord Willingdon

1936–43 Lord Linlithgow

1943–47 Lord Wavell

1947 Lord Mountbatten

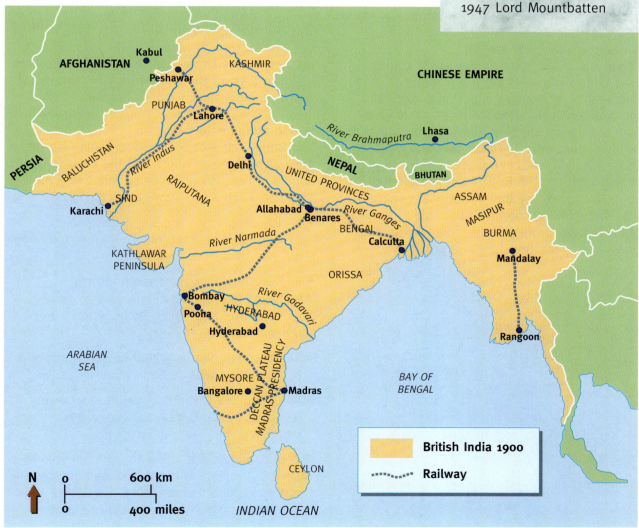

▲ Map of India in 1900.

The top person in the British Empire's government in India was the **Viceroy**, who was appointed by the government in Britain. He was the Queen's representative in India and behaved like it! He had over 700 servants and was paid twice as much as the British Prime Minister. Because India was so important, it also had its own minister in the British government to look after it. This was the Secretary of State for India.

The Viceroys worked hard in India. With the help of the Imperial Legislative Council and 70,000 civil servants, they began to make improvements in agriculture, education and transport. For example, by 1900 irrigation had been brought to 14 million acres of land which previously had suffered from shortages of water.

A country with great variety

In 1900, just like today, India was a country with great variety. It had 300 million inhabitants, at least 15 major languages and many different religions. At most, there were just 70,000 British people in India to govern the territory. That tells you that the great majority of Indians must have been prepared to accept British rule – or the British would have lost control. In 1885 the Indian National Congress was set up to try to end British rule in India. Many Indians protested that this was an act of disloyalty to the British.

The princes

In actual fact, the British never really governed much more than half of India. The rest was governed by princes, who were like kings in their area. There were 562 areas in India governed by princes. Some were very small but others were huge. Hyderabad had 14 million inhabitants. The British were happy to allow the princes to rule as long as they signed treaties promising to support the **British 'Raj' (Empire)**.

Rich trading

The British had originally come to India hoping to make money. They did this by taking raw materials, such as cotton, from India and selling manufactured goods, such as machinery, back to the Indians. This was a very profitable trade.

The Indians were very loyal to the British. When the First World War broke out in 1914 some of the first troops to be sent to Belgium were from India. In each of the two World Wars the Indians provided more than 1 million soldiers for Britain.

British attitudes to Indians

The British felt that their role in India was clear. They were there as rulers and the Indians should know their place as people being ruled. This had several important consequences:

- British people and Indians lived apart and worked apart. Except for official functions, they did not mix.

- Any Briton who was considered to be behaving like an Indian was said to have 'gone native' and risked being ignored by other Britons.

- Some British people would not even attend a court where there was an Indian judge.

- Anglo-Indians (people of mixed race) were regarded by the British as second-class citizens.

The British were not trying to be offensive. They were just convinced that they were superior. This was the attitude they adopted throughout their huge Empire, which in 1900 made up about a quarter of the world!

The religions of India in 1900

Hindus	210 million
Muslims	75 million
Sikhs, Christians, Buddhists Jains and others	about 15 million

It is not surprising that, as time went on, the Indians began to resent their treatment at the hands of the British, and set up organisations to try to improve their position.

The Congress Movement

The India National Congress was set up in 1885. The leaders believed in non-violent protest as a way to obtain more say in how India was governed. At first they did not go as far as demanding **Home Rule** (Indians governing themselves). But, from 1907, there was a great division in the movement. The Moderates wanted to work with the British; the Extremists wanted to get Home Rule for Indians.

The All India Muslim League

This organisation (usually just called the Muslim League) shows how the religious divisions in India led to difficulties. It was set up in 1906. It did not campaign to get rid of the British. Instead, its main aim was to protect Muslims who lived in areas of India where the majority of people were Hindus.

A good example of the problems created by religion was seen in 1905. Bengal had mostly Hindus living in it. But there were areas where large numbers of Muslims lived. Viceroy Curzon decided to split the state into two – to make a Hindu state and a Muslim state. The Hindus objected to this because previously they had controlled all of Bengal. There was rioting and violence. They even refused to buy British goods. So, in 1911, Curzon had to reverse his decision.

Tata Iron and Steel Works

One important change in India's relationship with Britain was the setting up of the Tata Iron and Steel Works in 1907. This showed that India was now beginning to produce goods which previously Britain would have made and sold to India. So as this change gathered pace, Britain found that India was not as profitable as it had been. By the 1930s India was selling more things to Britain than it was buying. (Today Tata builds most of India's lorries and most of its cars.)

The Morley-Minto reforms

The changes that were taking place in India made the British think again about how India was governed. Perhaps the time had come to make reforms (changes) which would give the Indians a greater say in how their country was run. If the British did this, then it would help make the Indians more satisfied with British rule and stop riots and violence.

So the Secretary of State for India, John Morley and the Viceroy came up with changes. An Indian had tried to assassinate Lord Minto in 1909, so he had even more reason to try to keep the Indians happy with British rule.

Source A

▲ Tata is a familiar name in India today.

Problems with the changes

Despite the attempts to give the Indians a greater say in how their country was run, the Morley-Minto reforms were soon criticised by many Indians.

- Although members of the Imperial Legislative Council and the local councils could be elected, very few Indians could vote. The qualifications necessary to vote meant that only 2 per cent of Indians could vote.

- Reserving seats for Muslims was a dangerous thing. It increased the divide between Hindus and Muslims in India. The British government looked like it agreed with **communalism** (the idea that different groups should be treated in different ways). Once this idea started it would be very difficult to stop. Eventually it led to India being split up.

Questions

1 How was India governed by the British at the beginning of the twentieth century?

2 Why did relations between Britain and India begin to change from 1905?

3 Why was the Indian Councils Act (Morley–Minto reforms) passed in 1909?

4 In what ways did the Indian Councils Act change the government of India?

The Morley-Minto reforms

These reforms were introduced in the **Indian Councils Act** of 1909. They gave the Indians much more say in running their own country.

- The Imperial Legislative Council was increased to have 60 members. Of these, 27 were to be elected, and Indians could be on it for the first time.

- Local councils would now also have elected members, many of whom would be Indians.

- Muslims complained that, as most Indians were Hindus, other people could not get elected. So there were now to be six Muslims on the Imperial Legislative Council. This was the first time special arrangements had been made for religious groups.

But in 1909 no-one realised how the future would turn out. King George V came to India in 1911 and held the great **Delhi Durbar** (meeting of leaders). The Indian princes expressed their loyalty to the King Of England (and Emperor of India) in a ceremony with great colour and celebration. All seemed peaceful and loyal in India – especially when George announced that the two parts of Bengal would be reunited. He also said that the capital of India would be moved from Calcutta to Delhi.

The impact of the First World War upon relations between Britain and India

In August 1914, Britain went to war with Germany. India immediately raised a force and sent it to Europe. Indian troops were part of the **British Expeditionary Force** sent to Belgium and they fought at the First Battle of Ypres at the end of October 1914. Soon more than 1.125 million Indians had volunteered to fight for Britain in the war.

India during the First World War

The war seemed to provide opportunities for India. There was a chance for the country's economy to prosper and, politically, to move much closer to Home Rule.

▲ **King George V and Queen Mary attended by young Indian princes at the Delhi Durbar.**

- In the early years of the war there was a great demand for Indian cotton and other raw materials. This brought more jobs and more prosperity in India.

- **Mohandas Gandhi** (see page 180) arrived back in India from South Africa. He told the Indians to support the British. Showing loyalty would help persuade the British to grant Home Rule.

- In 1915 Congress said India should move towards governing itself. The leader of the Extremists (Bal Tilak) set up the Home Rule League.

- Congress and the Muslim League signed the Lucknow Pact in 1916. This said that Muslims could have a certain number of seats in any parliament that was set up after Home Rule. The idea of the pact was to remove possible future problems before Home Rule was set up.

As the war continued many Indians were convinced that they would get Home Rule.

- The British said they were fighting to defend the rights of nations. So India must have the right to govern itself, thought many Indians.

▲ **Indian troops in France during the First World War.**

- British and Indian troops were fighting side by side as equals. So, if they were equal, Britain should not rule India.

- In August 1917 the Secretary of State, Sir Edwin Montagu, made a speech saying that Indians should have more say in their government. This **'Montagu Declaration'** seemed to show that Home Rule was not far off.

- In 1917 Montagu and the Viceroy, Lord Chelmsford toured India listening to public opinion. This seemed to show that they were thinking about Home Rule.

Unrest in India

But it would be wrong to think that all Indians were quietly waiting for the British to hand over Home Rule – or that if it came the different religious groups would live in harmony. The British were worried about what might happen in India.

Source B

▲ **Gandhi spinning cotton in 1919.**

In 1915 the British passed the **Defence of India Act** allowing them to arrest Indians without charge.

As the war went on, rising prices and the cost of war made life difficult and there were outbreaks of violence as people protested. These were very serious in an area in the Northwest called the Punjab. Here Hindus, Muslims and Sikhs distrusted each other. The British were very worried about India because most of the British troops had left to fight the war. So the British didn't want any trouble.

Source C

We must have more Indians involved in all parts of the government. We must also develop more ways for the Indians to govern themselves as part of the British Empire.

▲ The Montagu Declaration.

The Montagu-Chelmsford Report
At the end of the war the Indians waited to see what changes the British would make. Would they give the Indians Home Rule? The changes were announced in August 1918 and were made law in the **Government of India Act** in 1919. They were called the **Montagu-Chelmsford reforms** after the two men who suggested them. You can see full details of these reforms on page 182.

- The reforms gave a lot more say in running India to the Indians. This was welcomed by many Indians.

- But they did not go as far as giving Home Rule and this upset many other Indians who thought that the support they had given the British in the war would be rewarded with Home Rule.

- The failure to grant Home Rule came shortly after the Amritsar Massacre and the **Rowlatt Acts**. These had made many Indians even more determined to get Home Rule. So the Government of India Act was an even bigger disappointment.

The failure to grant Home Rule led to violence and demonstrations, particularly in the Punjab. At the same time, the end of the war had meant that there was no longer great demand for textiles for uniforms. So some textile factories had to close down and people lost their jobs. When influenza hit India in 1919, killing 13 million people, this seemed the last straw.

The Rowlatt Acts
Towards the end of the war the government in India had been frightened that it might lose control. So it passed the Rowlatt Acts in early 1919. These said that the Defence of India Act could apply in peacetime too. In other words, the British could arrest and imprison without trial anyone who they thought was a troublemaker. If they did put people on trial, judges could make decisions without needing to have a jury (so they usually decided what the government wanted).

The effect of the Rowlatt Acts
The Indians were very angry about the Rowlatt Acts. Special laws in wartime were one thing. But to have the same laws in peacetime was unjust.

The passing of these laws showed that the British would use force to bully the Indians into obedience. It was all very well Montagu and Chelmsford trying to give Indians more say in their government, but these laws showed that the British intended to keep power.

The Rowlatt Acts were never used and the government soon scrapped these laws. But the damage had been done. The Indian people realised that the British had no intention of relaxing the grip they had on India.

Enter Gandhi

It was around this time that Mohandas Gandhi became an important figure in India. Gandhi was born in India in 1869. He studied law in London and set up a law firm in Bombay (Mumbai). He believed that violence achieved nothing and that change would only come through peaceful protest.

In 1893 he left India for South Africa where he spent 20 years fighting legal cases for Indians who were suffering persecution. Here he developed his idea of 'Satyagraha'. This was non-violent disobedience – something which was to prove very successful in trying to get the British to grant rights to Indians in India.

In 1920, the leader of Congress, Bal Tilak, died and Gandhi became the most important leader in Congress. He was soon to become the most-well known Indian not only in his own country, but across the world.

The Hindu caste system

In modern India, the **caste system** has been abolished, but it still has great influence on people's lives.

Brahmans: the highest caste, its members were priests and highly educated people.

Kshatryas: members of this caste were rulers, nobles and warriors.

Vaisias: members of this caste were landlords and businessmen.

Sudras: the biggest caste as far as numbers are concerned. Its members were peasants and workers.

Below the castes were the **Untouchables**. These performed 'unclean' tasks such as sewage disposal.

Each caste was sub-divided into '**communities**' and people from one community did not marry those from another.

Gandhi's return to India

Gandhi had returned to India from South Africa in 1915. He soon joined Congress, but made himself unpopular with some of the other Congress leaders.

- India was a country with a rigid class system. The Congress leaders were generally well-educated and middle-class. They wanted their Party to be limited to people like them. Gandhi wanted it to be open to all Indians – even the 'Untouchables'. Normally, other Indians had nothing to do with them.

- Gandhi also put forward his ideas of 'Satyagraha' or non-violent disobedience. Not everyone thought this was the best way of persuading the British to grant Home Rule.

When the Rowlatt Acts were passed on 18 March 1919, Gandhi decided to put his plans for non-violent disobedience into action. He announced a '**hartal**', a day of fasting and strikes. This was supposed to have been a peaceful protest, but some of Gandhi's supporters either misunderstood his ideas or ignored them. There was rioting across India, particularly in the Punjab. Then came an even more dramatic event.

The Amritsar Massacre

In April 1919, five Britons were killed in a riot in Amritsar, the holy city of the Sikhs. The British officer in charge of the area was General Dyer. He banned all public meetings to make sure that there would be no more trouble. The Indians ignored his orders and called a public protest meeting on 13 April. Dyer did not take any steps to cancel the meeting. He intended to teach the Indians a lesson.

Dyer's lesson

When the meeting took place on 13 April, 5000 Indians gathered in **Jallianwala Bagh**, an area near the sacred Sikh Golden Temple. The crowd (which was unarmed, and contained women and children) was surrounded by high walls in a park with just a few narrow entrances.

General Dyer marched a small force of soldiers into the park and ordered them to fire on the crowd. The troops fired for about six minutes until their ammunition ran out. In panic, men, women and children tried to flee through the narrow exits. British figures say that 379 people were killed and 1200 wounded. The Indians say that the death toll was over 2000.

The massacre had a dramatic impact. It showed the Indians that the British were prepared to use brutality and violence to put down opposition in India. And Dyer had not finished. In the next few days he arrested more than 500 students and teachers, and imprisoned some of them in a cage in the market place.

Source D

▲ **The Golden Temple, scene of the Amritsar massacre.**

Source E

▲ **The entrance to the Jallianwala Bagh at Amritsar where bullet marks can still be seen.**

When a British woman was assaulted and knocked from her bike, Dyer ordered that all Indians who wanted to pass down the street where she had been assaulted had to crawl on their hands and knees.

What were the effects of the Amritsar Massacre?

The main effect of the massacre was to upset the Indians. The actions of Dyer were bad enough, but the British did not seem to be going to punish him. This led many Indians to decide it was time for the British to leave.

If the British had disciplined Dyer straight away, the Indians might have been less angered. But they did not. Instead, he was called back to Britain and the Hunter Committee was set up to investigate the incident. Dyer told them that, if the entrance to the Jallianwalla Bagh had been wider, he would have driven in armoured cars and used them to shoot the crowd.

Eventually Dyer was dismissed, but there was a great deal of support for him. Some British people thought that strong action like his was the only way to save India from rebellion. The British House of Lords voted 121 to 86 in support of what he had done. A British newspaper raised £23,000 to buy a jewelled sword for him. It was inscribed 'Saviour of the Punjab'.

Dyer never got his job back, but the Indians were greatly offended by what had been done. When the British introduced the Montagu–Chelmsford reforms by passing the Government of India Act in December 1919, many Indians refused to support them.

Opposition to the Act

The British hoped that the Indians would be pleased by the greater role in government that the Act gave them. Some were, but many were not.

- It was still true that only 2.8 per cent of Indians could vote in the elections.

- The Indians had more say in provincial government, but there was no money to allow them to put their ideas into practice.

The Government of India Act 1919

This said that the government of India was now a 'dyarchy'. This meant that power was split between two groups, the British and the Indians.

- The Viceroy remained in charge, but he was now advised by an Executive Council. This included the Commander-in-Chief of the Army and six other people – three of these were Indian.

- The Imperial Legislative Council (now called the Imperial Legislative Assembly) was to have 146 members, 106 of whom were elected.

- A Council of State was set up with 61 members. The British in it dealt with taxes, defence and foreign affairs. The Indians dealt with education, sanitation and agriculture.

- Indians would be given more power in the provincial governments (governments of provinces such as Bengal or the Punjab).

- The Act was opposed by Congress. Before the war, Congress had been a small Party with only limited influence. But by 1919 it had grown to have a great deal of support across India. The British were soon to find that, without the support of Congress, no changes could happen in the way India was governed.

Questions

1 In what ways did India help Britain during the First World War?

2 Why were the Rowlatt Acts passed in 1919?

3 Why did relations between Britain and India change after the First World War?

4 In what ways did the Government of India Act of 1919 (Montagu-Chelmsford Reforms) change the way that India was governed?

The Congress Movement and the Muslim League: Ghandi and Jinnah's campaign for independence

Why did Gandhi emerge as leader of the Congress after the First World War?

- We have already seen how Gandhi returned to India from South Africa in 1919 and how he became the most influential leader of Congress after Bal Tilak died.

- In 1920 he persuaded Congress to demand **swaraj** (Home Rule). This would be achieved by peaceful means.

- His policy of involving lower caste and poorly educated people in the movement upset many high-class Indians. But it also meant that support for Congress increased dramatically and it became a national Party.

- Gandhi began wearing Indian clothes instead of dressing in the western style as most educated Indians did. He encouraged other members of Congress to do the same.

Civil disobedience

In August 1920, Gandhi organised a massive campaign of civil disobedience by Indians.

- There was to be no violence. Instead the Indians would show their opposition to the British by refusing to co-operate with them.

- Congress members refused to work in courts and in schools. They also made a point of not buying British goods. Instead they had a policy of '**Swadeshi**', buying Indian goods in preference to British ones.

- Gandhi also persuaded them not to take part in the elections held after the Government of India Act. As a result of this decision, only one-third of those eligible to vote actually did so. The British were so angry at the opposition that they declared Congress to be illegal and arrested many of its supporters. By 1922 more than 30,000 Congress members were in prison.

▲ Gandhi's ashram in Gujerat.

- But, as had happened before, some of Gandhi's supporters did not follow his non-violent methods. In February 1922, 21 police were attacked and burned to death by rioters at Chauri Chaura.

- Gandhi was horrified by this action and immediately called off his campaign. Despite this, he was arrested by the British and imprisoned from 1922–24.

- When Gandhi was released from prison, he decided to make his protest against the British in a different way. He set up an '**ashram**' (or settlement) in Gujerat. At this settlement cotton was spun in a traditional way. This was illegal because the British had passed laws saying all raw cotton had to be sent to Britain to be spun.

Changing conditions

The violence at Chauri Chaura had persuaded Gandhi to call off his civil disobedience campaign. So it had not been as successful as he had hoped. But it did have several important effects in India.

- It was the first national campaign organised by Indians.

- It showed that Indians were no longer going to accept British decisions without question.

- It also made the British realise that they would have to change their views on India. No longer could they treat it as a place where they could get cheap raw materials and rely on the complete loyalty of the people to Britain. They would now have to treat Indians better and earn their loyalty.

Source B

▲ Motilal and Jawaharlal Nehru.

Motilal Nehru became one of the leaders of the Swaraj Party and co-operated with the British. His influence helped get the Rowlatt Acts abolished. To show his commitment to Home Rule he sold his legal practice and used the money to finance his campaigns. He died in 1930.

Britain and India in the 1920s

The British government had passed the Government of India Act (see page 182) to give the Indians more say in how their country was run. But they had kept important areas of government, like defence and foreign policy, in British hands.

The Nehrus

In 1922, Gandhi was imprisoned. Then he moved to his ashram in Gujerat. This meant that Congress did not have a leader. Soon the Party split into two. The 'Swaraj Party' supported co-operation with the British and the 'Non-Co-operation Party' rejected co-operation.

Soon two new leaders emerged. They were father and son, Motilal and Jawaharlal Nehru. The Nehrus were from Kashmir and were Brahmins, members of the highest Hindu caste. Both were trained lawyers. In the early 1920s both men were arrested and imprisoned several times for their work as members of Congress.

It is interesting that, despite the fact that they were father and son, the Nehrus did not see eye-to-eye on the best way forward for bringing Home Rule to India.

Jawaharlal Nehru became leader of the Non-Co-operation movement in Congress and, in 1929, was elected President of Congress. He supported Gandhi's ideas, but also felt that more extreme measures were needed.

During the 1920s the protests in India and changes in world trade made India less important to Britain. Britain was selling less and less to India and British business people were not investing as much money in the country. Now that it was no longer such a source of wealth to Britain, attitudes to India began to change. The number of Britons going to work there fell dramatically. Some British people were beginning to think that perhaps the time had come for Britain to leave India. But for most Britons this was out of the question. India was part of the British Empire and should remain so.

The Simon Commission

In 1927, the British government decided to have another look at how India was governed. It appointed Sir John Simon to head a Commission to make recommendations. There were no Indians on the Commission. This led to mass protests throughout India and Congress members refused to have anything to do with the Simon Commission.

When the Simon Commission had finished its work it recommended that:

- India should be a federal country (that is one where the individual provinces have their own government).

- There should also be a central government to control most of the important areas of government, like taxation, defence and foreign policy.

This was so much like the system that had been set up by the Montagu-Chelmsford reforms that, really, Simon was recommending no changes should be made.

Congress's reaction

Congress was angry at not having members on the Simon Commission and at the proposals to keep things as they were. Jawaharlal Nehru persuaded it to vote for something very important. For the first time ever, in 1928, Congress decided to call for **total independence** from Britain. It even went as far as drawing up a new Indian Constitution showing how India would be governed. It would have its own government, but would stay as part of the British Commonwealth. Congress announced that 21 January 1930 was 'Independence Day'.

The Muslim League's reaction

During the 1920s, Congress had been growing in importance. So had the Muslim League. Its leader Muhammed Ali Jinnah was also a member of Congress. Until 1927 he had supported Jawaharlal Nehru's policy of non-co-operation with the British. But in that year he decided to take a different approach.

Muslim co-operation with the British

Jinnah had two aims. He wanted to end British rule in India, but at the same time he wanted to make sure that Muslims had as much say as possible in how India was to be governed. Muslims were outnumbered three to one by Hindus and so Jinnah had to work hard to make sure that their interests were not neglected.

Source C

▲ M. A. Jinnah.

- The official policy of the Muslim League was to have nothing to do with the Simon Commission. But Jinnah thought this was a mistake. He could win benefits for Muslims if he co-operated with the British. He had great difficulty persuading the Muslim League to do this, but was eventually successful.

- In 1929 he published his ideas in the 'Fourteen Points'. This said that Muslims should have more say in how India was governed. This could be best done by agreeing to the British policy of having a federal India. Then, where the Muslims were in the majority (like in Hyderabad, Bengal or the Punjab), they would have control.

Source D

▲ Gandhi and Sarojini Naidu (politician, feminist and poet) leading the March to the Sea.

Gandhi and the 'March to the Sea'

In 1930 Gandhi decided that the time was right for a second 'Satyagraha' campaign. He knew that only the government was allowed to make salt in India, so he decided to organise a protest march to the sea and then to produce salt when he got there. This was typical of Gandhi's approach. It produced maximum publicity but he wanted absolutely no violence.

- But where Jinnah disagreed with the British was where the power should be. He wanted a weak central government and most of the power being in the hands of the provincial governments.

- As Jinnah did not approve of non-co-operation, he did not agree with Gandhi or with Congress. Not surprisingly he left Congress in 1930.

Questions

1 What tactics did Gandhi use in his campaigns against the British?

2 Why was the Simon Commission a failure?

3 In what ways did the Indian National Congress differ from the Muslim League?

4 What was the significance of the March to the Sea?

The march lasted 24 days from Ahmedabad in Gujerat to the coast. As soon as he arrived at the coast, Gandhi took a few grains of salt from the sea – and broke the law. The Viceroy, Lord Irwin, had Gandhi arrested and he spent much of 1930 and 1931 in prison. But his march had been a huge success. Soon 5 million Indians were making their own salt and selling it. Then people stopped buying British cloth and alcohol as another way of protesting. The British did not know what to do. So they began arresting people and soon 60,000 Congress members were in prison.

Source A

▲ **Gandhi in London, after attending a Round Table Conference.**

British policies and attitudes to India before the Second World War

Although the British imprisoned large numbers of Congress members, they also realised that they could not govern India just by force. There was a need to have discussions with the representatives of the Indian people to see if some agreement could be reached on how India should be governed. Then it would not be necessary to keep imprisoning people and getting such bad publicity for the British government.

The answer was to have what the British called '**Round Table Conferences**'. Representatives of all the political parties in Britain and in India would be invited to discuss a way of ruling India that suited everyone.

The decision by the British to call these conferences showed that it knew things weren't working.

- Congress was adopting a policy of non-co-operation.

- Gandhi was making the British look like brutal oppressors.

- The provincial governments could not act because they had so little money.

- No-one was quite sure what the position of the princes was. How much power should they have?

But there were two other important reasons for calling the conferences.

- In 1929 a Labour government was elected in Britain. The Labour Party did not support the idea of a British Empire as strongly as the Conservative government which it replaced. It was more willing to consider reducing Britain's role in India.

- There was also a need to reach an agreement on how India should be governed to stop violence in India.

By 1927 fighting between Hindus and Muslims (we call this 'communal' fighting) was causing 200 deaths each year. The government in India tried to make it an offence to insult the religion of other groups. Muslim members in the Legislative Assembly supported this. But Hindu members made sure it was not passed.

The Round Table Conferences
Between 1930 and 1933 there were three Round Table Conferences. Unfortunately they all ended in failure!

Failure one
The first conference was in London in 1930. Congress did not attend the conference because most of its leaders were in prison. So, even though the conference agreed to give the Indian provinces more power, it meant nothing because Congress had not agreed.

Failure two
The second conference was in 1931. The Viceroy, Lord Irwin, ordered Gandhi's release from prison so that he could attend the conference as the representative of Congress. There were high hopes that the friendly relations between Gandhi and Irwin would lead to success. But they did not. Gandhi recommended a new Constitution for India, but the minority groups (e.g. Muslims and Christians) were not happy with it. The talks ended in failure.

Failure three
The third conference took place in 1932. By then the Labour government had stood down in Britain. It had been replaced by a National government of all parties to try to solve the problems created by the **Great Depression**. It was less willing to make changes and Congress also did not attend the conference.

The decision to hold the conferences had raised hopes in India. So the failure to reach agreement had caused great disappointment. Congress went back to non-co-operation and the British went back to arresting Congress leaders.

Between 1931 and 1935 Jawaharlal Nehru spent most of his time in prison.

The new system of government

- India was to have a parliament based in Delhi. It would have two chambers (parts) like the British parliament. Each chamber would have appointed and elected members. 250 Indian representatives would be elected and 125 seats were reserved for the Indian princes.

- India was divided into 11 provinces. Each had its own parliament. These would control all policies, except defence and foreign affairs.

- Defence and foreign affairs would be controlled by the Viceroy (still appointed by the British government), but he would have to take advice from an Executive Committee made up mostly of Indians.

- Seats were reserved in the central parliament and the provincial parliaments for the minorities. This was to make sure that they had a say and were not totally dominated by Hindus.

The Government of India Act, 1935

The Round Table Conferences had not brought about an agreed way of ruling India. But the British had been made to realise that more power had to be given to the Indian people. So it passed the Government of India Act in 1935. It meant that Indians now had real power in their own country. The Viceroy still ruled on behalf of the English Monarch, but even where he still had control, he had to take advice from Indians.

Congress objects

Congress rejected the proposals in the Government of India Act. It had two main objections.

1. The British still had a role in governing India. Congress wanted total independence for India and it did not look like the British wanted to give it.

2. It did not like seats being reserved for the minorities or the princes. It was going to be the future government and it did not want its power limited.

Nehru wanted Congress to take part in the elections but not to take up their seats in the provincial assemblies. This would show their power, but at the same time act as a protest against the fact that Britain was still involved in governing India.

However, he accepted the arguments of his colleagues that Congress should not waste the opportunity to gain influence. The election was a great success for Congress which won a total of 715 seats and was able to form the government in eight of India's 11 provinces. Although Nehru had felt that Congress should not take up its seats he was chosen to be the leader of Congress, replacing Gandhi.

The Muslim League

During the late 1920s the Muslim League and Congress had begun to drift apart. Jinnah believed that Congress was deliberately not working with him to achieve independence, because he was looking after the Muslim cause.

Like Congress the Muslim League did not approve of the Government of India Act. It felt that it did not do enough to help Muslims. Jinnah believed that most of India's provinces would be ruled by Congress and there would be no protection for Muslim minorities.

He hoped, however, that in some provinces Congress would agree to let the Muslim League have a share of power. After all, there were many Muslims in Congress. But when he made these suggestions to Nehru, they were rejected.

Congress and the Muslim League

There were two main reasons for Nehru's decision not to share power with Jinnah.

1. The Muslim League claimed to speak on behalf of the Muslim people of India. But in the elections it won only 5 per cent of the total Muslim vote. It also won only 22 per cent of the seats that were reserved for Muslims. So Congress thought that it was not really a very important rival.

2. Congress also wanted India to be strong. It felt that it should try to win power in every province. So sharing power with a minority like the Muslim League would be going against this plan.

So the split between Congress and the Muslim League which had been growing for some years now became much wider.

- Jinnah was angry at his treatment by Congress and began working to build up the Muslim League. It grew rapidly in the late 1930s.

- There were many Muslims in Congress, but Nehru's refusal to share power caused many of them to leave and join the Muslim League. This helped make Jinnah an even more important person in India.

- For the first time the Muslim League began campaigning for Muslims to have their own country.

India was becoming more and more split between Hindu and Muslim.

Questions

1 Why were the Round Table Conferences held?

2 Why did the Round Table Conferences fail to reach agreement?

3 Why was the Government of India Act passed in 1935?

4 In what ways did the Government of India Act change the ways that India was governed?

5 Why did Congress and the Muslim League both reject the Government of India Act?

Source A

The Hindus and Muslims do not intermarry, nor dine together. They belong to two different civilizations. To join together two such nations under one single state must lead to growing discontent and the final destruction of such a state.

▲ Part of a speech made by Jinnah at a conference held by the Muslim League in 1940. The speech became known as the 'Lahore Declaration'.

The impact of the war on India and Britain

In September 1939 Britain went to war with Germany. Shortly afterwards the Viceroy, Lord Linlithgow, announced that India had declared war on Germany. This angered the people of India. According to the Government of India Act, the Viceroy was supposed to consult the Executive Committee before making important decisions on foreign affairs. Perhaps the Indians wanted to go to war to support Britain. Perhaps they didn't. But they never got a chance to say!

The Muslim League

The Muslim League continued its policy of co-operation. It backed the declaration of war and supported the British throughout the fighting. Jinnah also now began to talk about how a separate Muslim state should be set up called **Pakistan** (the Land of the Pure). In a speech made in March 1940 he explained why Hindu and Muslims could not live together in the same country (see Source A).

The Muslim League was continuing to grow and now had a membership of over 2 million. Jinnah was, therefore, a man the British were glad to have supporting them.

Source B

▲ Jinnah addressing the world press at a conference in London, December 1946.

Congress and the war

Congress was not so enthusiastic about the war. Gandhi was a man who did not believe in violence and wanted Britain to negotiate with Hitler rather than go to war. Nehru felt that it was right to go to war, but that India should have been allowed to make the decision for itself.

Congress was so angered by the British declaration of war that it felt it had to take steps to show its disapproval:

- It would not accept that India was at war with Germany if the Indian people had not been asked.

- All Congress state governments resigned in protest at the Viceroy's actions.

- In July 1940 Congress said it would support the war if the British set up a government for the whole of India with free elections.

- When the Viceroy said he could not do this, Congress began civil disobedience once more. So the British arrested Nehru and nearly 1700 leading Congress members in 1940.

Some historians think that Congress made a mistake in 1940. For much of the next five years Congress leaders were either in prison or refusing to co-operate with the British. But their great rival, the Muslim League, was becoming more influential by supporting the British in the war.

The Cripps' Mission

In December 1941 the Japanese attacked Pearl Harbor and joined the war on Germany's side. They were so successful in 1942 that it looked possible that an invasion of India might soon happen. The British were concerned that they did not have the full support of the Indian people. So they sent Sir Stafford Cripps to India to make a proposal to Congress. He said:

- India could have Home Rule as part of the British Empire.

- At the end of the war India could leave the Empire if it wanted.

▲ Jawaharlal Nehru and Sir Stafford Cripps in India.

- Any province that did not want to be part of India could become a separate country.

Congress rejects the offer

Nehru and Congress rejected the offer. They said they wanted full independence. They also did not want provinces to have the right to opt out of an independent India. That would allow the Muslims to set up Pakistan. What Congress wanted was a united India with one government.

The British would not give them this, so in August 1942 Congress decided to launch a non-violent 'Quit India' campaign.

Source D

I want freedom immediately, this night, before dawn, if it can be had. Congress must win freedom or be wiped out in the process.

▲ **Gandhi announcing the 'Quit India' campaign in 1942.**

The Quit India campaign

Gandhi wanted immediate independence. He told the British that troops needed to fight the Japanese could stay, but all other British people had to leave. This was an impossible demand for the British in the middle of a war.

Demonstrations began almost immediately in Indian cities. Once again Gandhi preached non-violence, but many of his followers did not follow his instructions. Police stations, government offices, railways and telephone lines were all attacked. Supplies for troops fighting the Japanese were held up.

Britain retaliates

The British could not allow this situation to continue. They sent 30,000 troops to restore order and more than 1000 people died in the fighting that followed. Then they arrested many leading Congress members and imprisoned them (including Nehru and Gandhi). Congress was declared an illegal organisation and its funds were confiscated. So from 1942–44 Congress virtually ceased to exist.

Subhas Chandra Bose and the Indian National Army

Congress was not the only problem facing Britain in India during the war. Far more threatening was the opposition of Subbas Chandra Bose. He had resigned from Congress in 1939 because he did not approve of Gandhi's non-violent methods. He wanted Indians to rise up and use violence to throw the British out of India.

When war broke out Bose declared his support for Germany. Not surprisingly he was arrested and imprisoned by the British. But he escaped and fled to Germany. After Japan entered the war Bose was sent to Singapore. His task was to speak to Indians in Singapore who had been taken prisoner of war and persuade them to join an **Indian National Army** to help the Japanese. Soon he had a force of 20,000 volunteers. He even went as far as to form the Provisional Government of Free India. The British were relieved when he was killed in a plane crash in 1945.

The end of the Indian National Army

In 1945 the Allies defeated both Germany and Japan. The Indian National Army was disbanded. Really, there had been very little support for it amongst Indians. Its leaders were arrested and found guilty of treason. However, after a plea from Congress they were not heavily punished.

Source E

▲ **Subhas Chandra Bose.**

There had not been much support for the Indian National Army, but many of the soldiers fighting for Britain had learned some interesting lessons. The Japanese had captured huge areas in the Pacific region. Wherever they went they encouraged the local people to set up nationalist organisations and reject rule by the old powers like Britain and France. Many of the Indian soldiers returning after the war brought back these ideas with them. They thought it was time to support Indian nationalism and reject Britain.

How did the Second World War change the political situation in India?

- Congress had been the dominant force in Indian politics before the war. It had won most of the seats in the 1937 election. But during the war, its opposition to the declaration of war had meant tough measures by the British. Its leaders were in jail and, for the moment, it had lost its influence.

- On the other hand the Muslim League had grown from a party which won only 5 per cent of the Muslim vote in 1937 to one with 2 million members. It had also been able to introduce the idea of a separate Muslim state, Pakistan.

The progress that the Muslim League had made was clearly shown in 1945. It won 90% of the seats reserved for Muslims. It had won just 22% in 1937. So Congress could no longer try to ignore the Muslim League as it had done in the 1930s.

Although the Muslim League had co-operated with the British during the Second World War, it too expected that they would now withdraw from India. In this they were supported by many other Indians. During the war Britain had needed support. Now the war was over that support quickly disappeared. It was time for Britain to leave.

Independence and partition: the role of Mountbatten

Britain in 1945

Britain had won the war, but at a terrible cost. It had spent huge sums and was financially exhausted. Since 1939 it had spent £1000 million on India. It simply could not afford to carry on spending such sums. Leaving India seemed to make good financial sense.

In July 1945 the Labour Party won an election in Britain. The previous, Conservative, Prime Minister (Winston Churchill) had opposed Indian independence. The new Prime Minister (Clement Attlee) was not in favour of Britain having an empire. So he supported Indian independence.

Questions

1 Why were many Indians angry at the declaration of war by the Viceroy in 1939?

2 How did Congress and the Muslim League react to the declaration of war?

3 Why did Gandhi begin the 'Quit India' campaign?

4 Why did the Muslim League become more influential during the Second World War?

India in 1945

By 1945 Britain was losing control of India. During the war Indian armed forces had remained loyal to Britain, but in February 1946 there was a mutiny in the navy which soon spread to the Army. Britain could not control India if it did not want to be controlled.

The question was, if Britain was going to leave India, how would the country be governed then? Congress wanted a unified India and the Muslim League wanted an independent Muslim Pakistan.

Source A

▲ Winston Churchill did not believe in granting India independence.

Source B

▲ Clement Attlee did not believe in Britain's right to an Empire.

The Cabinet Mission

The British government sent a **Cabinet Mission** to India and asked it to come up with proposals. It said:

- It did not agree with Jinnah's demands for a separate Muslim state.

- Instead India should stay as a unified country, but there should be protection for the Muslim minority.

- Provinces should be grouped together so that some had a Hindu majority and some a Muslim majority.

- The provinces should run all aspects of government except foreign affairs, defence and communications. These would be run by a central government formed from representatives of the provinces.

- A new Assembly would be elected and based in Delhi.

Reactions in India

The Cabinet Mission's proposals did not meet the demands of either Congress or the Muslim League. But both sides regarded them as a fair compromise. Gandhi said they were 'the best the British government could have produced'. It looked like both sides would agree to them. Elections were held for the new Assembly. Congress won 205 seats and the Muslim League 73.

Then it all went wrong. Congress decided that it did not want to support the proposals. (Perhaps it was surprised by the number of seats the Muslim League had won.) So the Muslim League also withdrew support.

Direct Action

Jinnah felt that he had been betrayed by Congress. It had agreed to support the new proposals and then had changed its mind. He decided to put pressure on Congress and the British by calling for '**Direct Action**'.

Direct Action was intended to be nationwide peaceful demonstrations by Muslims. In most places it was, with Muslims taking part in protest marches. But in some areas, Calcutta in particular, things got out of hand. Muslims attacked Hindus who then retaliated. In Calcutta alone there were 5000 deaths and the violence rapidly spread across India.

Jinnah was horrified at what had happened and the British seemed powerless to stop the violence. In the end Gandhi fasted to the point of death until the two sides stopped attacking each other.

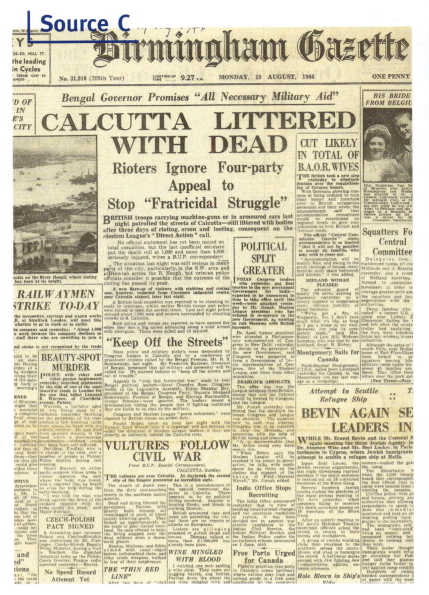

▲ **Violence in Calcutta was headline news in Britain.**

Source D

▲ Jinnah called for peaceful protests, but violence erupted in some areas, including Calcutta. Here, a Hindu lies dead in the street.

What were the effects of Direct Action?
- The action showed how deep the split was between Hindus and Muslims in India.

- Congress and the Muslim League agreed to join a government set up by the Viceroy and to try to reach an agreement on how India should be governed in the future.

- But they found that they simply could not work together. Violence started again and soon spread throughout Northern India.

- In late 1946 the Viceroy, Lord Wavell, told Clement Attlee that the British might have to just leave and let the Indians sort out the mess.

- Attlee would not do this. But he did announce that Britain would leave by June 1948. The two sides would have to sort things out by then.

The appointment of Mountbatten

Lord Mountbatten was chosen to be Viceroy in February 1947. He had served in the area in the war and understood the problems in India. His job was to get agreement on how India was to be governed after the British left. He insisted that he must have full power to do whatever he thought best. The British Cabinet was not to interfere.

His first piece of advice to Attlee was that a firm date should be fixed for withdrawal. Attlee decided that the British would leave at midnight on 28 August 1947. This surprised the Indians as it was nearly a year earlier than had at first been suggested.

▲ Nehru, Ismay, Mountbatten and Jinnah.

The partition of India

Mountbatten soon discovered that the violence and hatred between Hindus and Muslims was growing. This convinced him that a unified India would not work. So on 3 June 1947 he announced to Nehru and Jinnah that two countries would be created, India and Pakistan.

- Congress did not approve of the plan because it wanted a unified India, not **partition** (division). But it could not see any alternative. If the British were going to leave in less than three months they had to agree.

- The Muslim League wanted partition, but Mountbatten's plan involved splitting Bengal and the Punjab between the two new countries. Jinnah wanted all of both provinces in Pakistan, but he also saw that he had to agree.

Mountbatten now decided to bring forward the date of British withdrawal by two weeks to 14 August 1947. This would help stop the violence between the two sides, but it meant there was so much to do in so short a time. Officials had to divide up finances, the Army, the civil service and all government departments in about 10 weeks!

Setting the border

When the British left they had to decide where India stopped and where Pakistan began. This task was given to a British judge, Sir Cyril Radcliffe. He had less than three months to draw a border which put as many Hindus in India and as many Muslims in Pakistan as could possibly be done.

Radcliffe completed his task on time, but it was not possible to avoid problems:

- 5 million Hindus ended up in Pakistan and 5 million Muslims in India.

- Sikhs, who had argued for special treatment and an independent country of their own, were ignored altogether.

Violence and war

The events immediately following the partition of India were horrific.

- Millions of refugees crossed from India into Pakistan, and vice-versa. During this movement there was widespread violence. In the Punjab alone over 600,000 people were killed. Trains carrying refugees were stopped and their occupants slaughtered by 'the other side'. Neither of the two new governments had the power to stop this violence.

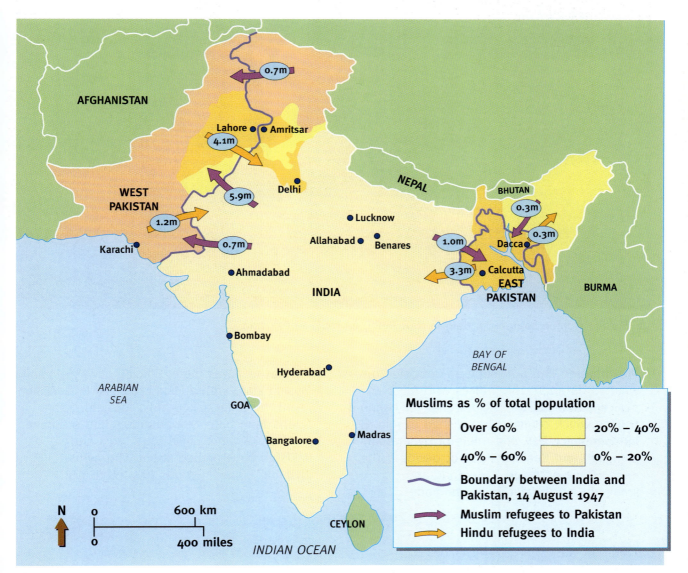

▲ Map showing the partition of India and Pakistan.

▲ Muslim women boarding a train in New Delhi, en route to Pakistan.

- Mountbatten had not made any decision on what to do about the princes who ruled 40 per cent of India. He decided that they should choose which country they wished to join. By **Independence Day**, the rulers of Hyderabad, Junagadh and Kashmir had not decided. The Indian Army occupied Hyderabad and Junagadh, so the decision was made.

But Kashmir was more difficult. It was a mainly Muslim state with a Hindu ruler. After a Muslim revolt, the ruler asked India for help. Soon troops from both new countries had occupied parts of Kashmir. Since 1947 India and Pakistan have argued about who owns Kashmir. Sometimes this has led to war.

▲ Independence Day celebrations in India, 15 August 1947.

Questions

1   Why did the British government decide to make India independent after the Second World War?

2   Why was the Cabinet Mission sent to India in 1946?

3   Why did Jinnah call for Direct Action?

4   Why did Attlee decide to send Mountbatten to India?

5   Why was India partitioned in 1947?

6   Why did Partition lead to widespread violence in parts of India?

A divided union?
The USA: 1941~80

Introduction

This chapter sets out the history of the USA in the second half of the twentieth century. It was a time when the USA became one the strongest countries in the world.

The chapter begins by looking at how the Second World War helped the US to become the world's richest nation. But at the same time there were great divisions within the country. Black Americans, for example, had few rights and it was only as a result of the work of black leaders such as Malcolm X and Martin Luther King that changes came about.

The chapter also considers the great fear that the USA had of communism and how McCarthy was able to use that fear. The darker side of politics is also covered in the assassination of President Kennedy and the resignation of President Nixon after the Watergate Scandal.

To the outside world the USA appeared a united country ready to dominate world affairs. A closer study, however, shows it to be a 'divided union' in this period.

The USA and the Second World War

The USA had decided after the First World War not to become involved in disputes in Europe. This policy of **isolationism** was popular with the US people. In 1937 an opinion poll showed that almost two-thirds of Americans thought that the USA should not have taken part in the First World War. So, during the 1930s, the US government introduced laws to make the USA's isolation from Europe even stronger.

A change in policy

However, the warlike actions of Japan and Germany in the 1930s (see Chapter 5) worried President Roosevelt and he persuaded Congress to provide money to build up the USA's armed forces – just in case. Then when the war in Europe started in 1939, Roosevelt introduced **conscription**. He also transferred 50 US destroyers to Britain to help it in the war.

This pleased US citizens whose families had come from Britain, but angered those from Germany, Italy and Japan.

Pearl Harbor

On 7 December 1941 the Japanese launched an attack on the American fleet in its base at Pearl Harbor. The attack resulted in 2400 American deaths, and President Roosevelt declared war on Japan. Soon the USA was involved in the war against Germany and Italy too. This war lasted for almost four years and brought major changes within the USA.

The impact of the war on American society

Although the war was not fought on US soil, it had a major impact on the lives of the average American citizen.

Source A

▲ The damage caused at Pearl Harbor by the Japanese fleet.

- By 1945 almost 16 million Americans had served in the armed forces. Many of these saw life outside their home town for the first time ever.

- For men who did join the Army there were new job opportunities, particularly in the defence industry.

- Nearly 700,000 black Americans moved to the North hoping for better jobs and an escape from the poverty and racial discrimination they experienced in the South.

- Almost 1.5 million **migrants** (mostly farm labourers) moved to California to work in the arms industry.

Women and the war

The war brought increased opportunities for women too.

- In 1941 they made up only 27 per cent of the workforce, but by 1945 this had risen to 37 per cent. Nearly 350,000 women served in the armed forces.

- Like the men, almost all the women stationed abroad experienced life outside the USA for the first time.

- Also like men, many women worked in the defence industry.

Many men found it difficult to accept women in the workplace, since there was still a general belief that a woman's role was to be at home looking after children. However, the country needed women workers and the government launched **campaigns** to encourage them into the factories. The poster of the determined looking 'Rosie the Riveter' became very popular.

The greatest change came for black women. There was a shortage of labour and so many of them were able to get employment for the first time. Some black women joined the armed forces as nurses, but they were only allowed to nurse black soldiers. Racial **segregation** was still strong in the USA.

Young people and the war

For young people the war provided the opportunity to find work. Many college students dropped out and started work. The number of 16–19 year olds in work rose from 1 million to 3 million between 1941 and 1944. Younger children were also affected. Many of them became '**latch-key kids**' as a result of their parents being at work. There was also more juvenile delinquency.

'Doing your bit'

The government set up schemes such as the Office of Civilian Defence to encourage people to 'do their bit' for the country. One way was to start 'victory gardens' growing vegetables, or to recycle scrap metal or paper. The government also introduced food rationing.

After the war

When the war ended in 1945 the men returned home and wanted their jobs back. The government now had to persuade women to give up their jobs. It used slogans such as 'go back home' and 'give your job to a veteran'. Of course, many of the jobs simply disappeared because there was no longer any need for war goods.

Source B

We must begin the great task ahead of us by forgetting the idea that we can stay isolated from the rest of the world.

All countries are under threat from powerful aggressors who sneak up in the dark and strike without warning.

▲ **President Roosevelt explaining why the Japanese attack on Pearl Harbor led the USA into war.**

Some women were happy to give up work and return to being 'homemakers'. Others, however, resented giving up their jobs. Their weekly pay packet had given them independence for the first time. Most women did lose their jobs, but it was true that in 1950 there were still more women in work in the USA than in 1940. Women had taken a small step towards equality.

Source C

▲ An encouragement to all women, Rosie the Riveter.

Source D

The men resented the women workers. But after a while they realised that the women were doing a pretty good job.

However, I always felt that they thought it wasn't your place to be there.

▲ A woman working as a riveter in an aircraft factory remembering how men had treated her.

Questions

1 How were the following affected by the war?

   a Men
   b Women
   c Young people

Chapter 9 *A divided union? The USA: 1941~80*

205

The impact of the war on black Americans

Roughly 1 million black Americans served in their country's armed forces in the war. The segregation which existed in US society also happened in the armed forces. Black soldiers were usually placed in all-black units with white officers. Black soldiers were also often expected to act as labourers or cooks instead of being sent into combat.

Black Americans were fighting for 'democracy and freedom' against Japan and Nazi Germany. Hitler's racial policies in Germany were widely condemned, but these black soldiers lived in a country where they were treated as second-class citizens. Many of them were not permitted to vote and found it difficult to get good jobs.

Progress made

The US Commander-in-Chief, General Eisenhower, supported the idea of racially integrated units and, as the war developed, they became more common. The number of black officers also increased. There were also several units of black pilots, whereas in 1941 there had been none.

The war also gave black Americans the chance to campaign for better treatment at home. Black newspapers talked about the '**Double V**' campaign. This meant victory in the war and victory at home in winning **civil rights**.

Source E

▲ Black American soldiers in action in the Second World War.

We loyal US citizens demand the right to work and fight for our country.

▲ One of the slogans used by black Americans in their campaign for civil rights

Modern World History

Source F

▲ A black victim of the 1943 race riots.

Questions

1 How did the position of black Americans improve during the war?

2 Why were there race riots in some American cities in 1943?

3 **a** Why do you think Japanese-Americans were treated worse than black Americans?

b Why would 'Nisei' have been particularly angry about their treatment?

Government reaction

The government responded positively to the campaign. In 1941 President Roosevelt ordered that discrimination in government agencies must stop. He also set up the Fair Employment Practices Committee to ensure his instructions were obeyed.

Black leaders set up their own campaigning groups such as CORE (the Congress of Racial Equality), and membership of NAACP (National Association for the Advancement of Coloured People) rose dramatically during the war.

Resistance to change

The movement of black Americans from the South to Northern towns caused problems in some areas. For example in Detroit there were race riots in June 1943 in which 25 blacks and nine whites were killed. There were also riots in black training camps where soldiers resented their inferior treatment. Later in the year, six blacks were killed in riots in Harlem in New York.

President Roosevelt sympathised with the black Americans' problems, but did not feel he could do any more to help. It was not until the 1960s that real change came.

Japanese-Americans

Although black Americans were treated unfairly during the war, Japanese-Americans suffered much worse treatment. The government thought they were a threat to the country, and so rounded them up and put them in special camps. Over 100,000 Japanese-Americans were sent to live in bleak conditions. This applied not only to **Issei** (people born in Japan), but also to **Nisei** (children of Issei, who had been born in the USA).

Chapter 9 *A divided union? The USA: 1941–80*

207

Source G

▲ Graffitti on the home of a Nissei family in May 1945.

The US government feared that the Japanese-Americans might carry out acts of **sabotage**, spy for the Japanese or even help them to invade the USA. This was why they were sent to camps. The Japanese-Americans were forced to sell their belongings, and often their homes were vandalised or seized illegally. It has been estimated that they lost US$500 million as a result of their treatment.

Yet, at the same time as many Nisei were placed in camps, others were conscripted into the Army to fight and 9000 Nisei volunteered to fight for the USA. The unit in the US Army which won the most medals in the war was made up almost entirely of Nisei!

Source H

What'd you get, black boy,

When they knocked you down in the gutter.

And they kicked your teeth out,

And they broke your skull with clubs,

And they bashed your stomach in?

What'd you get when the police shot you in the back,

And they chained you to the beds

While they wiped the blood off?

What'd you get when you cried out to the Top Man?

When you called to the man next to God, as you thought,

And you asked him to speak out to save you?

What'd the Top Man say, black boy?

Mr Roosevelt regrets ...

▲ A poem written by a black student in 1943. He is complaining that 'the Top Man' (President Roosevelt) is not doing enough to help black Americans.

Questions

1 Look at Source G.
   Why do you think this might have happened?

2 Read Source H.
   Explain in your own words what the black student was saying. Use quotations from the poem to back up your answer.

The impact of the war on the US economy

During the 1930s President Roosevelt had spent billions of dollars creating jobs. He wanted to bring the USA out of the **Depression**. The spending on war goods after 1941 finally brought unemployment down to the level it had been before the **Wall Street Crash** in 1929.

- The war created 17 million new jobs in the USA. It also provided overtime and extra pay. So US citizens had money to spend. When they spent it, they produced a demand for goods and so more jobs were created.

- For the first time for a generation, US farmers did well as they sold their produce to Europe where farming was disrupted by war.

- The US government spent billions of dollars on equipping the armed forces. It did this by selling **bonds** to the people. People buying bonds got their money back after a set time – plus an extra payment of interest.

- The government set up the War Production Board which encouraged industries to stop making 'non-essential' goods like refrigerators and to concentrate on vital goods like tanks and airplanes. By the end of 1942 one-third of the US economy was devoted to producing war goods. The USA was producing as much war equipment as Germany, Italy and Japan put together.

- The war gave the government a bigger role in running the US economy. Some Americans complained about this. They said that the **rugged individualism** which made the USA great was being lost as people began to rely more and more on the government.

- Whatever the rights and wrongs of this argument, the war lead to the USA becoming the richest country in the world. Unlike other countries, such as the Soviet Union, Britain and Germany, it did not have to spend huge sums on repairing damage caused by the war. So it was able to keep its wealth.

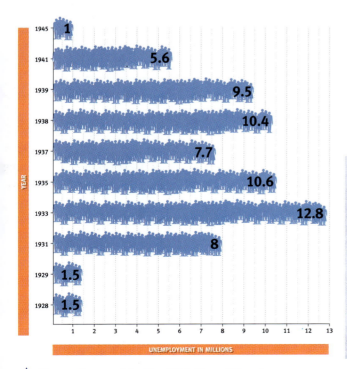

▲ Unemployment in the USA (in millions).

Source I

The USA was the only great power to emerge from the war stronger than it went into it. Its cities and farmlands, its oil wells and mines were all undamaged. Between 1939 and 1947 US production trebled and the numbers employed in industry doubled.

▲ A modern historian describing the economic benefits of the war to the USA.

Chapter 9 *A divided union? The USA: 1941–80*

209

1 What was the Cold War?

2 If the USA and the Soviet Union did not trust each other, why did they fight on the same side in the Second World War?

3 Why do you think the US government cared whether Hollywood writers and directors had been members of the Communist Party?

Source A

▲ An American cartoon showing the Russian bear spreading Communism throughout the world.

McCarthyism and the Red Scare

The Cold War

Although the USA and the Soviet Union had fought on the same side during the war they did not trust each other. The Soviet Union believed in **communism** and the USA was convinced that the Soviets wanted to spread their beliefs around the world. The Americans believed in **capitalism** and the Soviet Union was convinced that the Americans wanted to destroy communism. So, soon a war of words called 'the **Cold War**' began.

The Hollywood Ten

The US government was determined to make sure that the US people did not have political views which were 'unacceptable'. It set up the House Un-American Activities Committee. In 1947 it asked 10 well-known Hollywood writers and directors to confirm that they had once belonged to the Communist Party. The 'Hollywood Ten' refused to answer the question. They had been members, but that was not a criminal offence. They used the USA's **Fifth Amendment** to refuse to answer a question which might mean incriminating themselves. It did not matter. They were still imprisoned. The Red Scare was underway.

The scare grows

There was a growing feeling amongst some Americans that there were people working for the government who were really Soviet sympathisers, or even agents. President Truman (who replaced Roosevelt in 1945) asked the FBI to check this out. It carried out investigations between 1947 and 1950. It did not find a single case of government employees carrying out acts of **espionage**, but 212 people were forced to resign because they were thought to be 'security risks'.

The Alger Hiss Case

Alger Hiss had worked for President Roosevelt. Allegations had been made that he was a communist sympathiser, but they were proved to be unfounded. Then, in 1948, he was accused of being a high-ranking member of the Communist Party. He vigorously denied the charges. However, tests showed that government secrets had been typed onto microfilm on Hiss's typewriter and, in January 1950, he was imprisoned for five years. Most people today believe Hiss's protests that he was an innocent man.

The scare took hold of the country and later in 1950 the **McCarran Act** was passed. It said:

- It was illegal for Americans to try to create a communist government in the USA.

- All communist organisations had to register with the government.

- No communist could have a US passport or work in defence factories.

President Truman said the Act went against the idea of free speech in the USA, but anti-communist hysteria was developing in the USA and Congress passed the Act.

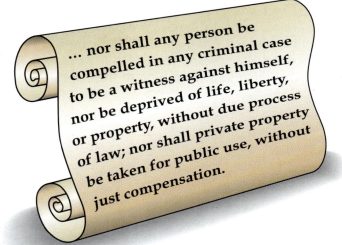

... nor shall any person be compelled in any criminal case to be a witness against himself, nor be deprived of life, liberty, or property, without due process of law; nor shall private property be taken for public use, without just compensation.

▲ Part of the Fifth Amendment.

Source B

▲ Alger Hiss.

Chapter 9 *A divided union? The USA: 1941–80*

211

Shortly after the imprisonment of Hiss, an engineer called Julius Rosenberg and his wife, Ethel, were charged with passing secrets about the atomic bomb to the Soviet Union. They were found guilty and executed. Both of them had denied the charges and refused to make a deal that was offered to them to save their lives.

Source C

I have in my hand a list of 205 men who are known to the Secretary of State as being members of the Communist Party. They are still working for and helping decide the policy of the State Department.

▲ Part of a speech made by McCarthy in 1950.

Source D

▲ Senator McCarthy showing 'evidence' to the House Un-American Activities Commission.

Enter McCarthy

Soon the anti-communist scare had a politician to lead it. In February 1950, Senator Joseph McCarthy of Wisconsin claimed to have a list of 205 communists who worked in the State Department (an important part of the US government). When he was questioned, McCarthy's numbers tended to vary. Sometimes it was 205 communists, sometimes 81, sometimes 57, or sometimes just 'a lot'. A Senate committee investigated McCarthy's claims and decided they were a 'fraud and a hoax'.

McCarthy responded by accusing the chairman of the committee, Senator Tydings, of being a communist himself. The accusations were unfounded, but the anti-communist feeling in the USA was so high that in the elections to Senate in the autumn of 1950 Tydings was defeated by a supporter of McCarthy. This made people think twice about criticising McCarthy!

McCarthy on the attack

McCarthy was soon accusing a wide variety of people of being part of a communist plot. He never produced a shred of evidence to back up his claims but it did not matter. Millions of Americans saw him as a crusader against evil communism. Those accused found it impossible to clear their name and were usually either sacked or they resigned from their jobs.

Soon the list of accused had grown until it included scientists, diplomats, writers, actors and members of the Democratic Party (McCarthy was a Republican). McCarthy always claimed to have evidence and the press seized on his allegations with great enthusiasm.

The evidence didn't really exist, but even someone as powerful as President Truman did not want to call McCarthy a liar. It was dangerous to oppose someone with so much public support.

In 1950 Eisenhower took over from Truman as President. He ordered a fresh investigation into government officials and nearly 7000 of them lost their jobs – though none was ever put on trial. McCarthy was made Chairman of the Senate Committee on Government Operations and appeared almost untouchable. Then he went too far.

McCarthy exposed

In 1954 McCarthy accused 45 Army officers of being communist agents. A series of televised hearings was held. In these McCarthy was shown as rude and bullying. His popularity soon declined and, in December 1954, the Senate condemned him for 'improper behaviour'. He was now finished as a leading politician and he died three years later. What the McCarthy era had shown, however, was how frightened the USA was of communism. McCarthy had no real evidence – it was enough just to accuse people to cause hysteria.

McCarthy had been exposed as a fraud, but the fear of communism continued. In 1954 the Communist Party was banned in the USA and as late as 1960 you could not get a job in some states without swearing an oath of loyalty to the USA.

Source E

I do solemnly swear that I will oppose the overthrow of the government of the USA ... I am not a member of the Communist Party.

▲ State of Massachusetts Oath of Loyalty, 1960.

Questions

1 Why was there fear of communism in the USA after 1945?

2 If McCarthy did not produce evidence about alleged communists in the government, why do you think some workers were dismissed from their jobs?

3 Why did President Truman dislike the McCarran Act?

Chapter 9 *A divided union? The USA: 1941–80*

213

The civil rights movements and their impact on American society

We have read how there were attempts to improve conditions for black Americans during the Second World War, but how progress had been very limited. In 1948 President Truman introduced a plan to end **lynching** and to help blacks ensure they were able to vote. He had to drop his plans, however, because of opposition within his own Party.

Education

In the 1950s only 16 of the states of the USA required their education system to be **integrated** (with blacks and whites educated in the same schools) and often this was not enforced. Then, in 1950, the Supreme Court (the highest court in the USA) made two important decisions:

1. In a school with both black and white students, black students must not be taught in separate classes.

2. Black students were entitled to the same facilities as white. This meant not only buildings and books, but also the quality of teaching should be the same.

Challenging desegregation

The NAACP was encouraged by these decisions to challenge segregation. At this time it was acceptable to have separate schools for whites and blacks, as long as they had equal resources (in theory at least). In 1954 the NAACP took the school board in Topeka, Kansas to court. Seven-year-old Linda Brown wanted to go to her nearest school (a few blocks away).

▲ An example of discrimination in the USA. Often coloured people were not allowed to use the same facilities as white Americans.

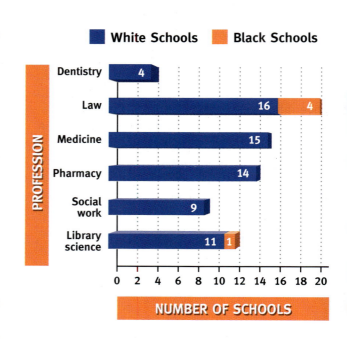

■ White Schools   ■ Black Schools

PROFESSION / NUMBER OF SCHOOLS

Profession	White Schools	Black Schools
Dentistry	4	
Law	16	4
Medicine	15	
Pharmacy	14	
Social work	9	
Library science	11	1

0 2 4 6 8 10 12 14 16 18 20

NUMBER OF SCHOOLS

▲ The number of schools where certain professions could be learned in the 1950s.

Source B

▲ Elizabeth Eckford, one of the 'Little Rock Nine', arriving at school in September 1957. Notice the hatred on the faces in the crowd.

The school board wanted her to go to an all-black school several miles away. The Supreme Court said that having different schools for blacks and whites was no longer acceptable. It said that the individual states of the USA should change their systems 'with all deliberate speed' to set up schools where both black and white students attended.

Resistance to change

It was one thing to pass laws, but another to ensure that change really happened. Some states introduced integration almost immediately. Others found ways round the ruling by introducing unfair tests, for example. Many black students were simply too afraid to go to previously all-white schools in case they were beaten up.

Little Rock

One of the most famous incidents happened in Little Rock Central High School in Arkansas. In September 1950 nine black students were due to start at the school, which had previously been all-white.

Source C

The mob was jeering and spitting. It had to be the most frightening thing, because she had a large crowd of white people threatening to kill her. And she had nobody. There wasn't a black face anywhere. Then this white woman came out of the crowd and guided her on to the bus and got her home safely. Elizabeth was in tears.

▲ One of the 'Little Rock Nine' explaining how Elizabeth Eckford was refused entry to the Little Rock Central High School.

The Governor of Arkansas, Orval Faubus said that he feared there would be trouble, so he surrounded the school with troops to stop the black students entering.

After a court ruling, Faubus was forced to remove the troops and the students turned up for school. They were met by a hostile crowd of 1000 demonstrators and, at lunchtime on their first day, had to be escorted home under police protection. President Eisenhower was so determined to ensure integration that he sent troops to stay in the school to protect the nine students until they were accepted.

Questions

1 Why do you think some politicians in the USA were not keen to support President Truman's plan to improve civil rights for black Americans?

2 What is the difference between 'integrated' schooling and 'segregated' schooling?

3 Why were people so concerned about whether their schools were integrated or segregated?

4 What can you learn about attitudes in Arkansas from Sources B and C?

Chapter 9 *A divided union? The USA: 1941–80*

215

Faubus fights back

Then in 1958 Faubus shut all the schools in Arkansas to prevent integration. The Supreme Court ruled that his actions were against the constitution and, eventually, the schools reopened for both black and white students. Faubus had lost his case, but in December 1958 in a nationwide opinion poll of the most admired men in the world he finished in the top ten!

The Montgomery Bus Boycott

The Linda Brown case showed that black Americans were beginning to win the fight against racial discrimination. In Montgomery, Alabama they used another method to try to win equal civil rights.

In Alabama, as in most states, blacks were only allowed seats at the rear of the bus. They were also expected to give them up if a white person was standing. In Montgomery, Alabama, in 1955 a black woman, Rosa Parkes, sat in the middle of the bus and refused to give up her seat when asked to by a white person. She was thrown off the bus and arrested.

Don't use the bus

Rosa's arrest was the spark that some black leaders had been waiting for. It gave them a chance to stand up for their rights. Black people were outraged and immediately organised a boycott of the bus company. It would have to change its policy – or go broke.

Source D

We are tired of being segregated and humiliated. We are tired of being kicked about. But if you protest courageously and with dignity, historians will have to pause and say 'there lived a great people'. They brought a new dignity into civilisation.

▲ Martin Luther King explaining why he believed in non-violence.

Martin Luther King

One of the leaders of the protest was a local Baptist Minister called Martin Luther King. He had a policy called **non-violent civil disobedience**, which he had learned from studying what Gandhi had done in India. He believed that black people should simply refuse to obey laws which were based on discrimination. They should not be violent, even if attacked. This would show their dignity – even in the face of the brutality of the white authorities.

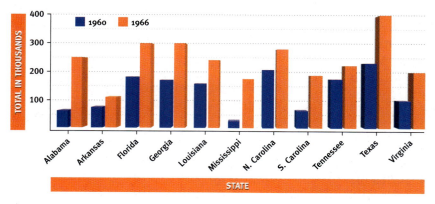

▲ Percentage of blacks registered to vote in the Southern states of the USA.

Questions

1 Why do you think black Americans always gave up their seats on buses before Rosa Parkes' action in 1959?

Another victory

The black community in Alabama gave full support to the bus boycott. For over a year they refused to ride on the buses and the bus company lost 65 per cent of its income. Then, in December 1956, the Supreme Court ruled that segregation on buses was against the American Constitution and had to end. This applied not only to Montgomery, but to all of the USA.

The campaign continues

Civil rights campaigners were encouraged by the successes in Little Rock and Montgomery. They kept civil rights in the news by holding marches, demonstrations and boycotts. They wanted to end segregation in public places.

They particularly objected to sandwich bars which would not serve blacks and organised '**sit-ins**'. This was a very brave thing to do, because often they suffered humiliation and violence. But they tried, not always successfully, not to react violently and to follow King's policy of non-violence.

By 1960 the civil rights campaign had spread across the USA. Many Americans were shocked to hear about the treatment that blacks received in some states. It was to be some time, however, before there were major changes in the law to try to end discrimination.

Source E

▲ **Black demonstrators at a sit-in at a sandwich bar. Note how they try to maintain their dignity even when food and drink is tipped on them.**

Chapter 9 *A divided union? The USA: 1941~80*

217

More support

Martin Luther King appealed to students to help fight discrimination. In April 1960 the Student Non-Violent Coordinating Committee (SNCC) was formed. Many students dropped out of college and began working to end discrimination. Some students moved to the Southern states to work for civil rights for black Americans. This was a very brave thing to do as there were very strong feelings in some states. Some students were beaten up and several of them were murdered.

The Freedom Riders

A group of campaigners working for the Congress of Racial Equality (CORE) wanted to make sure that the ban of segregation on buses was enforced. During 1961 this group, calling themselves 'Freedom Riders', toured the Southern states refusing to give up their seats on buses. They were often arrested for disturbing the peace. But the publicity they received led to the government body which supervised trade in the USA announcing that there must be no segregation on buses or in bus stations.

President Kennedy

President Kennedy was keen to improve civil rights for blacks. He and his brother Robert, the Attorney-General (an important job in the government), had regular meetings with black campaigners. They introduced the Voter Education Project, which led to many more blacks registering to vote. In response, in some areas, there were attacks on black homes and churches. There were even shootings of black people as some whites fought desperately to keep their advantages.

Birmingham 1962

An example of resistance to change was seen in Birmingham, Alabama. In 1962 the city authorities decided that they would not allow integration in their parks, swimming pools and other places. Instead they simply closed them. In 1963 Martin Luther King organised marches and demonstrations in the city to publicise this example of discrimination.

He was lucky because the Birmingham authorities acted so appallingly that the protest was soon broadcast nationwide. The police commissioner was so determined to take strong action that he set dogs on the demonstrators and, when they refused to disperse, turned fire hoses on them.

Source F

The boys dared Emmett to speak to a white woman in the store. Emmett walked in confidently, bought some candy from Carolyn Bryant, the owner's wife, and, as he left said, 'Bye, baby.' The store owner was so outraged that he and his half-brother took Emmett away. His body was found three days later with a bullet in his skull and his head crushed. The store owner and his half-brother were tried for murder. Local people raised money to pay for their defence and at the end of the trial the all-white jury took just one hour to find them not guilty.

▲ An example of racial discrimination. Emmett was from Chicago and was visiting relatives in Mississippi in 1955.

Source G

I have a dream that one day this nation will rise up …

I have a dream that one day on the red hills of Georgia sons of former slaves and sons of former slave-owners will be able to sit down together at the table of brotherhood.

▲ Part of the famous 'I have a dream' speech. It was made by Martin Luther King in 1963.

Source H

▲ **A black girl caught by a fire hose in Alabama.**

Nationwide publicity

The Birmingham demonstrations were broadcast across the USA, and there was outrage at the brutality of the police and the fact that Martin Luther King was jailed. The campaign was successful in ending segregation in Birmingham, but it was successful in other ways too. The publicity had made the rights of black people a major issue in the eyes of many US citizens. President Kennedy announced that he would ask Congress to pass a **Civil Rights Bill** to increase the rights of black Americans.

'I have a dream'

King continued to campaign for civil rights to ensure that Congress passed the Bill. In the summer of 1963 he made a speech in Washington in front of over 250,000 demonstrators (many of them white). His 'I have a dream' speech has become world famous (see Source G). In December 1964, King was awarded the Nobel Peace Prize for his work in trying to bring about 'brotherhood among men'.

Kennedy's assassination prevented the passing of the Civil Rights Bill. But the next President, Johnson, ensured it was passed in 1968.

Questions

1 Read Source F. Are you surprised by what it says? Think carefully about the people involved in this event and where they came from.

Chapter 9 *A divided union? The USA: 1941~80*

219

Black Power

Martin Luther King believed in non-violent civil disobedience. It seemed to be bringing improvements, but not fast enough for some black Americans. They argued that non-violence made black people appear just like 'nice' white people but with different coloured skins. This was degrading. They wanted to take what was theirs by right, using force if necessary. They also didn't want integration. They wanted blacks to be separate and to celebrate their blackness. It was a symbol of superiority.

One such group was the Black Muslims, the most famous of whom was **Malcolm X**. He disliked King's methods and thought that non-violence simply encouraged racism amongst white people. In 1965 he said,

> 'The white people should thank Dr King for holding black people in check.'

One of Malcolm X's supporters, Stokely Carmichael, was elected chairman of the SNCC. He believed in **Black Power**. He said blacks should take full control of their lives, even if it meant breaking away from society as it was. The **Black Panthers** went even further. They urged blacks to arm themselves and use violence to achieve equal rights.

Riots

Influenced by such views, in 1965, blacks began rioting in many US cities. In the Watts district of Los Angeles, 34 died and over 1000 were injured in six days of rioting. Riots continued through the summers of 1965, 1966 and 1967. In the first nine months of 1967 more than 150 US cities were affected by racial disorders.

Source I

Our enemy is the white man!

If we must take violence to get the black man his human rights in this country, then I am for violence.

We are the only black organisation that black people support. These other organisations insult your intelligence, claiming they are fighting on your behalf.

▲ Some of the views of Malcolm X.

Source J

▲ The results of rioting in Los Angeles in 1965.

The Kerner Report

President Johnson was so concerned about the riots that he set up a Commission of Enquiry, headed by Governor Kerner of Illinois, to find out why they had happened. Kerner's report said that black people in the USA were so frustrated by their treatment that:

'The nation is rapidly moving towards two Americas'.

(He meant a black America and a white America.)

The report recommended that all race discrimination in areas such as employment, education and housing should be stamped out and that the government should listen more carefully to the complaints of the black community.

More riots

But the report did not end the rioting. In April 1968 Martin Luther King was assassinated and rioting broke out across the country. His death followed that of Malcolm X who had also been assassinated in 1965.

The black community had lost two great leaders and found it more difficult to make progress as other issues, like drugs and Vietnam, caught the attention of the US public. But they had made progress in achieving more equality. Source L, however, shows that they had a long way to go.

Source K

POWER TO THE PEOPLE

FREE THE NEW YORK PANTHER 21

▲ A Black Panther poster from the 1960s.

Source L

Mississippi whites were responsible for at least twelve separate lynchings of blacks in 1980. On 12 October 1981, the body of Douglas McDonald was pulled from a lake in Eastover, Mississippi. The black man's ears had been hacked off.

▲ A recent book telling how mistreatment of black people continued.

Questions

1 What were the differences between King's approach to winning more civil rights and those of Malcolm X?

2 Do you think that the rioting in US cities in the 1960s helped black Americans win more rights or made it harder for them? Explain your answer.

Chapter 9 *A divided union? The USA: 1941–80*

221

The New Frontier and the Great Society

Kennedy's plans

In 1960 John F. Kennedy became the Democratic Party candidate for the Presidency. He said that he had a personal vision 'to get the country moving again'. He wanted to improve the US economy, have better education and housing, and raise the image of the USA abroad. This idea became known as the '**New Frontier**'. When he was elected, Kennedy had a chance to put it into operation.

The economy

Kennedy introduced a series of measures:

- Firms were given help with buying new equipment.
- Inflation was kept under control to keep prices down.
- Jobs were created in the defence and space industries.

- A minimum wage of US$1.25 an hour was introduced.
- Tax cuts were proposed to give people more spending money and increase demand for manufactured goods. (Though these were not introduced until after Kennedy's death.)

Welfare

Kennedy wanted to reduce poverty and took steps to help those in need:

- An Area Redevelopment Act made it possible for the federal government to give loans and grants to states like Tennessee and Kentucky, which had long-term problems with poverty.
- A Housing Act providing money for redevelopment and extra housing in towns.
- The Manpower Development and Training Act of 1961 helped jobless workers by retraining them.
- The government set up a US$900 million public works campaign to provide jobs for retrained workers.

Source A

▲ Kennedy speaking in the 1960s.

Source B

This is a great country, but I think it could be greater. This is a powerful country, but I think it could be more powerful. Economic growth means strength.

▲ An extract from a speech made by Kennedy in 1963.

Modern World History

Source C

Every American ought to have the right to be treated as he would wish to be treated.

But this is not the case.

▲ President Kennedy speaking on US television in June 1963.

Source D

EXTRA
PRESIDENT SLAIN
Texas Assassin Hits Kennedy in Automobile

PRESIDENT JOHN F. KENNEDY

News Call Bulletin
SAN FRANCISCO'S EVENING NEWSPAPER

Volume 5, No. 90   FRIDAY, NOVEMBER 22, 1963   Phone EX 7-5700   Price 10¢

DALLAS --- President John F. Kennedy is dead. He died after an assassin fired on his car leading a motorcade into Dallas, third stop on his Texas tour.

DALLAS (UPI)—President John F. Kennedy and Gov. John B. Connally of Texas were cut down by an assassin's bullets as they toured downtown Dallas in an open automobile today.

Mystery San Carlos Gun Battle
Gunfire blazed in a quiet residential section of San Carlos early this morning as

▲ The terrible news announced. A US newspaper front page on 22 November 1963.

Civil rights

You have already read that President Kennedy was interested in bringing about better civil rights for black Americans. He did not find this easy. Every President has to have the support of other politicians. Kennedy was a Democrat and many other Democrats from the Southern states did not support major changes to improve civil rights for blacks, as it would cost them votes. So Kennedy had to be careful.

- He appointed black Americans to several important government jobs. A black man called Robert Weaver became Home Finance Administrator.

- He set up the Committee on Equal Employment to try to improve job opportunities for black Americans.

- He encouraged his brother, Robert Kennedy, the Attorney-General, to help end inequality. Robert Kennedy took four of the US states to court because they denied the vote to black Americans.

- When James Meredith, a black student, was prevented from attending the University of Mississippi, President Kennedy stationed soldiers in the university until Meredith had finished his degree course. Troops were also sent to allow black students into the University of Alabama.

In June 1963 Kennedy put forward plans for a civil rights law that would ensure equal voting rights, ban discrimination in employment and provide all US citizens with equal access to public housing. Before it could be passed, Kennedy was assassinated in Dallas, Texas. However, the next President, Lyndon Johnson, made sure that the Civil Rights Act was passed.

Chapter 9 *A divided union? The USA: 1941~80*

223

1964	**Civil Rights Act** Banned discrimination in public accommodations, in federally assisted programmes, and in employment; gave federal government new power to enforce desegregation and prosecute voting rights violations
	Economic Opportunity Launched the 'war on poverty,' creating nationwide federal programs such as Head Start, the Job Corps, and VISTA, within the Office of Economic Opportunity
1965	**Elementary and Secondary Education Act** First major federal aid package for education in US history
	Medical Care Act Federally funded health care for the elderly (Medicare) and for welfare recipients (Medicaid)
	Voting Rights Act Ended literacy tests for voting; allowed federal agents to monitor registration
	Immigration Act Ended discriminatory ethnic quotas
1966	**Minimum Wage Law** Raised the rate from $1.25 to $1.40 an hour
	Model Cities Act Funded the clearing of slums and building of new housing projects, recreational facilities and mass transit

▲ **Some of the Acts passed as part of President Johnson's attempt to create a 'Great Society'.**

Source E

In the past we have waged war against foreign enemies. Now we have to declare war on a domestic enemy.

▲ **Johnson talking about the need to defeat poverty in 1964.**

The Great Society

President Johnson was keen to continue the improvements Kennedy had made. Johnson talked of establishing a **'Great Society'** in which poverty and racial discrimination had been wiped out. In a speech at Michigan University in 1964 he said that he wanted 'A Great Society where there is abundance and liberty for all'.

The 'Honeymoon Period'

President Johnson had one great advantage. The USA had been so shocked by Kennedy's assassination that it had immediately given its support to Kennedy's Vice-president, Johnson. He won the 1964 election easily and knew that, for a short period, he would have a great degree of support from other politicians. This was out of respect for President Kennedy.

So, Johnson pressed ahead with measures as quickly as he could. As you can see from the chart on this page he made reforms in a number of areas, including civil rights, education and housing. But his reforms were expensive and the USA was short of money because it was spending billions of dollars on the Vietnam War.

The end of Johnson

When the 1968 election came Johnson decided that he did not want to stand for re-election. He had been worn down by criticisms of his policies, in particular over the Vietnam War. In his place, the USA elected a Republican, Richard Nixon.

Source A

▲ A mother in a traditional 'stay at home' role.

Women's rights

One of the influences behind these changing attitudes was the black civil rights movement. Many women who campaigned against discrimination of black people came to realise that they suffered similar discrimination (see Source B).

In 1963 Betty Friedan wrote a book called *The Feminine Mystique*. It soon became a bestseller. Friedan wrote that women should have equal rights to men in politics, education and employment. It was wrong to give women low-paid jobs and judge them simply by how good they were as wives or mothers.

Women

During the Second World War many women had gone out to work for the first time. They had enjoyed the independence that having their own income brought. However, after the war, the majority of them returned to what most men thought was their proper role – as housewives.

As the USA became increasingly prosperous in the 1950s, more and more women began going to college, getting degrees and taking up skilled or professional jobs. They began to question whether it was right that they should be seen as people whose job it was to make a nice home, whilst the husband went out to work.

Changing attitudes

This change in attitudes really took off in the 1960s. A major reason was the introduction of the contraceptive pill. Once 'the pill' became widely available, women could decide when they had children and so could plan lives and careers to suit them. It also meant that women could be sexually active without the fear of pregnancy. This changed their attitudes to sexual relations.

Source B

Women experience discrimination as widespread and deep-rooted and every much as crippling as the assumptions of white supremacy are to the black Americans. We need to come to understand that this is no more a man's world than it is a white world.

▲ An SNCC publication supporting equal rights for women.

Questions

1 What do we mean when we say President Johnson had a 'honeymoon period' when he first became President?

2 Pick two of the Acts passed as part of President Johnson's attempt to set up the 'Great Society'. Explain why they would be important in changing America.

3 Why did so many women begin to think differently about their place in society?

Chapter 9 *A divided union? The USA: 1941~80*

225

Source C

▲ **Women campaigning for equality in August 1970.**

Equality for women

In 1961 President Kennedy appointed Eleanor Roosevelt (the widow of President Roosevelt) to chair the Presidential Commission on the Status of Women. Its report in 1963 showed how far women were behind men. It found that:

- Only 35 per cent of undergraduates in the USA were women.

- Women made up only 5 per cent of mangers and administrators, and just 12 per cent of the professions in the USA.

- Where men and women did the same job, on average men earned almost twice what women were paid.

Across the USA many states set up their own commissions – and found similar results. Soon two new laws helped improve the position of women.

These laws were:

1. The Equal Pay Act 1963. It said men and women doing the same job should be paid the same money.

2. The Civil Rights Act 1964. It made it illegal to discriminate on grounds of gender.

Of course, the Acts did not lead to full equality for women and the campaigning continued. In 1966 the National Organisation for Women (NOW) was set up. It had 40,000 members by the early 1970s. Other women's groups were formed, such as the National Black Feminist Organisation and the Women's Liberation Group. Soon these groups became known by opponents as 'women's libbers'.

In July 1972 the magazine *Ms* was launched. It sold 300,000 copies in just eight days. More extreme measures were also taken to promote the women's cause. For example girdles, bras, hair curlers and false eyelashes were burned in public as examples of 'female enslavement'. Sometimes men failed to understand what they were doing and ridiculed them. The 1968 Miss World Contest was also attacked as degrading to women.

A mixed reception

These actions annoyed many men and a large number of conservative women were also put off supporting the women's cause. They considered that the extreme behaviour of the feminists was 'unwomanly' and that they were showing themselves up in front of men. However, there was a need for extreme action to change people's attitudes and win equal rights for women. As a result of the women's action, change did come.

For example, in 1972 the Educational Amendment Act outlawed sex discrimination in education and ensured that the school curriculum did not stereotype women as people whose place was only in the home. The teaching of a more positive image had an important long-term effect on how women felt about themselves and how they were treated.

Source D

▲ **A positive role model. A successful 1980s career woman.**

Occupational Group	1950	1960	1970	1980
All workers	28	33	38	44
White-collar	40	43	48	55
Professional	40	38	40	46
Managerial	14	14	17	28
Clerical	62	68	74	81
Sales	34	37	39	49
Blue-collar	24	26	30	34
Crafts	3	3	5	6
Operatives	27	28	32	34
Labourers	4	4	8	11
Private household	95	96	96	97
Other services	45	52	55	61
Farm Workers	9	10	10	17

▲ **This chart shows how a higher percentage of women worked in various occupations between 1950 and 1980.**

Chapter 9 *A divided union? The USA: 1941~80*

227

Source E

Even those of us who have achieved success are still looked on as freaks in a man's world.

▲ Betty Friedan commenting on women succeeding in a 'man's world'.

Source F

It's obvious why there's so much delinquency now – working women. They should stay at home and look after the kids. Men should go out to work; women are the home-makers.

▲ The views of a man in his 60s in 1959.

The student movement

The 1960s was a time when many people were challenging society and wanted to see changes. This applied to black Americans and women, and also to students in the USA's colleges and universities. By the mid-1960s many students across the country were heavily involved in demonstrations. There were several reasons for this:

- The civil rights campaigns and the feminist movements had encouraged people to challenge existing beliefs and demand changes where they saw injustice.

- President Kennedy's assassination had shocked the US people and led to a belief that their society was corrupt.

- The stories of atrocities carried out by US soldiers in Vietnam served to reinforce the belief that something was wrong with the USA.

- The 1960s was a period when there was an explosion in rock and pop music. Many of the sixties bands attacked the injustices in society. Most famous of these was the singer/songwriter Bob Dylan. He wrote protest songs criticising politicians, the Vietnam War and racism, amongst other things.

- The 1960s was also a time of worldwide student unrest. In the UK there were 'sit-ins' and strikes at universities such as the London School of Economics. In France student demonstrations became so serious that they almost overthrew the government.

Student action

One of the first student protest groups in the USA was Students for a Democratic Society (SDS). It campaigned strongly for the USA to leave Vietnam, especially after President Johnson announced bombing raids on North Vietnam and thousands of innocent civilians were killed.

Questions

1 Why do you think not all women supported the women's movement in the 1960s?

2 Do you think the chart on page 227 proves that women had achieved equality by 1980? Explain your answer.

3 List the reasons why students began to take action in the 1960s.

4 'Students at university should just get on with their studies and not become involved in demonstrating.' Explain whether you agree with this view.

Source A

▲ One of the students shot dead at Kent State University.

Source B

Come senators, congressmen
Please heed the call,
Don't stand in the doorway
Don't block up the Hall.
For he that gets hurt
Will be he who has stalled.
There's a battle
Outside and it's ragin'
It'll soon shake your
windows
and rattle your walls
For the times
they are a changin'

▲ The words of a Bob Dylan
song.

By the end of 1965 SDS had 10,000 members in 150 colleges and universities. In April of that year 20,000 students marched on Washington in a demonstration against the Vietnam War. Over the next five years demonstrations and protests grew. Usually these demonstrations were peaceful, but sometimes feelings ran so high that they got out of control.

At Kent State University, Ohio, in 1970 students were campaigning peacefully against President Nixon's decision to bomb Cambodia as part of the Vietnam War. Soldiers were called in to disperse the students. The students refused and tear gas was used. The students still refused to disperse and, in the confusion, shots were fired. Four people were killed and 11 injured.

Some of the dead had not even been in the demonstration and were innocent bystanders. The US people were stunned to hear that soldiers were shooting students at university.

Student protest did not bring an end to the Vietnam War, but it helped highlight the weaknesses in the government policy and make the US withdrawal from Vietnam more likely. This was especially true because most students were from middle-class homes. They were the very people who had previously been supporters of their country in war. It was almost unheard of for such people to oppose the government in such times.

Chapter 9 *A divided union? The USA: 1941–80*

229

▲ Travelling 'Hippy-style' in the 1960s.

Flower power

The student youth movement believed in protest and changing society. Other young people became involved in developing what is now called 'an alternative lifestyle'.

These people were known as 'hippies'. Their major centre was in San Francisco and they had a form of dress which was easily recognisable. They had flowing, highly colourful clothing, and both men and women wore their hair very long. Sometimes they wore flowers in their hair and talked about 'flower power'. One of the best known hippy songs was a worldwide hit in 1967. It was called 'San Francisco' and said that if you were going to San Francisco you had to 'be sure to wear a flower in your hair'.

Hippies were associated with drugs such as LSD and marijuana. They also followed such groups as Jefferson Airplane, the Grateful Dead and the Doors. One of the most famous of all rock festivals, at Woodstock, in 1969 was a great hippy celebration.

Hippies also had very strong anti-violence views. Their slogan was 'Make love, not war' and so they were strongly opposed to the Vietnam War.

1950	1 million
1960	4 million
1970	8 million

▲ **The growth in student numbers 1950–70.**

The Watergate scandal

The hippies might have supported love, but there was little love between the major political Parties in the USA at this time.

On 17 June 1972, five burglars were arrested in the offices of the Democratic Party in the **Watergate building** in Washington. The burglars had some unusual things with them, including two cameras and an address book. In the address book was a name, a telephone number and a note saying 'W. House'. This was no ordinary burglary and it was eventually to lead to the resignation of the President, Richard Nixon.

CREEP

The men arrested in the Watergate building were part of a campaign to get Nixon re-elected. He had set up the Committee to Re-elect the President (CREEP). It was headed by John Mitchell, a close friend of Nixon. Soon it had US$60 million to use (which was against US law). Around US$350,000 of the money was to be used in dirty tricks against Nixon's opponents, the Democrats. One idea was to bug the Democrats' offices, and this is what the 'burglars' were doing.

None of this was known when the burglars were caught, but two newspaper reporters, Carl Bernstein and Bob Woodward, decided to carry out their own investigation. To the embarrassment of the White House, the two men found that the burglars were employed by CREEP and that CREEP had a fund controlled by the White House. They also discovered that CREEP was involved in several illegal activities at the time.

Source A

▲ The Watergate building in Washington.

Nixon's denial

In August 1972 President Nixon said that no-one at the White House was involved in this 'bizarre incident', but he was lying. At the same time, US$460,000 of CREEP's money was paid to the Watergate burglars. If Nixon was found out, he would be in terrible trouble.

Questions

1 Why do you think people were so shocked by what happened at Kent State University in 1970?

2 Most Americans did not take the hippies seriously. Why do you think that was?

3 **a** What was CREEP?
  b Why was it set up?

Chapter 9 *A divided union? The USA: 1941~80*

231

Nixon in trouble

Nixon won the election and seemed to have got away with the Watergate affair. But when the five burglars were put on trial, one of them, James McCord, told an amazing story. He said that White House officials had lied about their involvement in the burglary. They had also pressurised the burglars to 'plead guilty and keep quiet'.

The US Senate held an inquiry into the Watergate Affair. Nixon's closest advisors, John Dean, Bob Haldeman and John Erlichman resigned. But Nixon said he knew nothing about the affair. He ordered an enquiry of his own saying 'there can be no whitewash at the White House'. The enquiry was led by Archibald Cox.

Twists and turns

In the summer of 1973 Dean said that there had been a cover up and that Nixon knew all about the burglary. Nixon denied it. Then a White House official told the Senate that all Nixon's conversations in the White House were taped. The Senate asked for the tapes, but Nixon refused claiming **'executive privilege'**.

He also said that the information on them would endanger national security if it became known.

Nixon then decided to sack Cox. He told his Attorney-General to do so, but the Attorney-General refused and resigned. So did his deputy! Finally Cox was sacked, but the man chosen to replace him, Leon Jaworski, still demanded to hear the tapes. Finally Nixon was forced to issue some transcripts, but most of the incriminating material was left out.

'Expletive deleted'

Even so, the tapes shocked the nation as the phrase 'expletive deleted' appeared regularly. In other words, the President's swearing had to be taken out before they were considered readable by other people. The tapes also showed Nixon to be petty and vindictive. As Source B shows, Nixon knew about the bugging that was happening and was not in the least bit concerned that it was against the law.

Source B

Meeting between President Richard Nixon, Chief of Staff H. R. Haldeman and Counsel to President, John W. Dean at the Oval Office on 15 September 1972.

Nixon: Boy, you never know when those guys get after it – they can really find it.

Dean: The resources that have been put against this whole investigation to date are really incredible. It is truly a larger investigation than was conducted against the after inquiry of the JFK assassination.

Nixon: Oh.

Dean: Good statistics supporting the finding.

Haldeman: Isn't that ridiculous – this silly thing.

Nixon: Yes (expletive deleted). Goldwater put it in context when he said '(expletive deleted) everybody bugs everybody else. You know that.'

Dean: That was priceless.

Nixon: It happens to be true. We were bugged in '68 on the plane and in '62 even running for Governor – (expletive deleted) thing you ever saw.

▲ Part of the Watergate tapes published in the *Los Angeles Times* in May 1974.

Nixon defeated

Nixon still refused to release the unedited tapes, so Jaworski took him to the Supreme Court which ordered their release. Then the Senate threatened to **impeach** him. That meant that he would be tried by Congress. Congress found three reasons for impeaching Nixon (see Source D).

In desperation, Nixon released the tapes. They showed that he had tried to get the CIA to stop the investigation into the Watergate affair. Yet he had told the Senate and the people of the USA that he had not. Now it was no longer relevant whether Nixon had known about the original burglary. He had been caught lying.

The only way he could avoid impeachment was to resign. On 7 August 1974 he went on US television and announced his decision.

Source D

1 Obstructing justice by trying to cover up the role of the White House in the Watergate burglary.

2 Violating the rights of US citizens by using the FBI, CIA and IRS (Internal Revenue Service) to harass critics of the President.

3 Defying Congressional authority by refusing to hand over the tapes.

▲ The three reasons why Congress decided to impeach President Nixon.

Source C

▲ President Nixon announcing his resignation on American television.

Chapter 9 *A divided union? The USA: 1941–80*

233

After Watergate

One month after his resignation, Nixon was pardoned by Congress, though 31 of his advisors went to prison. Steps were taken to make sure that the powers of the President were restricted in the future.

- The War Powers Act 1973 said that the President could not send troops to war without consulting Congress.

- The Congressional Budget and Impoundment Control Act 1974 said that the President could not use government money for his own purposes.

- The Election Campaign Act 1974 limited how much individuals could contribute to a party's election campaign.

- The Privacy Act said that the public could have access to any files the government had on them.

In summary, in the period after 1945 the USA suffered a series of blows which took away much of its confidence.

- Its President (J. F. Kennedy) was assassinated in 1963.

- It was defeated in war in Vietnam.

- President Nixon was shown to be dishonest.

- From 1973 the economy went into recession as oil prices soared.

Source E

▲ Front cover of an English newspaper reporting Nixon's resignation.

Questions

1 Why do you think CREEP wanted to burgle the Democratic Party headquarters?

2 Why do you think Nixon lied about his role in the Watergate affair?

3 What was the impact of:
a Nixon releasing transcripts of edited tapes?
b Nixon releasing unedited tapes?

Overview

Do you agree that by 1980 the USA was still a very divided society? Explain your answer.

The rise and fall of the communist state. The Soviet Union: 1928~91

Introduction

By 1928 Joseph Stalin had established himself as leader of the Soviet Union. During the next 10 years he brought about changes in the Soviet Union to make it a major industrial nation. By the time the country became involved in the Second World War in 1941, Stalin's reforms had made the country strong enough to resist attack from Nazi Germany, but at an enormous cost in human lives. Stalin's work had also cost Soviet citizens their personal freedom as he extended his control across many aspects of people's lives.

Following Stalin's death, he was condemned by Nikita Khrushchev, who tried to allow more personal freedom in the Soviet Union. His successor, Leonid Brezhnev, blocked any further reforms, however and it was not until Mikhail Gorbachev came to power that real freedom was given to Soviet citizens.

But by then it was too late. The Soviet Union was bankrupt and Gorbachev could not prevent the Communist regime from being overthrown – both within the Soviet Union and across Eastern Europe.

Chapter 10 *The rise and fall of the communist state. The Soviet Union: 1928~91*

235

Lenin and Trotsky

In May 1924 Lenin's '**Political testament**' was published. In this statement Lenin set out how he thought the country should be run after his death. He thought the General Secretary of the Communist Party, **Joseph Stalin**, should be dismissed. Instead the new leader of the Soviet Union should be **Leon Trotsky**, who had played a big part in helping win the Civil War. You can see why Lenin didn't like Stalin in Source A.

Stalin survives

Stalin had spent many years building up his influence in the Communist Party and was not prepared to give up power so easily. Fortunately for him, the other Communist leaders decided to stand by him, even though many of them agreed with Lenin's criticisms of him. But they disliked Trotsky even more.

Stalin establishes himself in power

So Stalin became the new Soviet leader. He began by destroying the evidence which showed that Lenin had wanted him dismissed, and by getting rid of people who knew what Lenin had written (even though many of these people had actually helped Stalin come to power).

From 1924 to 1928 Stalin removed almost all of the senior Party members who had helped Lenin run the country. (These were known as '**Old Bolsheviks**'.) Some were simply dismissed. Others were accused of crimes against the country. They were given trials in which they never stood a chance of convincing the judge of their innocence and then they were executed.

Stalin was determined that his decisions would be accepted without question. To help him achieve this he used the **NKVD**, which was a secret police force. Any Soviet citizen daring to criticise Stalin's rule faced the terrifying prospect of arrest by the NKVD – often late at night, so that the sleepy victims were even more terrified.

Source A

Stalin has too much power in his hands and I am not sure he always knows how to use it wisely.

I propose that Stalin should be replaced by a man who is more patient, more polite and more attentive to his colleagues.

▲ **What Lenin said about Stalin in his Political Testament.**

Source B

We are 50 to 100 years behind the advanced countries. We must catch this up in 10 years. Either we do it or we go under.

▲ **Stalin explaining the purpose of his Five-Year Plans.**

Changes in industry and agriculture

In 1928 Stalin decided that the time had come to modernise the Soviet Union to make it able to compete with the West.

The Five-Year Plans

To improve Soviet industry, Stalin used an organisation called **Gosplan**. It set targets for the amounts that factories and mines had to produce. Star workers were used as examples of how to work. The most famous of these was Alexei Stakhanov who dug 102 tonnes in a single shift instead of the usual 7 tonnes. Of course, he had access to the best part of the mine, the best equipment and good support – not things the other workers had. Soon expert workers became known as '**Stakhanovites**'.

Propaganda posters talked of how every worker should be like Stakhanov. To help build up industry, huge new cities were built. One of these was **Magnitogorsk** where 50,000 workers slaved in appalling conditions.

Meeting targets

Stalin said that **production** had to double in the first Five-Year Plan. The figures showed that, in many industries, production did increase dramatically. But often these figures were faked by managers to avoid getting in trouble. And the quality of goods was sometimes so low that they were useless.

Source C

▲ Men like these Stakhanovite miners were praised as great workers.

Chapter 10 *The rise and fall of the communist state. The Soviet Union: 1928~91*

237

More Five-Year Plans

Stalin was not satisfied with the improvements made during the first Five-Year Plan. In 1933 he started a second plan, which had more realistic targets. The third plan began in 1938, but was cut short by the German invasion in 1941.

The table below shows how the plans went. Soviet figures show the percentage of the targets met (they beat the targets!). Western economists think they did much less well.

Industrial production	First 5-Year Plan	Second 5-Year Plan
Official Soviet figures	100.7	103.0
Western estimates	65.3	75.7

▲ Percentage of targets met in the First and Second Five-Year Plans.

Why did Stalin introduce the Five-Year Plans?

Stalin had two main reasons for introducing the plans:

1. He knew that countries in the West, like Britain, France and the USA, hated **Communism** – the type of government in the Soviet Union. So Stalin had to make the country as modern as possible in case it came under attack from the West.

2. Lenin had set up a plan in 1921 called the **New Economic Policy** (NEP). This was a temporary measure to help win the war and went against the ideas of Communism. Some individual citizens had become very rich. Stalin did not approve of this as Communism said that it was the state, not individuals, which should make profits.

Source A

НЕ ПОСТУПИМОСЬ У ЛЕНІНОВІЙ СПРАВІ

▲ A Soviet poster encouraging people to support the first Five Year Plan.

Legend:
- Canals built by forced labour
- Railways built by forced labour
- Trans-Siberian railway
- Main areas of forced labour camps
- Main industrial areas
- *Karaganda* New industrial cities

▲ This map shows the growth in the Soviet industry. Notice that some of the growth was due to 'forced labour'.

Kulaks

Stalin particularly hated the richer peasants who had made money out of the NEP. These '**Kulaks**' had to be destroyed. They were not good Communists as they had gained individual wealth. Stalin thought they must be disloyal and should be wiped out.

When Stalin said the Soviet Union was under threat, it gave him an excuse to take more and more power to help build up the country. By 1934, many Soviet people no longer even had the right to change jobs without permission.

Questions

1 What are the following:
   a Lenin's Political testament;
   b The Five-Year Plans;
   c Kulaks?

2 How many different reasons can you find for Stalin introducing the Five-Year Plans? Explain your answer as fully as possible.

Chapter 10 *The rise and fall of the communist state. The Soviet Union: 1928~91*

239

What went wrong with the Five-Year Plans?

Problems set in

At first the Soviet people liked the idea of the plans. They wanted the Soviet Union to be powerful. But soon problems set in and people became discontented.

- Many of the targets set were not realistic. Gosplan officials often didn't know what realistic targets were, so they just set figures that would make Stalin happy.

- The first Five-Year Plan was brought to an end after just four years, but targets stayed the same – as if there were five years to meet them.

- There was no chance for any criticism. If targets were not met, someone was always blamed. Engineers and managers were sometimes arrested or imprisoned for not meeting targets. Often this was just so that they could be replaced with less experienced men who did not know that the targets were unrealistic.

- The new workers were usually peasants who had come into the cities looking for work. They were not good at operating the new machinery and made many mistakes, resulting in machinery breaking down.

- When machines broke down workers were accused of deliberately wrecking them. In the Dombass area, more than half of the engineers and skilled workers were arrested and tried for supposedly wrecking machinery.

- Really these arrests were just part of the plan to frighten workers into obedience. Other measures included the death penalty for theft of state property, instant dismissal for one day's absence and restrictions on travel for work. Workers were told where to work and how much to produce.

The end result

With so much pressure on workers, it is not surprising that production did go up. It is estimated that by 1939 the Soviet Union was producing four times what it had produced in 1928. You can see this in the tables on this page.

But quality remained a problem. Tractors are a good example. Stalin wanted more tractors built to help boost agriculture. According to the first Five-Year Plan 170,000 tractors were to be built each year. Only 50,000 were actually built and half of these soon broke down.

Pig iron	3.2
Steel	4.0
Coal	35.0

▲ Production figures for the Soviet Union in 1928 (in millions of tonnes).

	Pig iron	Steel	Coal
Soviet Union	14.8	18.4	164.6
USA	31.9	47.2	359.0
UK	6.7	10.3	227.0
Germany	18.3	22.7	186.0

▲ How production in the Soviet Union compared with other countries in 1940.

Questions

1 Why did the Soviet people grow to dislike the Five-Year Plans?

2 Look at the production figures on this page. How can you use them to show that the Five-Year Plans were both successful and unsuccessful?

Collectivisation

As part of the Five-Year Plans Stalin wanted to bring about **collectivisation** in agriculture. This involved the state creating huge collective farms where machinery and skilled labour could be used more efficiently. Tractors were also made available at state tractor stations. There were two types of collective farm:

1 **Sovkhozy** were farms owned by the state. All produce went to the state and workers were paid wages.

2 **Kolkhozy** were collective farms made up of a large number of smaller farms. Workers kept plots of land for themselves and had to sell fixed amounts of produce to the state at agreed prices. If any food was left they could keep it. If none was left, they starved.

No choice

At first Stalin tried to persuade peasants to join the collective farms, but in 1928 and 1929 there was a shortage of food for industrial workers. The government seized food from the peasants to feed the workers. The kulaks led opposition to this policy and so Stalin decided to take stronger action.

He introduced a policy of '**dekulakisation**'. Across the Soviet Union kulaks were arrested and sent to labour camps in the North. Sometimes whole villages were arrested by the NKVD. Their land was used to make collective farms. Any opposition was met with execution. All those arrested were labelled as kulaks. No-one quite knew what the precise definition of a kulak was. So it was decided that any peasant who made a profit fitted the bill.

Source B

▲ **This Soviet poster was designed to encourage Soviet women to play their part in the Five-Year Plans. Notice the variety of tasks which Soviet women were encouraged to be involved in.**

Chapter 10 *The rise and fall of the communist state. The Soviet Union: 1928–91*

241

Famine

Stalin had originally guessed that there were 6 million kulaks in the Soviet Union, but more than 10 million were arrested. They were so angry at what was happening that many of them destroyed their livestock, crops and property before they could be seized.

The result was a terrible **famine**. There were often food shortages in the Soviet Union and nearly 5 million people had died of starvation in the famine of 1919–20. But the famine of 1932, brought about by enforcing dekulakisation, may have cost as many as 20 million lives.

The successes of collectivisation

Despite the terrible loss of life, Stalin was convinced that his policy was successful.

- The kulaks had been destroyed and could not stand in his way.

- By 1932, 62 per cent of farms had been collectivised and by 1940, 400,000 collective farms had been set up.

- By 1937 wheat production was one-third higher than it had been in 1928.

	Cattle	Pigs	Sheep
1928	70.5	26.0	146.7
1933	38.4	12.1	50.2

▲ This chart shows how the numbers of animals dropped as a result of the kulaks' action (numbers are in millions).

The failures of collectivisation

But it is very difficult to say that the policy was really successful.

- Food shortages remained and were made worse by the kulaks' destruction of crops and livestock.

- Since peasants did not own the new farms, they did not feel motivated to work hard on them. In places where they were allowed to keep small plots for themselves, they worked much harder on these than on the state-owned land.

Source C

We must smash the kulaks, eliminate them. We must strike so hard that they will never rise up again.

▲ Part of a speech by Stalin attacking the kulaks.

Questions

1 a What were collective farms?
   b Why do you think Stalin wanted to introduce them?
   c Why did many peasants resist what Stalin was doing?

2 Do you think that Stalin's policy of collectivisation was a success or a failure? Explain your answer.

Source A

▲ This type of painting was used to encourage Soviet citizens to support Stalin's policies. The painting is called 'Higher and Higher' and represents Soviet achievement.

How did life change for the people of the Soviet Union?

It was not only industrial production which improved during the 1930s.

- Education and housing were improved.
- The number of doctors increased and medical treatment improved.
- There was higher pay for some workers.
- Social security benefits were introduced.

Women

The position of women also improved. The government had declared equality for women in 1917 and now they were expected to play their part in the modernisation of the country. Nurseries and crèches were provided in factories, and between 1927 and 1937 the number of industrial workers who were women rose from 28 per cent to 40 per cent.

But the reason why women played such a major part in the Soviet growth was only partly because Communism taught equality. A more important reason was that, since so many men had been arrested, the women were needed to take their places. When war broke out in 1941 the situation became even worse. Deaths through execution, overwork and war meant that by the 1950s women outnumbered men by three to two in some parts of the Soviet Union.

The down side

As more workers moved into the cities, **living standards** fell. Flats which were ideal for one family, had two or more families crammed into them. Pay did not keep up with price increases and crime soared. Alcoholism became common.

Of course those in the higher ranks of the Communist Party had special privileges like luxury goods and holidays at exclusive resorts on the Black Sea.

Chapter 10 *The rise and fall of the communist state. The Soviet Union: 1928–91*

243

Source B

▲ A workers' canteen in Moscow. Overcrowded conditions and poor food were common.

It was true that there was now no unemployment in the Soviet Union, but there was also little freedom. People were told where to work and what to produce. They lost their ability to act as individuals and think for themselves. Perhaps this was what Stalin had wanted.

Questions

1 Look again at the pages you have read about Stalin.
   a Make a list of all the ways in which you think he improved the Soviet Union.
   b Make a list of all the ways in which he made it worse.

2 If you were asked to give Stalin's work in the 1930s a mark out of 10, what would you give? Explain why you chose this mark.

Source A

▲ Stalin with his closest associates in 1934. Of the seven people shown with Stalin, only three were still alive four years later. One was executed, two murdered and one died of natural causes. Sergei Kirov is seated in the front row, on the far right of the picture.

Stalin's dictatorship

Although Stalin kept a tight control on the Soviet Union, he still faced opposition. In 1934 Stalin came close to being voted out as General Secretary of the Party. Sergei Kirov was elected to a senior position within the Party and some people spoke of him as a possible successor to Stalin.

Then, in December 1934, Kirov was murdered. It is possible that Kirov was killed on Stalin's orders. Stalin used Kirov's death in a very clever way. It showed, he said, that there was disloyalty amongst Party members and steps needed to be taken to stamp out opposition to the leader.

Source B

My communism was defective and became a form of Trotskyism.

▲ Part of the confession of Zinoviev, a senior Communist official on trial for taking part in Kirov's murder.

Chapter 10 *The rise and fall of the communist state. The Soviet Union: 1928~91*

245

The purges

Kirov's death was the starting point for a huge campaign against Stalin's supposed enemies. This became known as the **'purges'** and it applied to all sections of Soviet society. The most fortunate of Stalin's victims spent ten or more years in labour camps. The unlucky ones were executed.

- **Politicians** More than 1100 of the 1966 delegates to the 1934 Congress were executed. More than three-quarters of the members of the Central Committee (which helped Stalin rule) were also to lose their lives.

- **Members of the armed forces** 90 per cent of the generals and more than half of the officers of the Red Army were executed in 1937–38.

- **Scientists and engineers** who Stalin mistrusted were purged. So were managers of industries or collective farms who did not meet their targets.

- **Poets, writers, artists and musicians** also suffered. If Stalin did not approve of their work, or considered it **anti-Soviet** they were purged. The composer Prokofiev fled to the West, though he was allowed to return to write the sort of music which Stalin approved of.

- **Ordinary people** Stalin's purges also extended to the ordinary people of the Soviet Union. For example in Leningrad 30,000 people were arrested and sent to labour camps. In 1937–38 alone, 682,000 people across the Soviet Union were shot by the secret police, and the age at which the death penalty could be given was lowered to 12 years.

Source C

▲ A Soviet drawing of Lenin and Stalin working together. Notice how they appear to get on so well.

The impact of the purges

From Stalin's point of view the purges served a very useful purpose:

- They removed all opposition to him.

- They gave him the opportunity to fill vacant jobs with his supporters, e.g. he was able to put the loyal Beria in charge of the secret police.

- They frightened Soviet citizens into working harder.

But they also created many problems in the Soviet Union:

- The Red Army lost so many of its officers that it stood no chance when the Germans invaded in 1941.

- Industry suffered because managers were frightened to try new ideas in case they didn't work.

- The loss of scientists and engineers prevented new inventions being developed.

- The loss of huge numbers of workers hit industry.

- Literature, art and music failed to develop.

Show trials and gulags

These were two of the more appalling aspects of Stalin's rule.

Show trials were public trials in Moscow where political leaders of the Soviet Union admitted that they were working with Trotsky to carry out crimes ranging from arson to plotting to overthrow Stalin. Leaders such as Zinoviev and Kamenev confessed to their crimes and were executed. Of course they had not committed these crimes, but knew that if they did not plead guilty they would still die and their families would also be executed.

The gulags were slave labour camps where ordinary Soviet citizens were sent to carry out work projects. They were usually in the frozen far North, and millions of workers died from exhaustion, starvation or by simply freezing to death.

Perhaps the saddest aspect of these camps is that many of those in them had been arrested after accusations were made about them to the NKVD by neighbours or workmates – often to get revenge after arguments or simply to get their jobs after they were arrested.

Questions

1 What were the purges?

2 Who were the victims of them?

3 Why do you think Stalin cared about what music was composed or what poetry was written?

4 Why do you think Stalin carried on the purges even though they seemed to be harming the country?

Chapter 10 *The rise and fall of the communist state. The Soviet Union: 1928–91*

247

Changing history

Stalin wanted all his opponents (real ones and suspected ones) removed from power. He also wanted to get rid of any suggestion that they had played a major part in converting the Soviet Union from the rule of the Tsar to Communism.

This was one of the reasons why **Trotsky** became a target. He had organised the Red Army during the Civil War and helped the Communists defeat their enemies. He had also been Stalin's rival for power after Lenin's death. Now he was accused of being a traitor, and anyone seen as a possible threat to Stalin was said to be working with him.

What Stalin wanted was for people to think that he, Stalin, was their hero. So during the 1930s he began rewriting history to show himself in an even better light. Stalin's role in Soviet history was exaggerated and he was shown as being responsible for winning the Civil War. Textbooks and encyclopedias were rewritten to show this. They were also edited to take away any reference to the victims of the purges.

Stalin and Lenin

Stalin knew that Lenin was the real hero of the Soviet Union and would not have dared to try to rewrite the history of Lenin's part in the revolution.

Instead he decided to show himself as the politician closest to Lenin (remember Lenin had not even trusted him!) Pictures such as those on page 246, showing the two men working together, became common. Stalin had a huge mausoleum built in Moscow where his 'close friend's' body could be put on permanent display.

'The wisest man of the age'

Stalin not only wanted people to see him as Lenin's true heir, he also wanted them to respect and love him. So a massive propaganda campaign was launched.

- Throughout the Soviet Union mass **rallies** were held in his honour.

- Photographs showed him as a loving man, caring about children or ordinary citizens.

- Artists painted him as a happy smiling man meeting cheerful and adoring workers. (Actually he rarely met ordinary citizens, most of whom were more scared of him than adoring.)

- In books, films, plays and newspapers Stalin was described as the '**Father of the Soviet Union**' and 'the wisest man of the twentieth century'. Nothing he did could be wrong.

Source D

Thank you, Stalin. Thank you, because I am joyful. Thank you, because I am well.

Generations of people still to come will think of us as the most fortunate of men because we were privileged to see Stalin, our inspired leader.

▲ **Part of a speech given in 1936 to honour Stalin.**

Source E

▲ A photomontage showing Stalin being joyfully received by the children of the Soviet Union. It is an excellent example of how Stalin liked to be shown. In the montage he is portrayed as the father of the Soviet people.

Yet more power

Stalin's **propaganda** and his use of the secret police made him untouchable in the Soviet Union. After the Second World War he planned more purges to remove 'supporters of the West who opposed communism'. He did introduce a new **Constitution** (set of rules about how the country should be run) in 1936. It said that there should be freedom of speech, freedom of the press and freedom of religion. But there was no such thing. It was merely another example of what Stalin wanted people to believe was true. It wasn't.

Questions

1 Why did Stalin want to be closely linked to Lenin?

2 Study Source C on page 246. Explain how it gets across a message which Stalin would have liked.

3 Do you agree that it is a waste of time rewriting history because people will remember the truth?

▲ A map showing how the Germans invaded the Soviet Union in 1941.

The impact of the Second World War on Soviet society

On 21 June 1941, the Germans launched **Operation Barbarossa** – their invasion of the Soviet Union. At the time, Germany and the Soviet Union were **allies**, but Stalin had suspected that one day Hitler's forces would invade.

Even so, he was shocked when he heard that German troops were advancing at great speed across the Soviet Union.

Stalin was so stunned that it was almost a week before he worked out what needed to be done. He decided to appeal to the peoples of the Soviet Union to defend their **motherland**. He didn't tell them to defend communism. Instead he mentioned the different areas of the Soviet Union by name and appealed to the patriotism of the people.

Source A

▲ A German soldier attacking a Soviet village with a flame thrower.

Source C

The Fuhrer has decided to wipe the city from the face of the Earth. We will use artillery fire and non-stop bombardment from the air to destroy the city. Even if people in the city decide to surrender, they will be ignored.

▲ An announcement made by German forces which had surrounded Leningrad in 1941.

Divided loyalties

At an Anniversary of the Revolution Parade in 1941 Stalin called on the people to resist the invasion from the West, just as they had resisted Napoleon and other invaders in the past. The war became known as the **Great Patriotic War** and all citizens were encouraged to unite to resist the Germans.

But Stalin was a worried man. He had treated some of the Soviet people so badly that they were not keen to fight to save him. So in parts of the Ukraine and the Crimea, the Germans were welcomed and even given gifts. Hitler, however, had little time for people of **non-German** races. He shipped millions of Soviet citizens back to Germany to work in labour camps and killed thousands of others. Almost 3.5 million prisoners of war died in German hands. It soon became obvious that Hitler was an even worse prospect than Stalin.

Scorched earth

As the Germans advanced in 1941 Stalin ordered a **scorched earth policy**. As people retreated they took what they could carry (even some factories were transported East) and destroyed the rest. Hitler's forces would find no crops, no livestock, no food and no useful equipment.

Of course the invasion also meant that the Soviet people could not grow crops in the invaded areas and agricultural production fell by two-thirds. Hunger became common.

Source B

Comrades, citizens, brothers and sisters, men of our Army and Navy. It is to you I am speaking, dear friends.

▲ Part of Stalin's appeal to the people to defend their motherland.

Source D

One day an actor just fell dead on the stage. We shuffled in front of him to hide him and someone pulled him off. You had to keep going.

▲ The show must go on in a Leningrad theatre in 1941.

Leningrad: a case study

As you read on page 251 the city of Leningrad soon came under attack from the Germans. Hitler knew that destroying the city named after the great Communist leader would be a huge blow to Soviet pride.

So, for almost three years, the city came under attack from German artillery and bombers. In September 1941, the Germans had surrounded the city and cut off food supplies. Soon the people were reduced to eating cats and dogs as food supplies ran out. Death from starvation was common. The people were too weak to bury the dead and disease set in. Source E tells the sad story of what happened to the Savicheva family.

The German attack on the Soviet Union eventually failed. The lack of supplies, the huge distances the Germans had to travel and the appalling cold cost Hitler 200,000 men. Some say this campaign used up so many resources it cost him the war.

It cost the people of Leningrad even more. Over 600,000 of them died from disease and starvation.

How did the war affect the Soviet Union?

- There were terrible casualties. It is estimated that some 28 million people died – 9 million soldiers and 19 million civilians.

- Over 1700 towns and 70,000 villages were destroyed.

But in some ways the invasion worked in Stalin's favour:

- He was able to use the war as an excuse to transport groups he distrusted to Siberia (over 3 million people were sent there).

- When the war was won, Stalin could claim to be the saviour of the Soviet Union and would get even greater loyalty from the people.

Source E

Z – Zhenya died on 28 December, 12.30 in the morning, 1941.

B – Babushka died on 25 January, 3 o'clock, 1942.

L – Leka died on 17 March, 5 o'clock in the morning, 1942.

D – Dedya Vasya died on 13 April, 2 o'clock at night, 1942.

D – Dedya Lesha died on 10 May, 4 o'clock in the afternoon.

M – Mama died on 13 May, 7.30 in the morning, 1942.

S – Savichevs died. All died. Only Tanya remains.

▲ Tanya Savicheva, a Soviet schoolgirl, wrote this account of her family's death in her school notebook in 1943. Shortly afterwards she too was dead. Most of her family had died from starvation. She died from the disease dysentery which was brought on by her sufferings in the siege.

The war also had an impact on relations with the West. Britain and the USA had become Stalin's allies once Germany invaded. But Stalin thought that these countries had not done enough to help him. He thought that they would have liked Hitler to defeat the Communist Soviet Union. As you can read in Chapter 11, this had an impact on relations between the Soviet Union and the West after the war.

Stalin after the war

After the success in the war, Stalin had total control in the Soviet Union. The Communist newspaper, **Pravda**, used the term '**Stalinist**' to describe correct behaviour. Those who showed **dissent** (disagreement) were dealt with severely. Artists, poets, musicians and now Jews became victims of more purges. In November 1952 details of an alleged '**Doctor's Plot**' were published. This was an imaginary plot by Jewish doctors to kill Stalin.

On 2 March 1953 Stalin had a brain haemorrhage. He had dismissed his doctor the previous year, so no-one was on hand to treat him. The only man who could call a doctor to treat Stalin was Beria, head of the NKVD. By the time he was found, Stalin could not be saved. He died three days later.

Source A

▲ Stalin's body lying in state shortly after his death.

Source B

A man is invited to visit Stalin as a friend. But he never knows where he will be sent next. It could be home or to jail.

▲ Nicolai Bulganin, Prime Minister from 1955–58 remembering the fear that an 'invitation' from Stalin caused.

Questions

1 What was the impact of the war on the Soviet Union (including the position of Stalin)?

2 What does Source B tell us about life in the Soviet Union under Stalin?

3 What might the Soviet people have thought if they had been shown the picture in Source A in March 1953?

Chapter 10 *The rise and fall of the communist state. The Soviet Union: 1928~91*

253

De-Stalinisation

For almost 30 years Stalin had ruled the Soviet Union. Now he was gone. He was replaced as Prime Minister and Party Secretary by Georgi **Malenkov**. Malenkov was persuaded, however, to give up the post of Party Secretary to Nikita **Khrushchev**. These two men formed part of a committee which governed the country until 1956. By then it was obvious that Khrushchev was in control.

Why Khrushchev?

- Just like Stalin, Khrushchev was able to use his position as Party Secretary to gain support and 'freeze out' those who opposed him.

- He was popular with the Army because he had played a major part in the war.

- He promised to make changes to improve the standard of living in the country.

Stalin denounced

Shortly after Stalin's death, Beria was arrested and shot. His name was taken out of the *Great Soviet Encyclopedia* and replaced by 'Bering Sea' (which fitted in the same place). Then something even more extraordinary happened.

In February 1956 Khrushchev made a speech (the **'Secret Speech'**) at the Twentieth Party Conference. He said Stalin was a **dictator** and enemy of the people, that he had been cruel and had ignored the laws of the land. Other Soviet politicians were horrified and criticised Khrushchev for his speech.

But Khrushchev knew that the Soviet Union had to change and it could only do so if attitudes changed. Of course, by criticising Stalin, he got himself off the hook. He had been a leading figure under Stalin and might have been accused of cruelty himself. Now he could not – and if anyone opposed him, it would look like they supported Stalin's cruelty.

How did de-Stalinisation change the Soviet Union?

- There was no longer 'hero-worship' of Stalin. His body was removed from Lenin's mausoleum in Moscow, Stalingrad was renamed Volgograd and street names were changed, removing his name.

- The role of the secret police was reduced, the death penalty abolished and millions of political prisoners set free.

- Exiled politicians returned and minority groups sent to Siberia were allowed to return to their homeland.

- Restrictions on poets, writers, artists and musicians were relaxed.

Source A

Stalin made up the idea that there was 'an enemy of the people'. This allowed him to take cruel actions against anyone he suspected. Many abuses were carried out on Stalin's orders. He paid no attention to the laws of the Soviet Union. His behaviour affected life in the Soviet Union and our relations with foreign countries.

▲ **Some of Khrushchev's criticisms in the Secret Speech.**

Source B

▲ The actor Omar Sharif in the film Dr Zhivago, which was based on Pasternak's novel.

Not so different

But Khrushchev was not really changing the Soviet Union, just relaxing things a little. Criticism of Stalin was acceptable, but not criticism of the Soviet system.

- In 1958 Boris Pasternak won the Nobel prize for literature for his book *Dr Zhivago*. As the book was an attack on the Soviet system, Pasternak was forced to make a public apology and refuse the prize.

- In Poland and Hungary, Soviet forces were sent to deal with **uprisings** when the people thought that the end of Stalin meant more freedom for them.

- The **death penalty** was reintroduced and 10,000 churches closed down.

- In 1957 Khrushchev removed all his political opponents from power after they tried to remove him.

But there was a major difference between Stalin's rule and Khrushchev's. When one of his opponents begged not to be executed, Khrushchev told him, 'You will be given a job and will live in peace if you work honestly.' This was de-Stalinisation in action.

Chapter 10 *The rise and fall of the communist state. The Soviet Union: 1928~91*

255

Khrushchev's attempts at modernisation

Why did Khrushchev want change?

Khrushchev knew that the Soviet Union had to produce more food and goods for the people. He once said, 'What sort of Communism is it which cannot produce a sausage?'

The time had come to reduce control from Moscow and let local leaders run their industries and agriculture. They would know better what was needed and what could be done.

Agriculture

Khrushchev had three main policies to improve agriculture.

1. The **Virgin Lands** scheme. This involved ploughing up large areas of previously uncultivated Kazakhstan, Western Siberia and the Urals. Around 13 million hectares of new farmland would create 20 million tonnes of grain. The country's food problems would be solved in just two or three years.

2. Joining together **collective farms**. This would make them more efficient. Debts were written off and tractors given to the new, larger farms. These farms would be more independent and able to prosper.

3. **Growing maize**. This would be used to feed animals instead of grain, which could be used solely for human consumption.

Industry

Khrushchev also tried to give more power to local people in industry. He set up **sovnarkhozy** (regional economic councils) which had the power to make decisions about what could be produced. A seven hour day was introduced and workers were allowed to change their jobs.

Year	Amount
1954	86 million tonnes
1955	104 million tonnes
1958	135 million tonnes
1961	133 million tonnes
1963	109 million tonnes

▲ **Grain grown in the Soviet Union 1954–63.**

Questions

1 Why did Khrushchev become leader of the Soviet Union after Stalin?

2 Why was his Secret Speech such a shock to many people?

3 In what ways was the Soviet Union:
   a Different from
   b The same as
   how it had been under Stalin?

▲ **A map showing Kazahkstan and the area selected by Stalin to launch the Virgin Lands scheme.**

What went wrong in industry?

The sovnarkhozy did not work because, under Stalin, local managers had been frightened to make decisions. They could not believe that they had any real power. Khrushchev combined some of the sovnarkhozy into regions, but still no effective decision-making took place.

What went wrong in agriculture?

Khrushchev's ideas sounded very good but there were many problems. Some of these were because Krushchev thought he was an expert on agriculture and would not listen to advice.

- Not enough money was spent on **fertiliser** for the newly ploughed lands.

- In 1963 hurricanes blew away the top soil on 6 million hectares of land in Kazakhstan. It was destroyed forever.

- Transport was too inefficient to get crops from distant Kazakhstan to the cities. When crops were successfully grown they sometimes rotted on the roadside before they could be transported.

- Maize was sometimes planted in areas where the climate was not suitable.

Why did Khrushchev's reforms fail?

- Despite his plans, Khrushchev was not really able to break away from the Soviet custom of **government control**.

- There was no real incentive to workers to produce more. They could not gain individually from the profits made and often saw no reason to work harder.

- From 1956 huge sums of money were diverted into the **space race** to prove Soviet supremacy over the USA. Money was also spent on foreign aid and sport to promote the image of Communism in the world. This money was badly needed to help make consumer goods for the Soviet people.

Chapter 10 *The rise and fall of the communist state. The Soviet Union: 1928~91*

257

Opposition to Khrushchev

By 1962 food prices were rising and opposition was growing. Khrushchev had made many promises, but had not been able to keep them. Although there was a small improvement in living standards, there were still shortages of many day-to-day necessities.

Krushchev's resignation

By October 1964 Khrushchev had failed in too many areas to keep his job.

- In June 1962, many people were killed (including children) when he ordered armed troops to stop people marching in protest about price rises.

- His agricultural and industrial policies were failing.

- In 1962 he took on the USA in a power struggle over **nuclear missiles** in Cuba (see page 282). Despite Soviet propaganda, it was Khrushchev who eventually backed down. Other Soviet leaders were angry at this failure.

- Khrushchev was also a rather rude man whose behaviour, such as taking his shoe off at a meeting of the United Nations, embarrassed his countrymen.

So in October 1964 Khrushchev was sacked and allowed to retire to the suburbs of Moscow to write his memoirs.

The decline and fall of the Soviet state

Tougher policies

The Communist Party leaders decided that Khrushchev had tried to make too many changes and had been too critical of Stalin. So they appointed a hard-line Communist, Leonid **Brezhnev**, in his place.

- Brezhnev opposed change and began to reverse most of Khrushchev's changes.

- In particular, he tightened up on dissidents. Thousands of writers were arrested and imprisoned.

- Yuri **Andropov** was put in charge of the **KGB** (as the secret police was now called).

Andropov locked dissidents up in mental hospitals to break their spirits. He also began a campaign against **corruption**. Many Party officials had been taking bribes or using their positions to gain property and favours. A major problem here was that Brezhnev's family were amongst the worst offenders, so little could be done whilst he was in power.

Source A

His policies were based on harebrained scheming, rash decisions, wishful thinking and empty words. He ignored the achievements of science and practical experience.

▲ The Communist paper, *Pravda*, criticising Khrushchev.

Questions

1 What three policies did Khrushchev have for agriculture?

2 Why did they fail?

3 What other reasons were there for Khrushchev failing to change the Soviet Union?

4 Do you think there is any way in which Khrushchev can be said to have been a success as leader of the Soviet Union?

Source A

▲ Leonid Brezhnev.

Source B

Lack of skilled labour and problems created by alcoholism, absenteeism and lack of effort by the civil servants responsible for planning.

▲ Reasons for the failure of the Tenth Five-Year Plan.

Source C

▲ Yuri Andropov.

In a speech in 1981 Brezhnev listed the reasons for the lack of success in improving living standards in the Soviet Union (see Source B). It was so difficult to obtain some consumer goods and foods that a huge black market had grown up in the Soviet Union. This was hardly surprising when the alternative was queuing all day for goods or paying the equivalent of seven years' wages for a car (for which there would be no spare parts).

Chapter 10 *The rise and fall of the communist state. The Soviet Union: 1928–91*

259

The decline continues

- The major problem which the Soviet Union faced was that it could not afford to play the role of a **superpower**. It had spent huge sums on the space race, on nuclear weapons and on providing help to countries in Eastern Europe and elsewhere. Then, from 1979, it found itself at war in Afghanistan.

- To pay for all this, the Soviet Union tried to sell goods abroad. But its manufactured goods, such as cars, were considered a joke in the West. So it had to sell raw materials and grain – and it did not have enough of these for its own people.

No settled leadership

In 1982 Brezhnev died and was succeeded by Andropov, but he fell ill and died shortly after taking over. His successor, Konstantin **Chernenko** lasted just 13 months before he died.

Mikhail Gorbachev

Unlike the previous leaders, the next leader Mikhail Gorbachev wanted a completely different approach to government. The government could no longer bully the people into supporting it. He had not been brought up under Joseph Stalin and this may explain why he felt differently to other hard-line communists.

Gorbachev's policies

Gorbachev was horrified by what he found out about the Soviet economy. More than half of state controlled businesses were running at a loss and 10 per cent of workers regularly arrived at work drunk. What was needed was a new approach to the economy called '**Perestroika**' (see box). Linked to this should be a new approach to government. This would be '**Glasnost**' (openness). Soviet citizens and foreign powers would see less secrecy, less state control and more acceptance of Western ideas.

Gorbachev's policies

Perestroika was designed to change the Soviet economy. Gorbachev wanted to reduce state control and introduce more competition – as in the West. Prices would no longer be kept low by government subsidies and **enterprise** would be encouraged.

Glasnost meant the end of press censorship and the entry of Western ideas and music into the Soviet Union. Religious freedom was allowed and the Orthodox Church was no longer controlled. The KGB had its powers reduced and free elections were held. A 'McDonalds' even opened in Moscow.

Gorbachev hoped that Perestroika and Glasnost would benefit the Soviet Union and improve his relations with the West. Then he could reach agreement with the USA to **reduce arms**. That would enable him to cut spending on defence and to stop the Soviet government from spending millions of roubles more each year than it raised in taxes.

He wanted to keep the Soviet Union as one united country, but was determined to make changes.

Why did Gorbachev fail?

Despite his efforts, Mikhail Gorbachev was not successful and he was eventually overthrown in 1991. Why was this?

- His reforms had come too late. The problems were so deep that changes needed time to take effect. Gorbachev had promised improvements, but the people were not prepared to wait.

- Gorbachev expected that his changes would win support in the West, and countries such as the USA and Japan would provide financial help. But he was wrong and the West was not prepared to help him out. A Soviet Union in difficulty was less of a threat to them.

- As Gorbachev began to introduce changes, he actually created problems for himself. In 1989 the countries of Eastern Europe broke free from Soviet control. Soon parts of the Soviet Union itself, such as Estonia, wanted their freedom too.

- Glasnost allowed people to complain about the government. Once they realised this, the floodgates opened. Gorbachev expected his reforms to make him popular. Instead he was abused in the street by people making demands for more changes.

- In the end, Glasnost and Perestroika revealed the terrible state of the Soviet Union. It also showed that it was a collection of unwilling partners. Once control from Moscow was relaxed, the minority nationalities in places like Chechnya and the Ukraine wanted their freedom from the Soviet Union.

Source A

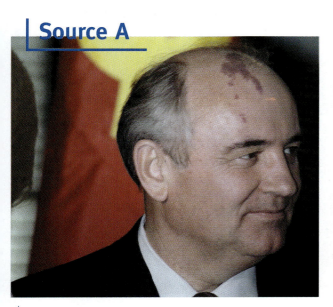

▲ **Mikhail Gorbachev.**

Questions

1 Gorbachev was trying to improve the Soviet Union. Why did his attempt fail?

The end of the Soviet Union

In August 1991 Gorbachev was arrested by Communist Party hard-liners who disapproved of his changes. Did this mean the old style Soviet system would return?

No, because Boris **Yeltsin**, the leader of Russia (the richest and most powerful of the republics making up the Soviet Union) appeared outside the home of the Russian parliament and dared the military (which was supporting Gorbachev's arrest) to attack him.

When it became obvious that the people of Russia supported Yeltsin's move, the Army withdrew and Gorbachev was saved. But, of course, the real power in the Soviet Union was now in the hands of Yeltsin. The 14 republics of the Soviet Union now began to take advantage of the weakness of Gorbachev's position. By 1992 the Soviet Union had ceased to exist. The team in the Olympic Games of that year did not participate as the Soviet Union, but instead as a group called the **Commonwealth of Independent States**.

The republic of Russia, which contained the Soviet capital, Moscow, also had difficulties. It was made up of a collection of over 50 smaller groups. They now took the opportunity to break away from the control of Moscow. From being one of the most controlled and disciplined of countries, the Soviet Union had collapsed into chaos.

Source B

▲ **Yeltsin leads members of the Russian parliament in opposing the coup of August 1991.**

▲ Map showing the states which made up the new Commonwealth of Independent States.

Source C

▲ Boris Yeltsin.

Questions

1   Which of the following do you think is a
    reason for the break up of the Soviet
    Union? Explain your choice or choices.

    a Mikhail Gorbachev did not make
    enough changes.

    b Stalin was too cruel during his rule.

    c Communism did not bring a high
    enough standard of living.

    d The Soviet Union had too many
    different nationalities in it.

Chapter 10 *The rise and fall of the communist state. The Soviet Union: 1928~91*

263

CHAPTER 11

Superpower relations: 1945~90

Introduction

The Soviet Union had fought alongside the Western powers in the Second World War, but when the war ended so did the friendship between the West and the Soviet Union. Soon the two 'superpowers' (the USA and the Soviet Union) had become deadly rivals.

Stalin was convinced that the West wanted to destroy his country and stamp out Communism. He was particularly concerned that the USA now had an atomic bomb with which to threaten his country. So he made sure that the countries which were between the Soviet Union and the West were Communist, acting as 'buffer states' to protect him from the West.

This marked the beginning of the Cold War, a war of words and propaganda between the West and Eastern Europe. This was a war which, on several occasions, almost led to direct military conflict. Fortunately such devastating warfare was avoided.

When the Soviet Union invaded Afghanistan in 1979 relations between East and West deteriorated once more, but this was the final conflict of the Cold War. The Soviet Union was close to bankruptcy and was keen to scale down its spending on armaments. As the Soviet Empire began to break up, Mikhail Gorbachev met the then US President, George Bush in December 1989. Together they declared that the Cold War was over.

The origins of the Cold War and the partition of Germany

In the Second World War the Soviet Union had been in an alliance with the USA and the countries of Western Europe. After the war, this alliance split up and relations worsened. They became so bad that historians have labelled this period of history the '**Cold War**'.

What was the Cold War?

The Cold War was a war of words and propaganda. The West (Western Europe and the USA) tried to show that it was superior to Eastern Europe (the Soviet Union and its allies). It did so by using propaganda, spying, building up weapons to show its strength and emphasising the faults in the way the Soviet Union behaved. Of course, the Soviet Union acted in exactly the same way towards the West. Although the Cold War did not involve fighting, perhaps one day it would. So it was vital to maintain strong armed forces to be ready for war. Source A shows how, between 1945 and 1983, each side built up its armed forces in what became known as '**the Arms Race**'.

There were several reasons why the Cold War came into being:

- The Soviet Union was a **communist** country and feared that the West wanted to attack it because of its fear of communism.

- The Western countries were **capitalist** and **democratic**. They feared that the Soviet Union wanted to spread communism and overthrow their governments.

So, although the two sides had been allies, they did not really trust each other. After the Second World War more and more countries gained their independence from European Empires. Both the USA (the leader of the West) and the Soviet Union tried to get these newly-independent countries to join their side in the Cold War.

Superpowers

- 1945: US atomic bomb.

- 1949: Soviet atomic bomb.

- 1949: The USA began the development of the hydrogen bomb, or H-bomb.

- 1952: US H-bomb.

- 1953: Soviet H-bomb.

- Mid-1950s: Nuclear weapons developed by the USA; began to be tested in the 1950s and became available in the early 1960s.

- 1957: The Soviet Union tested the first **Intercontinental Ballistic Missile** (ICBM). The USA responded by building its own ICBMs.

- Early 1960s: Nuclear weapons available.

- 1966: Soviet Union developed **Anti-Ballistic Missiles** (ABMs) that could shoot down ICBMs. These were almost immediately followed by **Multiple Independently Targeted Re-entry Vehicles** (MIRVs). These carried more than one warhead so they could hit more than one target and were, therefore, very difficult to shoot down.

- 1968: USA began to develop ABMs and MIRVs.

- 1982: USA deploys Cruise and Pershing missiles in Europe. Soviet Union deploys SS-20s.

- 1983: USA announces **Star Wars**.

▲ The Arms Race from the 1940s to the 1980s.

Not complete allies

Although the two sides had been allies in the war, relations had not been good since the Russian Revolution of 1917. The West had sent troops to fight against the communists in Russia in 1918. It had also done little before the Second World War to reach an agreement to work against Hitler. Everyone knew that Hitler hated communism and would attack the Soviet Union, but the West made only half-hearted efforts to reach an agreement with Stalin. Perhaps it didn't mind if Hitler attacked the Soviet Union. Then, during the war, the West ignored Stalin's appeals to invade mainland Europe in 1942 and 1943. This would have made Hitler withdraw troops from the Soviet Union. But the Allies were not ready for such an attack until 1944.

The Soviet view

It is interesting to see how people have different opinions. Stalin saw all the above events as examples of how the West did not want the Soviet Union to survive. So, after the war, he would have to take steps to ensure the safety of his country against the West.

The view of the West

The Allies thought that they were doing what they could to help the Soviet Union. But it was true that they did not trust Stalin. The British leader, Winston Churchill, said that as Germany was captured by Allied troops from the West, they should go as far East as possible. This would mean fewer places were left for the Soviet Army to flee from Germany – and fewer possible places for them to take over. After the war Stalin would try to spread communism in other countries and the West needed to stop this attempt to take over the world.

Source A

▲ The uneasy allies: Churchill of Britain, Roosevelt of the USA and Stalin of the Soviet Union at Yalta in 1945.

So, by 1945, Stalin was determined to expand communism in Eastern Europe to protect himself against the West. Meanwhile the West was determined to stop the spread of communism because they thought it was part of a plan to take over the world. These different ideas on what would happen were bound to cause problems.

Source B

One hell of a people who to a remarkable degree look like Americans, dress like Americans and think like Americans.

▲ A description of Soviet people in a US magazine in 1943. The US people would have been surprised to hear that the hated Communists were just like them really!

Why did rivalry develop between the superpowers after the Second World War?

The Yalta Conference 1945

By February 1945 Germany was close to defeat. Allied forces had marched across France and were about to invade Germany from the West. Soviet forces had marched through Eastern Europe and were about to invade Germany from the East. There was no doubt that Germany would be defeated, but what would happen then? After the First World War, Germany had recovered its strength and started another war. This must not be allowed to happen again. Therefore, the three countries met at **Yalta** in the Soviet Union to work out arrangements.

Dividing Germany

- It was decided to divide Germany into four zones. One would by occupied by the Soviet Union, one by France, one by the USA and one by Britain.

- Since the capital, Berlin was in the Soviet zone, it was agreed that it too would be split into four in exactly the same way.

This agreement sorted out what to do with Germany, but there were other decisions too.

- Poland would be given land taken from Germany in the West. But some of the land on its Eastern border would be given up to the Soviet Union.

- The Soviet Union would declare war on Japan within three months of the end of the war with Germany.

- Stalin agreed that the countries in Eastern Europe freed by his Red Army would have free elections (in other words, he would not put Communist governments in place against the people's wishes).

Yalta was a conference which had gone well, but it had not worked out full details. That was to be done at a second conference in **Potsdam**, near Germany, in July 1945. By the time the leaders met for this conference, relations had begun to get worse.

Stalin was already showing that he did not intend to keep his promise about free elections in Eastern Europe. President Roosevelt had died and been replaced with President Truman. Unlike Roosevelt, Truman did not trust Stalin and went to the Potsdam Conference determined 'to get tough with the Russians'. When the Soviet Foreign Secretary met Truman in April 1945, he came away from the meeting complaining, 'I have never been talked to like that in my life.' The Cold War was beginning.

Source A

We believed in our hearts that this was the dawn of a new day. The Russians had proved that they could be reasonable and there wasn't any doubt in the minds of the President or any of us that we could live with them peacefully.

▲ **One of Roosevelt's advisors remembering the optimistic feelings after Yalta.**

The Potsdam Conference 1945

When the three sides met some agreements were quickly reached:

- Germany and Berlin would be divided as agreed at Yalta.

- All decisions about how Germany should be governed would be taken jointly by all four countries – though it was agreed that, at some time in the future, the country would be reunited.

- The Nazi Party would be dissolved and war criminals punished.

- Germany would pay reparations.

- Britain, France, the USA and the Soviet Union would all join the United Nations.

- There would be free elections, a free press and freedom of speech in Germany. In other words, there would be no censorship of what people could say or write.

Source B

▲ The leaders at Potsdam. By now they were Attlee of Britain, Truman of the USA and Stalin of the USSR.

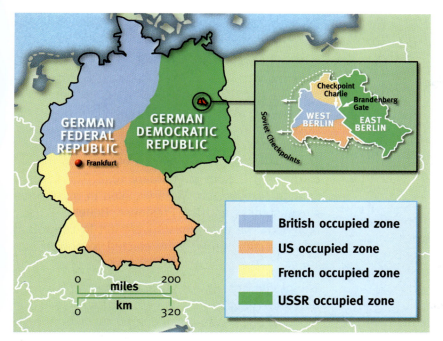

▲ The eventual division of Germany and Berlin.

Source C

The Soviet Union does not claim the right to interfere in matters relating to Belgium or Greece.

We understand how important these countries are to the security of Britain.

But Poland has borders with the Soviet Union, not Britain or the USA.

▲ Part of a letter from Stalin to Truman and Churchill explaining why the Soviet Union had a right to interfere in Poland.

Problems

Although there were agreements, there were also some serious disagreements. President Truman tried to force Stalin to allow free elections in the countries of Eastern Europe that had been occupied by Soviet forces at the end of the war. Stalin was now convinced that it was vital to the security of the Soviet Union to get communist governments in these countries.

So, when Truman asked why Stalin wasn't allowing free elections in Poland, Stalin asked what was happening in Greece. This was a difficult question. There was a civil war in Greece and Britain had sent troops to fight against the communist side. If Stalin wasn't supposed to interfere in Poland, why could the British interfere in Greece?

Another thing which bothered Stalin was the atomic bomb. Truman announced at Potsdam that the USA had this bomb. Stalin feared it might be used to threaten the Soviet Union after the war. He was angry that the Americans had not told him earlier about its existence. Obviously they were keeping it secret for a purpose (although Stalin's spies had told him about it long before the Potsdam meeting).

So, the Potsdam meeting ended with the two sides distrusting each other even more than they had before the meeting.

Questions

1 What was the Cold War?

2 Why did it break out after the Second World War?

3 What does the Potsdam Conference tell us about relations between the Soviet Union and the West after the Second World War?

What to do about Germany?

The allies had decided to split Germany and, at some stage, to reunite it. But they had not agreed how to govern their various zones. Soon a major difference in their approach became obvious.

The Soviet approach

Germany had invaded the Soviet Union in 1941 and 20 million Soviet citizens had died in the war that followed. So Stalin was determined to keep Germany weak to make sure this could not happy again. Machinery and equipment were taken from Germany back to the Soviet Union to help rebuild the country. This kept Germany weak and helped the Soviet Union recover.

The approach of the Western powers

The Western powers did not fear Germany in the same way. They wanted to rebuild their sectors and allow Germany to recover economically. The Second World War had been caused partly by Germany being treated so badly after the First World War that the people turned to Hitler for revenge. The Western powers wanted to avoid that by helping Germany get back on its feet – therefore saving the cost of having to run their sectors.

So, in December 1946, Britain and the USA (and later France) joined their zones together in an economic union called **Bizonia**. They also planned to introduce a new currency. This was the first step towards the recovery of Germany. But Stalin was furious. He had not been consulted and he did not want to see Germany strong again.

Spreading Soviet control

At the end of the Second World War most of the countries of Eastern Europe had been **liberated** from Nazi occupation by the Soviet Red Army. These countries were grateful to the communist Soviet Union and there was much support for communism in the region.

Stalin wanted to ensure that this support survived as he considered it vital to the security of his country. He tried to get communist governments elected in these countries by using

persuasion and also by placing communists in the civil service, police and trade unions.

In Poland Stalin had set up a communist government in 1944. The first countries to actually elect communist governments were Romania in March 1945 and Bulgaria in November 1945. But things were not always so straightforward. In Czechoslovakia the communists could not win an election so they carried out a **coup** in February 1948. The Czech Foreign Minister, Jan Masaryk, died in mysterious circumstances and the President, Benes, resigned. The communists were left in control. In Hungary communists were elected to power in 1949.

Things did not always go according to plan, however. A communist government was set up in Albania, but it was not prepared to take orders from Moscow. In Yugoslavia President Tito refused to co-operate with Stalin. Yugoslavia was communist, but was not going to do just what Stalin wanted either. In fact it was expelled from **COMINFORM** (see page 272) for failing to obey instructions from Moscow.

Source D

"IF WE DON'T LET HIM WORK, WHO'S GOING TO KEEP HIM?"

▲ **A British cartoon of 1946. It is saying that unless Germany is allowed to recover and look after itself, the Allies will have to pay to run it.**

The Iron Curtain

By the end of 1946 it was obvious that the Soviet Union and the Western powers were not going to get on. Stalin decided to build a 1600 kilometre fence cutting off the Eastern European countries from the West. In time this would mean a division between communist and non-communist countries. No contact would be allowed and barbed wire, dogs, control towers and remote-controlled weapons would ensure that this was the case. The British leader, Winston Churchill, talked of how this was like setting up an '**Iron Curtain**' and the name stuck.

The Truman Doctrine, the Marshall Plan and the Soviet response

President Truman believed that his country had a duty to support countries trying to stand against communism. He published his beliefs which became known as the **Truman Doctrine**.

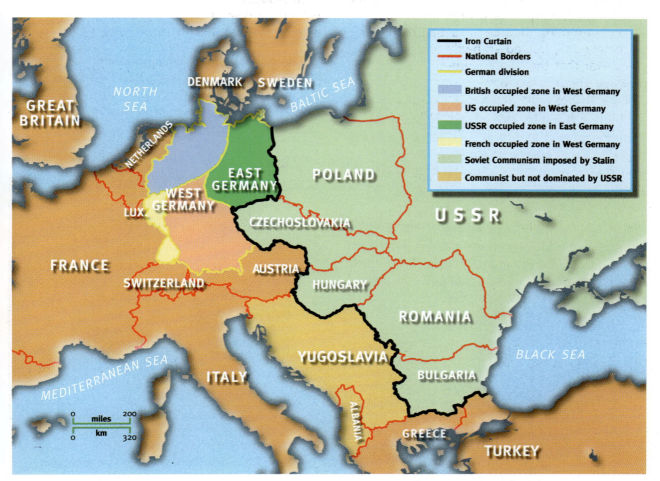

▲ **Europe during 1945–48, showing the Iron Curtain and the countries under Soviet control.**

He said he would give help to any country threatened by rebellion from within its borders or by an outside power. He didn't mention communism or the Soviet Union, but everyone knew what he meant. Stalin was angry and claimed that the Truman Doctrine was just a way to get bases in countries for US bombers (see Source B). Stalin set up COMINFORM, which brought together all the Communist Parties of Europe. It was designed to strengthen communism and counter the Truman Doctrine.

Why was the Truman Doctrine published?
Truman wanted to stop the spread of communism. He saw the devastation that the war had caused and the pressure that countries were under from the Soviet Union. So he hoped that by promising support he could persuade some of the Eastern European countries to break away from communism. The USA had already provided US$400 million of aid to Greece. Perhaps the promise of financial help would persuade other countries.

Marshall Aid
So, to back up the Truman Doctrine, the USA announced **Marshall Aid**. In June 1947 President Truman said that grants of US dollars would be available to all European countries to help rebuild their economies after the problems caused by the war.

A meeting was held in 1947 to discuss who should receive the grants. At first communist countries were looking to get grants, but when they realised that the money had to be spent in ways which would develop capitalism in their countries they became less keen.

Source B

The Truman Doctrine meant in reality the building of bases in countries for US bombers. This has been justified by making outspoken claims of defending democracy and peace.

▲ **The Soviet view of the Truman Doctrine. From a history book published in the Soviet Union.**

Once Stalin saw what the USA was up to he stopped the communist countries applying. Instead he set up **COMECON** (Council for Mutual Economic Assistance) to offer Eastern European countries aid from the Soviet Union – though it did not have anything like the wealth of the USA.

So the only countries which accepted Marshall Aid were those in the West. Between them 17 countries received US$13.75 billion, which allowed them to recover more quickly than the countries of Eastern Europe.

Source A

I believe that it must be the policy of the USA to support free peoples who are resisting takeover by armed minorities in their own country, or by outside countries.

▲ **An extract from the Truman Doctrine.**

The Berlin Blockade

Marshall Aid helped the three sectors of Berlin under Western control (West Berlin) to develop their economies more quickly than the Soviet controlled area (East Berlin). Since travel between the various sections was not subject to controls, many East Berliners crossed into West Berlin to work and saw how much better off the people living there were.

Berlin itself was in the middle of the Soviet controlled part of Germany and Stalin hated the fact that West Berlin was like a capitalist island in the middle of the communist zone. He also objected to the formation of Bizonia (see page 270) and proposals for a new currency.

(see page 270)

Source C

▲ A Soviet poster attacking the Marshall Plan.

Source D

Our policy is not directed against any country or belief. It is directed against hunger, poverty, desperation and chaos.

▲ George C. Marshall explain the reason for setting up the Marshall Plan.

Stalin did not want West Berlin becoming prosperous. He still thought that Germany had to stay weak to stop it ever being a threat to the Soviet Union again.

So, in June 1948, Stalin tried to persuade the Western powers to give up their sectors. He closed all the road and rail routes between West Berlin and the distant Western controlled parts of Germany. West Berlin would soon run out of food and other supplies. Stalin hoped that the Western allies would not try to break through his **blockade**, but would instead feel that it was not worth the trouble maintaining capitalist West Berlin in the middle of the Soviet sector of Germany. Instead, they would withdraw and leave Stalin to control all of Berlin.

The reaction of the West

The Western powers knew that Stalin was trying to bully them out of Berlin. They knew that, at Potsdam, they had agreed with Stalin how Germany should be governed, but they were fed up with his unco-operative attitude.

So they stood by their plans for West Berlin and were determined not to pull out of the city. As the US Commander in the city said, 'If West Berlin falls, West Germany will follow.' But the Western powers did not want to smash through Stalin's road and rail blocks because that might cause war. So, instead, they decided to supply West Berlin by air.

Airlift

This was a clever idea as it now meant that, if Stalin wanted to stop the supplying of West Berlin, he would have to shoot the planes down. He wouldn't look very good shooting down planes just because they were carrying food supplies to innocent civilians!

From June 1948 to September 1949 the Western powers made 277,264 flights and brought in an average 8000 tonnes of supplies each day. There were 79 pilots killed in accidents during this period.

Eventually Stalin gave up and lifted the blockade. The Western powers were not going to give up West Berlin, so there was no point carrying on with the blockade. What the blockade had proved to the West was that there was no point hoping that Stalin would co-operate and that he wasn't going to keep the promises he had made at Yalta and Potsdam.

THE BIRD WATCHER

▲ A British cartoon from 1948. Stalin is watching the birds supply West Berlin. But he does not dare shoot them down.

Questions

1 Explain in three or four lines what the following were:
   a the Iron Curtain
   b Bizonia
   c the Truman Doctrine
   d the Marshall Plan
   e NATO
   f the Warsaw Pact.

2 Explain why Stalin did the following:
   a Stopped East European countries receiving Marshall Aid.
   b Set up the Berlin blockade.
   c Formed the German Democratic Republic.

3 Look at Source E on page 274. What do you think the cartoonist was trying to say when he drew this cartoon?

NATO, the Warsaw Pact and the Arms Race

The Berlin blockade had convinced the West that it could not work with Stalin. It had to make sure it was protected against the Soviet Union. In April 1949 12 countries (including Britain, the USA and France) joined together in the **North Atlantic Treaty Organisation** (**NATO**). If any country was attacked, the others would declare war to support it.

In May 1949 the Western powers formally joined their sectors of Germany together to form the **Federal Republic of Germany** (West Germany). The new country received aid under the Marshall Plan. In return, in October 1949 the Soviet Union established the **German Democratic Republic** (East Germany). No matter what had been agreed in any conferences, Germany was now formally split in two.

The Death of Stalin

Stalin died in 1953. At first it seemed that his death would make no difference to the Soviet Union's relations with the West. For example, in 1955, the **Warsaw Pact** was signed bringing all the communist countries together in an alliance to compete with NATO.

Although there were eight members of the Warsaw Pact (the Soviet Union, Romania, Hungary, Poland, Czechoslovakia, Bulgaria, Albania and East Germany), really it was a military alliance run by the Soviet Union. Soviet troops were stationed in other East European countries and were used, when necessary, to keep control for the communists.

Coexistence

Although the new Soviet leader, Nikita Khrushchev, appeared to have the same approach to the West as Stalin, this was not quite true.

Stalin had built barriers across Europe to keep out Western ideas and to keep in the Soviet people. He felt that the Soviet Union needed protecting from the West and that there should be as little contact as possible. Khrushchev thought that contact was acceptable and that the Soviet Union should compete with the West to show that its communist system was better. This was called **coexistence**.

Some people thought that Khrushchev's approach meant that the Soviet Union would not be so tough an opponent for the West. But they were wrong. Khrushchev had no intention of threatening the security of his country. Whilst he was in power, he increased spending on weapons and made sure the Soviet Union competed fully in the **Arms Race**.

The Arms Race

At the end of the Second World War, the USA had developed an **atomic bomb** which it dropped on Japan. The Soviet Union was concerned that it did not have this bomb and its scientists worked hard to catch up with the USA. In July 1949 the Soviet Union exploded its first atomic bomb. It was now the equal of the USA in firepower. For the next 50 years the two sides took part in an arms race, trying to build bigger and better weapons than the other side. Huge sums of money were poured into research and weapon building.

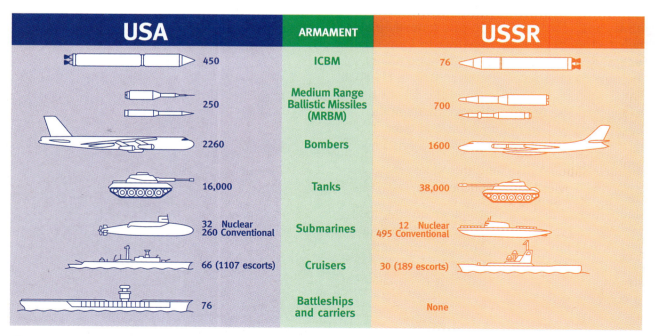

USA	ARMAMENT	USSR
450	ICBM	76
250	Medium Range Ballistic Missiles (MRBM)	700
2260	Bombers	1600
16,000	Tanks	38,000
32 Nuclear 260 Conventional	Submarines	12 Nuclear 495 Conventional
66 (1107 escorts)	Cruisers	30 (189 escorts)
76	Battleships and carriers	None

▲ The Arms Race between the USA and the Soviet Union showing the armaments each superpower had.

In 1952 the USA exploded a new hydrogen or **H-bomb**. Nine months later the Soviet Union had one too. Soon both sides were testing nuclear weapons. There were several other important developments:

- **Inter-Continental Ballistic Missiles** (ICBMs) – these were missiles which could carry a warhead from one continent to another, without using a plane to drop a bomb.

- **Anti-Ballistic Missiles** – these were missiles that could shoot down ICBMs.

- **Multiple Independently Targeted Re-entry Vehicles** (MIRVs) These missiles had more than one warhead and so more than one target.

Communism is better

Khrushchev wanted to show the world that communism was a better way of running a country. So he set about competing with the West in sport, in space and in helping newly-independent countries.

Sport

Khrushchev wanted his country to be the leading sporting nation. Large sums of money were put into developing sporting facilities and this approach soon paid off. The Soviet Union won a large number of medals at the Melbourne Olympics in 1956. By the Rome Olympics in 1960 it topped the medal table. This superiority continued into the 1980s.

Space

The USA and the Soviet Union were both determined to show the technological superiority of their nation by winning the 'space race'. In 1957 the Soviet Union launched the first satellite into space (**Sputnik 1**). In 1958 the USA sent monkeys into space and brought them safely back to Earth. Then, to their delight, the Soviets sent the first man into space (**Yuri Gagarin**). Just one year later John Glen became the first American in space.

In 1969 the first men on the moon were Americans, **Armstrong** and **Aldrin**. Although the space race allowed the Soviet Union to be a technological giant, the expense was one of the main causes of bankruptcy in the 1980s.

Aid to other countries

Khrushchev wanted to spread support for the Soviet Union. One way to do this was to provide financial help to countries which became independent from European Empires in the 1950s and 1960s. So loans and specialist workers were provided for countries in Africa and Asia. Of course, this also cost large sums of money and contributed to the bankruptcy of the Soviet Union in later years.

Source A

▲ Soviet athletes on the medal rostrum at the Rome Olympics in 1960.

Relations between the Soviet Union and the USA

The US government found Khrushchev a difficult man to deal with. His policy of coexistence seemed to suggest that he wanted to get on better with the West, but his actions showed that he was determined to make his country the most powerful in the world.

Khrushchev's character was also difficult to judge. On his travels he would deliberately go out of his way to attract newspaper attention. Sometimes he would ignore the agreed schedule and do something else – like go over to talk to factory workers. He was a lively and interesting character who made the more subdued President Eisenhower of the USA look dull. This was one of the reasons why, in 1960, the USA elected the younger and more lively John F. Kennedy.

Source B

▲ Sputnik. The first satellite launched into space. Satellite television would soon be available!

Source C

The Sputniks proved that the economy, science, culture and creative genius of the people was better in communist countries.

▲ Krushchev explaining how important the space race was to his country.

Source D

Americans were extremely concerned. Short-range rockets were installed in Turkey and Italy. Money was poured into missile and bomber programmes.

▲ A US historian explaining how his country's politicians reacted to the news that the Soviet Union had launched a satellite into space.

Questions

1 In what ways was Khrushchev's attitude towards the West different from that of Stalin.

2 Why were sport and space so important to the Soviet Union and the USA during the Cold War?

3 **a** What point was Khrushchev trying to make in Source C?
   b Why do you think the USA reacted as it did in Source D?

The nature of the Cold War: Poland, Hungary, Berlin, Cuba; the differences between communist and non-communist societies

In February 1956 Khrushchev made a speech which shocked the Soviet Union. In his '**Secret Speech**' at the Party Congress he criticised the way Stalin had treated the people of the Soviet Union and other communist countries.

In some countries, such as Poland and Hungary, people thought this meant that they would not be so controlled by the Soviet Union. They soon found out that this was not the case.

Poland

In June 1956 there was rioting in Poland and over 100 people were killed. The Polish people wanted more freedom than they were allowed by their communist leaders. On 21 October, Wladislaw Gomulka became the new leader of the Polish Communist Party. Khrushchev was not sure whether Gomulka was strong enough to govern Poland and deal with the rioting. The Polish Minister of Defence wanted Gomulka sacked and Soviet troops brought in.

In the end, Khrushchev sacked the Defence Minister and supported Gomulka. But he also made him promise that Poland would remain a loyal member of the Warsaw Pact and that there would be no changes to weaken communist control in Poland.

Hungary

The position in Hungary was very similar. The people thought that Khrushchev was weaker than Stalin and would let them bring changes to the way their country was run. In October 1956 they elected Imre Nagy as their Prime Minister. He was not a strong communist and favoured change.

Soon there was rioting in the streets and fighting developed between Soviet and Hungarian forces.

At first Khrushchev withdrew Soviet forces and left it to Nagy to deal with the rioting. But when he allowed non-communists into his government and said that Hungary would be leaving the Warsaw Pact, Khrushchev had to act. He could not allow any country to leave the Warsaw Pact because it was so important in defending the Soviet Union.

In Hungary thousands of people took to the streets in rebellion against Soviet control. Rumours spread that the USA was sending troops to help the uprising. But the USA knew this might lead to war and did not send troops. In November Khrushchev sent Soviet troops into Hungary. In bitter fighting 7000 Soviet soldiers and 30,000 Hungarians were killed. Nagy was arrested and later shot.

The uprising had been put down. The West protested, but took no action. The Hungarians felt betrayed.

Source A

▲ **Soviet tanks on the streets of the Hungarian capital, Budapest, in November 1956.**

Berlin – the hole in the Iron Curtain

By the end of 1949 many East Berliners and East Germans had come to believe that life was better in the West. The authorities would not let them leave East Germany to cross into West Germany, but there were no restrictions on crossing into West Berlin from East Berlin. So from 1949 hundreds of thousands of people crossed from East to West in Berlin. On average the number ranged between 20,000 and 25,000 each month.

Why did people cross?

Many of the **defectors** were well educated professionals, such as teachers, doctors, lecturers and engineers. These were just the sort of people that East Germany needed to help develop its economy. What made such people abandon their roots and move to the West?

- **Lack of freedom**. There were few freedoms in the East. Only one political party, the Communist Party, was allowed. There was censorship of newspapers, radio and television, so that only the official version of the news was reported. It was almost impossible to find out what was really happening both inside the country and outside. The secret police ensured that people did as they were told. Criticism of the government and the Communist Party was not allowed. Anyone publicly criticising the way the country was run was likely to be arrested and imprisoned.

- **Lack of consumer goods**. Compared with the West, East Germany was poor. Wages were low and there was a lack of opportunities for educated and skilled people to earn the level of wages that they could get in the West. The failure to invest in the country after the Second World War meant that East German industry was run-down. There were few consumer goods and owning a fridge or a car was just a dream to many East German citizens.

There were, of course, benefits to living in the East. All citizens had a job, prices of goods were kept low and rent, electricity, gas and telephone charges were only a fraction of what was charged in the West. Public transport was cheap and very reliable. But none of this compared with the opportunities for freedom and higher wages in the West.

Stopping defectors

The West wanted to reunify East and West Germany, but Khrushchev was not interested. What he wanted was to stop people defecting from East to West. If the country was reunited, it was bound to be dominated by the richer West Germany. In September 1960 he ordered that anyone wanting to cross from East to West Berlin had to obtain a police pass.

Then on 13 August 1961 he solved his problem. A border of machine guns and barbed wire was built between East and West Berlin. Three days later, work started on the 45 kilometre concrete **Berlin Wall**. It was announced that anyone trying to cross the wall would be shot. In its first year, 41 East Germans lost their lives trying to cross.

Why did Khrushchev decide to build the Berlin Wall?

Obviously, Khrushchev wanted to build the wall to stop defectors from East Berlin to West Berlin. But the decision to build it in August 1961 was the result of a series of events which made Khrushchev feel that he had gained the upper-hand over the USA.

- In 1959 **Fidel Castro** took over in Cuba. After the USA refused to give him financial help, he became an ally of the Soviet Union.

- In May 1960 a US spy plane, the U2, was shot down over the Soviet Union and its pilot captured. At the time Khrushchev was at a summit meeting with Eisenhower. When Eisenhower refused to apologise for spying on the Soviet Union, Khrushchev walked out of the summit.

▲ **Attempts to cross the Berlin Wall dividing East
and West Berlin usually resulted in death.**

- In 1961 the USA gave support to an attempt
  to overthrow the Cuban leader. There was an
  invasion at the **Bay of Pigs** that went so
  badly wrong that the Americans looked
  foolish.

- In June 1961 Khrushchev met the young new
  President Kennedy at a summit meeting in
  Vienna. Khrushchev thought Kennedy was
  inexperienced and weak.

All these events gave Khrushchev the confidence
to build the Berlin Wall – and take his next step
to try to outwit the USA.

Questions

1 Explain why the following things
   happened:
   a Soviet troops were sent into Hungary in
   November 1956.
   b People defected from East Berlin to
   West Berlin.
   c Khrushchev ordered the building of the
   Berlin Wall.

Source C

CHERRY PICKER

LAUNCH PAD WITH ERECTOR

LAUNCH PAD WITH ERECTOR

MISSILE READY BLDGS.

OXIDIZER VEHICLES

FUELING VEHICLES

▲ A photograph of the missile sites in Cuba with labels added by the US government.

Cuba

In 1959 Fulgencio Batista was overthrown as leader of Cuba by Fidel Castro. This was a blow to the USA. Cuba was only 150 kilometres from the USA and it was important that it was governed by someone friendly to the Americans. Batista had allowed the USA to invest heavily in his country and was a good friend.

The US President, Eisenhower, did not approve of Castro's takeover. He refused to give him aid and cut down the amount of sugar which the USA bought from Cuba. This meant that Cuba would have little income. So Castro asked the Soviet Union for help. Khrushchev was happy to agree to buy 1 million tonnes of Cuban sugar every year.

Castro had financial support and Khrushchev had a friend on the USA's doorstep.

The USA angered

The USA was extremely angry about what Castro had done – especially when he **nationalised** US businesses and property in Cuba. The Americans tried to assassinate him but failed. They also supported an invasion by anti-Castro Cubans at the Bay of Pigs in April 1961. The invasion was a disaster and President Kennedy, who had agreed to the attack, was made to look foolish.

Castro and communism

In December 1961 Castro announced he was setting up a communist government in Cuba. The USA was horrified. Khrushchev was delighted. Now he intended to take advantage of his new communist friend so close to the USA.

The Missile Crisis

On 14 October 1962 a US spy plane brought frightening news from Cuba. The Soviet Union was building missile bases in Cuba. Once missiles were in place on Cuba, then most of the USA would be within their range. The security of the country was at risk.

What to do?

Then came more bad news. Soviet ships, 20 of them, had been spotted on their way to Cuba, carrying what appeared to be missiles. Kennedy knew he had to act to stop the missiles. But what could he do? He called his advisors together and listened to what they said. Most of them suggested invading Cuba. But the USA was not at war with Cuba and it had not broken any international agreements. If the USA invaded, the Soviet Union would almost certainly help Castro. Then there might be a nuclear war. Of course, Kennedy could just sink the Soviet ships. Then there almost certainly would be a war!

Kennedy's solution

On 22 October 1962 Kennedy went on US television and told the US people what he intended to do. He knew that the message would soon get back to Khrushchev. He said that he would not allow missiles to be set up in Cuba:

'All ships bound for Cuba will, if found to contain cargoes of offensive weapons, be turned back'.

Then he called on Khrushchev to 'halt this reckless and provocative threat to world peace'.

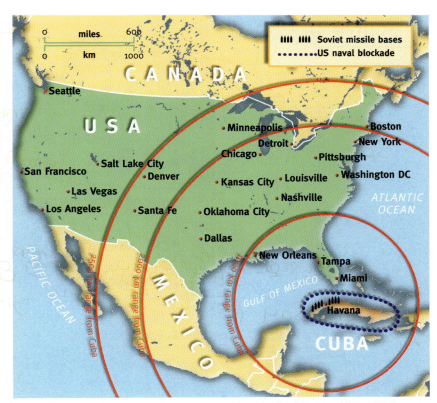

▲ **This map shows the cities that were threatened by missiles on Cuba.**

Kennedy's speech was a brave one. He intended to stop the Soviet ships and search them. But what if they refused to stop. Would he board them by force? Or sink them?

The next day (23 October) Kennedy had a reply from Khrushchev who warned the USA that 'its government is playing with fire and the fate of the world'.

First to blink?

Kennedy lined up his ships around Cuba and waited. At the same time he put his forces on full alert and got 156 ICBMs ready to fire. The world held its breath. Was this going to be the start of the war that everyone dreaded? Then, on 24 October, some Soviet ships turned around and the others stopped. Khruschev sent Kennedy two letters.

Source D

▲ A cartoon published in 1962 during the Cuban Missile Crisis. It shows Khrushchev and Kennedy.

- The first letter said that, if the USA withdrew its blockade and agreed not to invade Cuba, Khrushchev would withdraw any missiles on Cuba and send no more.

- But the second was more menacing. In it Khrushchev complained that US missiles were stationed in countries surrounding the Soviet Union. So what was the USA's problem with missiles in Cuba?

Kennedy decided to ignore the second letter and reply to the first. He sent a message to Khrushchev saying that he agreed:

1. The Soviet Union would remove the missile bases from Cuba.

2. The USA would remove the blockade and give assurances that it would not invade Cuba.

The world breathed a mighty sigh of relief. War had been avoided – though only just!

Further concessions

Several days after the crisis, President Kennedy's brother, Robert, met the Soviet Ambassador in the USA. Robert Kennedy made an informal promise that missiles in Turkey and Italy (which threatened the Soviet Union) would be removed. This could not be announced immediately because the USA's NATO allies would have to agree. Keeping it secret would also make it look more like Khrushchev had given in. Three months later the missiles were quietly removed.

Why did the Cuban Missile Crisis end like this?

- The good sense of the two leaders, Kennedy and Khrushchev, ensured that they stepped back when war seemed likely.

- Kennedy could have invaded Cuba or sunk the Soviet ships. Khrushchev could have kept his ships sailing until the USA was forced to sink them.

- Both leaders realised that it was important to allow the other to save face. So Kennedy publicly agreed not to invade Cuba and privately agreed to remove missiles from Turkey and Italy. Khrushchev agreed to remove the missiles from Cuba, but also gained more security for his country.

Historians have debated who 'won' the Cuban Missile crisis. Source F gives the US view and Source G the Soviet view. It is interesting to see different interpretations of the same incident.

Source F

John F. Kennedy had won. The Soviet government was backing down. The Russians did dismantle the bases. They took everything away.

▲ The views of a US historian.

Source E

It is not the first step that concerns me, but having to go on to a fourth or fifth step. And I don't want to go to the sixth step.

▲ President Kennedy talking about the dangers of the Cuban Missile Crisis.

Source G

Kennedy gave in.

It was a great victory for us, a spectacular success without having to fire a shot.

▲ What Nikita Khrushchev wrote about the Cuban Missile Crisis in his memoirs.

Questions

1 Why did the USA care about the fact that it had spotted Soviet nuclear bases on Cuba?

2 Why did Kennedy have to be very careful about how he reacted to what Khrushchev was doing?

3 Look at Source D. What do you think the cartoonist was trying to say?

4 Read Source E. What do you think Kennedy meant?

5 Read Sources F and G. Can you explain why these two sources say such different things?

Détente: Cuba to Afghanistan and the roles of Reagan and Gorbachev

Source A shows the way that many people saw the Cuban Missile Crisis – as a trial of strength between two men, Kennedy and Khrushchev. That trial of strength had almost brought the world to war. What was needed now was a way to prevent such problems happening again.

In his discussions with Khrushchev, Kennedy had talked about 'détente'. By this, he meant a lessening of tension and better relations between the two superpowers. Kennedy was pleased to discover that Khrushchev was keen to accept this offer.

After the Cuba affair, a 'hotline' was set up between the **White House** and the **Kremlin**. In times of crisis, the two leaders would be able to communicate directly and immediately.

In 1963 the **Test Ban Treaty** was signed stopping nuclear tests above ground. It was a tiny step in limiting the arms race, but it was a sign of the new spirit of co-operation.

Brezhnev, Vietnam and Czechoslovakia

Unfortunately the co-operation did not last long. In 1964 Khrushchev was replaced by Brezhnev. The new Soviet leader was determined to maintain the military strength of his country and to increase spending on arms. Then two events occurred which worsened relations between the two countries.

Firstly, in 1965 President Johnson of the USA decided to send US troops to Vietnam. Before this, the USA had only 'military advisors' in Vietnam, but from 1965 the number of troops rose until it reached a peak in 1969. Since the USA was helping South Vietnam fight communist guerillas and communist North Vietnam, sending troops did little for relations with the Soviet Union. It was not until 1973 that the last US troops left Vietnam. Some South Vietnamese civilians chose to leave too rather than live in the new communist country.

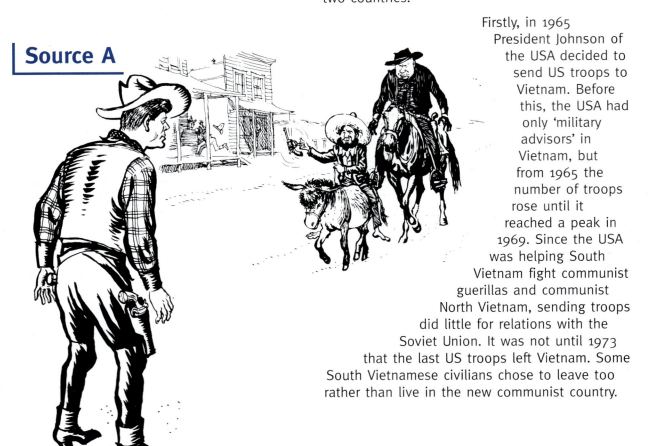

Source A

▲ How some people saw the Cuban Missile Crisis – a gunfight between Kennedy and Khrushchev.

Source B

American Presidents 1945-1990
Truman
Eisenhower
Kennedy
Johnson
Nixon
Carter
Reagan
Bush

▲ American Presidents
1945–1990

◄ South Vietnamese civilians
scrambling aboard a US
helicopter to leave South
Vietnam.

Secondly, in January 1968 the government of Czechoslovakia introduced a policy which became known as '**the Prague Spring**'. It promised freedom of speech for the public, the press and religion. Brezhnev was very concerned and ordered the Czech Prime Minister, Alexander **Dubcek**, to stop his reforms. Dubcek refused and appeared to be getting support for his changes from other Communist leaders, such as Presidents **Tito** of Yugoslavia and **Ceausescu** of Romania. Brezhnev knew he could not allow this weakening of Communism. He sent 20,000 Soviet troops into Czechoslovakia, dismissed Dubcek and reversed the changes. The USA complained bitterly about 'Soviet bully-boy tactics'.

Despite the worsening of relations, a **Nuclear Non-Proliferation Treaty** was signed in which the two superpowers agreed not supply nuclear technology to other countries.

Nixon and SALT talks

President Nixon wanted to improve relations with the communists. It was he who began withdrawing troops from Vietnam and he also made efforts to improve relations with communist China. He was helped by the fact that Brezhnev had come to the conclusion that the Soviet Union could not afford to keep spending huge sums on the arms race. The time had come to reduce military spending.

In 1970 the Soviet Union and the USA began the **Strategic Arms Limitation Talks (SALT)** and a treaty was signed in 1972.

The SALT Treaty said that:

- There would be a five year hold on building missiles.

- At the end of the five years a further agreement would be made.

Meetings were also held to discuss reducing the numbers in the armed forces. You can see how difficult this was when you realise that after 300 meetings no real agreement had been reached.

The spirit of détente, however, did lead to a trade deal between the two countries, greater artistic and sporting links; and Soviet and US astronauts linked up in space for the first time in 1975.

Détente extended

- In 1975 the USA and the Soviet Union, along with 33 other countries, signed the **Helsinki Agreement** on Human Rights. They agreed to guarantee basic human rights for all, regardless of race, sex, language or religion.

- In 1979 SALT II was signed in which further reductions in arms were agreed.

Détente destroyed

But even before SALT II was signed, relations had begun to break down again. In 1977 President Carter of the USA criticised the Soviet record on human rights. He wanted to discuss human rights at the same time as arms reductions. The Soviet Union was not prepared to do this. Then, in 1979, a series of events destroyed détente.

Source C

▲ Many civilians wanted arms reductions too. This protest is against US missiles in Britain.

Weapons Allowed	USA	Soviet Union
ICBMs	1000	1600
SLBMs	650	700

▲ The number of missiles agreed at SALT I.

Weapons Allowed	USA	Soviet Union
ICBMs	1054	1398
SLBMs	656	950

▲ The number of missiles agreed at SALT II.

- The ruler of Iran, the **Shah**, was overthrown and an Islamic republic set up. The US embassy was attacked and hostages were taken. The USA feared that the new government would be pro-Soviet.

- In Nicaragua in South America, communist guerillas were given help by the Soviet Union and the Cubans were helping rebels in Angola.

- In Europe new missiles were being put in place in communist countries.

These events made the USA distrustful of the Soviet Union. But where relations really broke down was over Afghanistan.

Afghanistan

On 25 December 1979 the Soviet Union invaded Afghanistan, executed the President and set up a communist government. Brezhnev said the action had been taken after an urgent request from the government of Afghanistan.

The West was shocked by the action. The USA broke off trade relations and refused to **ratify** SALT II. Even more damaging to Soviet pride was a US boycott of the 1980 Olympics, because they were being held in Moscow.

Questions

1 What do the following mean?
  a détente
  b ICBMs
  c SALT

2 **a** Make a list of the main events in the relations between the two superpowers in the years 1963–1979.
  b Beside each event say whether you think the event improved relations between the USA and the Soviet Union, made relations worse or had no effect on relations.

Source D

▲ **US citizens taken hostage when the embassy in Iran was attacked.**

The Reagan Years

In 1981 Ronald Reagan became US President. There were two major influences in his relations with the Soviet Union.

1. He hated the Soviet Union and did not trust what he called 'the Evil Empire'.

2. He believed in tax cuts, so if it was possible to cut arms spending he would be interested. But not if it weakened his country.

So what happened?

- In 1981 Reagan put forward his idea for the **zero-option** on Intermediate Range Missiles. Each side would dismantle all such weapons in Europe. Brezhnev refused.

- In Poland the communist government was having great difficulty controlling the trade union, **Solidarity**, led by **Lech Walesa**. When Walesa was imprisoned, Reagan stopped all technological exports to the Soviet Union to show his disapproval. Walesa was released in 1982, but Solidarity was banned by the Polish government. It did not, however, give up and it continued to campaign.

- In 1982 **Strategic Arms Reduction Talks (START)** began, but they came to nothing.

- Then Reagan announced his support for **Star Wars**. This was a plan to use lasers from space to destroy enemy missiles. The Soviet Union condemned this idea (though no-one knew if it would work).

- Relations continued to deteriorate. The Soviet Union condemned the US invasion of Grenada in 1983 and stopped the East European communist countries from attending the Los Angeles Olympics in 1984.

Problems with the Soviet leadership

By the late 1970s Brezhnev was seriously ill and it was difficult to get decisions made in the Soviet Union.

- When Brezhnev died in 1982 he was replaced by Yuri Andropov.

- Almost immediately Andropov contracted a serious kidney disease and died in 1984.

- His successor, Konstantin Chernenko, lasted only 13 months and died in 1985.

These changes in leadership meant that no decisive action was taken to bring about change in the Soviet Union. The economic position continued to decline and corruption continued to make good government harder.

Enter Mikhail Gorbachev

Gorbachev came to power in 1985. He knew that the Soviet Union was bankrupt and that there had to be rapid change. He quickly introduced two policies:

1. **Perestroika**. This involved a major change in the way the Soviet economy was run. Now there was to be competition and an end to rigid state control.

2. **Glasnost**. The government of the Soviet Union was to become more 'open'. The secret police had their powers restricted and criticism of the government was allowed. Free elections were to be held in 1990.

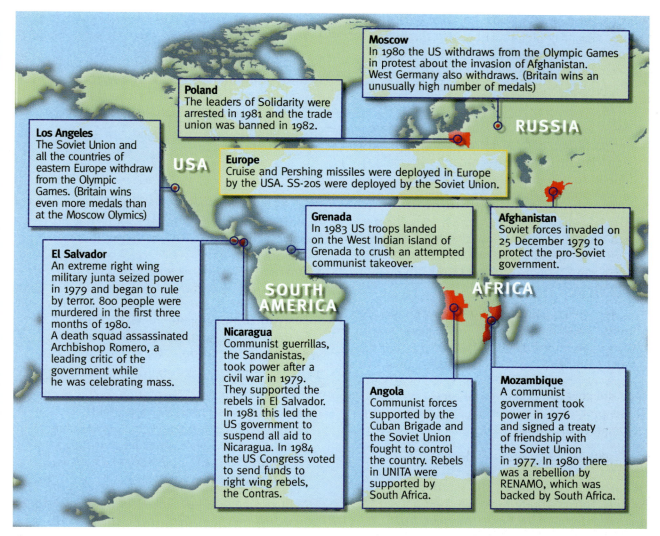

Moscow
In 1980 the US withdraws from the Olympic Games in protest about the invasion of Afghanistan. West Germany also withdraws. (Britain wins an unusually high number of medals)

Poland
The leaders of Solidarity were arrested in 1981 and the trade union was banned in 1982.

Los Angeles
The Soviet Union and all the countries of eastern Europe withdraw from the Olympic Games. (Britain wins even more medals than at the Moscow Olymics)

Europe
Cruise and Pershing missiles were deployed in Europe by the USA. SS-20s were deployed by the Soviet Union.

Grenada
In 1983 US troops landed on the West Indian island of Grenada to crush an attempted communist takeover.

Afghanistan
Soviet forces invaded on 25 December 1979 to protect the pro-Soviet government.

El Salvador
An extreme right wing military junta seized power in 1979 and began to rule by terror. 800 people were murdered in the first three months of 1980.
A death squad assassinated Archbishop Romero, a leading critic of the government while he was celebrating mass.

Nicaragua
Communist guerrillas, the Sandanistas, took power after a civil war in 1979. They supported the rebels in El Salvador. In 1981 this led the US government to suspend all aid to Nicaragua. In 1984 the US Congress voted to send funds to right wing rebels, the Contras.

Angola
Communist forces supported by the Cuban Brigade and the Soviet Union fought to control the country. Rebels in UNITA were supported by South Africa.

Mozambique
A communist government took power in 1976 and signed a treaty of friendship with the Soviet Union in 1977. In 1980 there was a rebellion by RENAMO, which was backed by South Africa.

RUSSIA

USA

SOUTH AMERICA

AFRICA

▲ The incidents around the world between 1976 and 1984 which killed off détente.

Gorbachev hoped that the changes he was making would make the Soviet Union more acceptable to the West. Then there could be agreements on arms reductions (and so a cut on what was spent), and possibly loans from the West to help rebuild the economy.

Why was the Soviet Union bankrupt?
- For 40 years the Soviet Union had been spending money supporting communist governments in Europe and around the world.

- Military spending had been enormous. The Soviet military was so powerful that none of the political leaders dared make cuts in case they were overthrown.

- In an attempt to show the power of the country the Soviet Union had put astronauts into space, but this had cost more than the country could afford.

- Inside the Soviet Union, the principles of communism meant that the government spent money to keep prices low. There were few consumer goods available and a large number of products had to be bought on the **black market**.

- Soviet exports were of a very low standard and so it was difficult to sell goods such as Lada cars or Qualiton records. As it was so difficult to sell goods abroad, the country earned little foreign currency with which to buy imports.

- Those imports were badly needed because the country could not grow enough food or manufacture 'high-tech' goods to run its industries.

- In the Soviet Union everyone was guaranteed a job, cheap housing and public services. So there was little incentive to work hard and raise standards.

How did this affect foreign affairs?

These problems made Gorbachev desperate to cut military expenditure. In the USA, President Reagan was also keen to cut the US$300,000 million spent each year on arms.

So, in 1987, they signed the **Intermediate Nuclear Forces Treaty** in which they agreed to remove Intermediate Range Missiles from Europe.

Then, before other agreements could be reached, Soviet control of Eastern Europe began to disintegrate.

The collapse of the Soviet Empire

- In Poland the banned trade union, Solidarity, had continued to campaign against the government. The communist government found it so hard to maintain its authority that it allowed free elections – and Solidarity was voted into power.

Source E

We are catching up with the USA in some of the old industries. But in newer fields, like computers and industrial research, we are not just lagging behind. We are also growing more slowly.

▲ A Soviet description of the backwardness of its industry in the 1980s.

- In September 1989 Hungary opened its borders with Austria – and many people began to leave. The same happened in East Germany. The communist governments appealed to Gorbachev for help, but he said there was nothing he could do.

- When the peoples of Eastern Europe realised that the Soviet Union was now helpless, they began demonstrating against their governments. Soon communist governments in East Germany, Czechoslovakia and Bulgaria resigned. In Romania, President Ceausescu was arrested and shot.

The Soviet Empire had fallen. In December 1989 Gorbachev met President Bush, the new US President. Together they announced that the Cold War was over.

▲ Gorbachev and Reagan meeting in Geneva in 1985. This meeting
was a sign of improved relations between the two powers.

Questions

1 Explain the following terms:
   a Zero option
   b Perestroika
   c Glasnost
   d START.

2 Why did the Soviet Union become
   bankrupt by 1985?

3 Why did **a** Ronald Reagan and **b** Mikhail
   Gorbachev want to cut spending on
   arms?

Overview
Do you agree that the breakdown of the
wartime alliance created a feeling of
mistrust which lasted from 1945 right
through to the end of the Cold War in
1989?

Use the information in this chapter to
explain your answer.

The collapse of the Warsaw Pact and the Soviet Union. The dates show the year in which each country became independent.

Why did the Cold War end so suddenly?

- The major reason for the end of the Cold War was simply that the Soviet Union could no longer afford to play its part as a superpower. Soviet industry was so outdated that it could not produce high quality goods to export and earn foreign currency. So the Soviets could not afford to subsidise other communist countries.

- The Afghan War was a major blow to the Soviet Union. After the invasion in 1979 the Soviet forces were opposed by Afghan guerillas. The cost of the war was huge – both in money and in lives. By 1989 the Soviet forces had to accept defeat and leave.

- The Soviet Union had become so poor that it could not pay its soldiers' wages. The West German government had to offer to pay the £30,000 million bill for removing Soviet troops from East Germany and rehousing them in the Soviet Union.

- Perhaps force could have prevented the fall of communism in Eastern Europe, but Gorbachev was not prepared to use it. Perhaps his troops would not have obeyed orders anyway. Since it was Soviet strength that kept the Warsaw Pact together, once it was gone, the Pact dissolved.